HOW TO BE A SMARTER INVESTOR

ANDREW FEINBERG
and the Editors of MONEY

Edited By Sheryl Hilliard Tucker

MONEY BOOKS
Time Inc. Home Entertainment / 1271 Avenue of the Americas / New York, New York 10020

MONEY MAGAZINE

MANAGING EDITOR Robert Safian EXECUTIVE EDITORS Eric Gelman, Denise B. Martin ASSISTANT MANAGING EDITORS Glenn Coleman, Alan Mirabella, Sheryl Hilliard Tucker EDITORS-AT-LARGE Jean Sherman Chatzky, Michael Sivy SENIOR EDITORS Marion Asnes, Jim Frederick, Jon Gertner, William Green, Scott Medintz, Ellen Stark, Teresa Tritch, Walter Updegrave SENIOR WRITER/COLUMNIST Jason Zweig ASSOCIATE EDITORS Katharine B. Drake, Michael J. Powe SENIOR WRITERS Peter Carbonara, Jerry Edgerton, Amy Feldman, Pablo Galarza, John Helyar, Amy Dockser Marcus, Pat Regnier, Penelope Wang, Suzanne Woolley STAFF WRITERS Jon Birger, Joan Caplin, Brian L. Clark, Lisa Cullen, David Futrelle, Leslie Haggin Geary, Lisa Gibbs, Laura Lallos, Jeanne Lee, Nick Pachetti WRITER-REPORTERS Alec Appelbaum, Adrienne Carter, Jeff Nash, Ilana Polyak CONTRIBUTING WRITERS Paul Lukas, Bethany McLean, Joseph Nocera, Andrew Serwer, Rob Walker ART DIRECTOR Syndi C. Becker DEPUTY ART DIRECTORS David E. McKenna, MaryAnn Salvato ASSOCIATE ART DIRECTORS Marci Papineau, Michael Scowden DESIGNER Semi Kang INFORMATION GRAPHICS DESIGNER Myra Klockenbrink TECHNICAL PROJECTS COORDINATOR Tommy McCall PICTURE EDITOR Jane Clark DEPUTY PICTURE EDITOR Cathy Mather FEATURES PICTURE EDITOR Betsy Keating ASSISTANT PICTURE EDITORS Melanie Skrzek, Shawn Vale SENIOR STAFF REPORTERS Judy Feldman, Roberta Kirwan STAFF Andrea Bennett, Erica Garcia, Grace Jidoun, Patrice D. Johnson, Katherine Zamira Josephs, Daphne D. Mosher (mail), Natasha Rafi, Stephanie D. Smith GROUP EDITORIAL PRODUCTION MANAGER Allegra-Jo Lagani COPY CHIEF Patricia A. Feimster OPERATIONS CHIEF Lionel P. Vargas STAFF Sally Boggan, Martha E. Bula Torres, John D'Antonio, Judith Ferbel, Emily Harrow, Carol Robinson, Eve Sennett, Libby Stephens PUBLIC RELATIONS DIRECTOR Patrick Taylor PUBLIC RELATIONS MANAGER Robyn Kenyon COORDINATOR FOR PERSONAL-FINANCE GROUP Jamie Ringel ASSISTANT TO THE MANAGING EDITOR Lysa Price ADMINISTRATIVE COORDINATOR, DESIGN Llubia Reyes STAFF Merrily Brooks, Maitreyah Friedman, Amy Wilson CORRESPONDENTS Linda Berlin, Barbara Hordern, Ann S. Knol, Stephen Marsh, Melanie J. Mavrides, Laura Mecoy, Marcia R. Pledger, Elizabeth S. Roberts, Carol F. Shepley, Nancy Stesin, Jeff Wuorio DIRECTOR OF IMAGING Richard J. Sheridan IMAGING STAFF Janet Miller (manager), Michael D. Brennan, Edward G. Carnesi, Jeffrey Chan, Janet Gonzalez, Marco Lau, Angel A. Mass, Kent Michaud, Stanley E. Moyse, Claudio M. Muller, Paul Tupay DIRECTOR OF TECHNOLOGY John J. Ruglio TECHNOLOGY STAFF Al Criscuolo, Arthur Wilson (technology managers), John Deer, Ken Klokel, Michael Sheehan, Marvin Tate EXECUTIVE PRODUCER, MONEY WEBSITE Craig Matters VICE PRESIDENT, INTERACTIVE DEVELOPMENT Mark Gilliland DESIGN DIRECTOR Caldwell Toll TECHNOLOGY DIRECTOR Mark Thomas SENIOR EDITORS Alexander Haris, Anthony Mitchell, Susan Price, Peter Valdes-DaPena SENIOR PRODUCER Waits May SENIOR WRITER Borzou Daragahi PROGRAMMERS Steve Leung, Kim Tan, German Todorov, Tim Ungs, Georgi Vladimirov PROJECT MANAGER Ainsley Fuhr PRODUCTION ASSISTANT Savy Mangru ADMINISTRATIVE ASSISTANT Patricia Egbert

TIME INC. HOME ENTERTAINMENT

PRESIDENT Rob Gursha VICE PRESIDENT, BRANDED BUSINESSES David Arfine EXECUTIVE DIRECTOR, MARKETING SERVICES Carol Pittard DIRECTOR, RETAIL & SPECIAL SALES Tom Mifsud DIRECTOR OF FINANCE Tricia Griffin MARKETING DIRECTOR Kenneth Maehlum PRODUCT MANAGER Dennis Sheehan EDITORIAL OPERATIONS MANAGER John Calvano ASSOCIATE PRODUCT MANAGER Sara Stumpf ASSISTANT PRODUCT MANAGER Linda Frisbie

Special Thanks to Victoria Alfonso, Suzanne DeBenedetto, Robert Dente, Gina Di Meglio, Peter Harper, Roberta Harris, Natalie McCrea, Jessica McGrath, Jonathan Polsky, Emily Rabin, Mary Jane Rigoroso, Steven Sandonato, Tara Sheehan, Meredith Shelley, Bozena Szwagulinski, Marina Weinstein, Niki Whelan

MONEY BOOK SERIES

DESIGNER Laura Ierardi, LCI Design

CONTENTS

INTRODUCTION

In these days of astonishing stock market volatility, it is more important than ever for millions of Americans to become smarter investors. Managing money wisely has always been important, of course, but the recent market gyrations make it an even more vital skill. After all, as too many investors discovered to their horror during the 2000-2001 bear market, it is now easy to lose a huge amount of money very quickly. One of the many goals of *How to Be a Smarter Investor* is to keep you from implementing any similar get-poor-quick strategy.

Naturally, we want you to build wealth instead. That's why we wrote a book to help you become a smarter, more successful investor. To the editors of MONEY, smart investing entails three specific requirements. First, you must understand how the market works. You need to know how market cycles normally proceed, and which types of stocks commonly move in a manner opposite to the prevailing trend. Second, you must learn how to use a wide variety of investment strategies and specific investing techniques. Like a golfer, you should know something about all the clubs you carry in your bag. However, simply learning when to use a sand wedge is not enough. Unfortunately, we've seen many investors torpedo savvy strategies with poor execution. (Example: paying an exorbitant price for the stock of a good company. Many of the largest Nasdaq stocks sold at ridiculous price/earnings ratios in 2000, and an investor who bought them near the peak may have to wait many, many years just to break even.) Which leads us to the final crucial component: You must learn to execute your strategies in an effective manner and to avoid the costly mistakes that undermine so many investors' returns.

How to Be a Smarter Investor is being published at a particularly important time. Many investors are still shell-shocked from the drubbing that stocks took following their early 2000 highs—and who can blame them? As you probably know all too well, in 2000-2001 the Standard & Poor's 500-stock index fell 28% from its peak and the Nasdaq crumbled 68%. Given such sharp—and in the case of Nasdaq, extraordinary—declines, how should people think about stocks now?

We think stocks should remain a significant, and even essential, part of most people's portfolios. If you look at history, we'll always be in a bull or a bear market, but no matter what we're in, shifting from stocks to cash can devastate your long-term returns.

Consider for a moment those long-term average stock gains of 11% or so that financial writers go on and on about all the time. Well, that figure masks a lot of fluctuation. And it's the rebounds from severe setbacks that produce sharp bursts of gains that prop up the long-term average.

From the fall of 1980 through the summer of 1982, for example, stocks suffered a 27% decline that lasted 21 months. In August 1982, however, that setback gave way to a new bull market that generated incredible returns. From the beginning of August through the end of the 1980s, stocks exploded for an annualized return of 22.2%—about twice their long-term average. But to get that blockbuster gain, you had to be there when stocks took off.

If you had been sitting in secure Treasury bills during the first year of the market's recovery and then switched to stocks, your gain would have dropped from 22.2% to 16%. That's right, six percentage points less each year. Make no mistake about it, that kind of return difference translates to significant bucks. An annualized gain of 22.2% would have turned a $10,000 investment into just over $44,000 during that period, while a 16% return would have given you a bit more than $30,000, or about $14,000 less.

But there is also danger in expecting that the outsize returns from 1982 to 2000—a period during which the S&P 500 rose at a rate of 18.5% per year—will be duplicated any time soon. It was easy to get spoiled by the abnormally wonderful returns of the stock market in the recent past. In the five record-breaking years from 1995 through 1999, the S&P 500 rose more than 20% each year, something that had never happened before in U.S. history.

It may never happen again.

IMPROVING YOUR RETURNS

How to Be a Smarter Investor is intended to be entertaining and informative, but if it doesn't improve your investment planning and performance it will have been a failure. Above all, we filled the book with practical advice that you can begin applying today to enhance your investment returns.

How, specifically, will the book help? It will help you avoid making moves that can sabotage your investment plan. It will give you rules to follow that can prevent you from overpaying for stocks, and provide strategies that will help you select winning mutual funds.

You'll also learn about the psychology underlying many investor mistakes. For instance, everybody knows the Wall Street mantra "buy low, sell high," but isn't it interesting that the human brain seems wired to do precisely the opposite? We'll show you techniques to overcome this psychological impediment, as well as many others. In addition, you'll receive comprehensive advice on how to cut your tax bill when you invest, which will be particularly valuable to anyone who currently holds a stock, or especially a mutual fund, that is underwater. Finally, the book will provide detailed information about goal setting, retirement planning, handling stock options, using online resources and investing for college.

And we'll help answer the question: Would I benefit from the services of a financial adviser? As helpful as good books and periodicals can be, for many people there is no substitute for a flesh-and-blood financial adviser who—theoretically, at least—tailors a plan precisely to meet your needs. But don't even think of hiring one until you read every word of Chapter 7.

That's just a brief overview of what you'll find in *How to Be a Smarter Investor.* The book contains dozens of specific pieces of advice that can transform your financial life. Granted, we're biased, but we think that handling your money in an intelligent manner is undeniably one of the most powerful things you can do for yourself.

Furthermore, we think that almost everyone who invests could learn to do so even more intelligently. (Okay, maybe there's a guy in Omaha who doesn't need this book.) Becoming a smarter investor means, in part, that you will keep learning about the markets, taking what amounts to continuing education "courses." Markets evolve and new investment vehicles—such as exchange-traded funds—are frequently introduced. And, alas, we all make mistakes, many of which are avoidable. (For a detailed analysis of how investors could have avoided losing billions of dollars in just one stock—Lucent—see Chapter 3)

So, if you want to become a smarter investor, dive in. We think you'll find it a profitable and enjoyable experience.

Chapter 1
THE NEW
MARKET REALITY

After five consecutive years of rock-and-roll market returns in the last half of the 1990s, it all ended as abruptly as the Spice Girls fad. The Nasdaq composite plunged almost 70% from its peak in little more than a year, a crash of epic proportions. The S&P 500 tumbled 28% from peak to trough. A perfectly booming New Economy slowed to a rather imperfect and old-fashioned stop. And growth stalwarts like Dell, Home Depot and Microsoft suddenly acted like yesterday's hit parade.

Call it the New Market Reality. Clearly, the tools that investors once used to profit from the roaring stock market no longer work. Attempts to value New Economy companies by new-age metrics—such as page views, eyeballs and mind share—have been utterly discredited and have gone the way of the hoop skirt. Yahoo, for example, has always been able to attract millions of eyeballs, but the owners of those peepers seldom pay Yahoo for anything and, increasingly, seem reluctant to pay attention to ads on its—or many other Internet companies'—sites. Small wonder that the stock has cratered.

The funhouse-mirror effects of the stock market in early 2000 have disappeared. No longer do the anointed market darlings seem far larger than life, nor have many value stocks remained at nearly half their normal valuation. It has been very painful, no doubt, but some rationality has returned to the stock market.

As recently as 2000, remember, the greatest investor of our time—Warren Buffett—was being ridiculed for his aversion to tech stocks. Some of his detractors depicted him as little more than a doddering old fool who was incapable of changing with the times. A good thing too, some of his shareholders might now be saying. From March 10, 2000 to April 19, 2001, Berkshire Hathaway Class A shares rose 66%, while the Nasdaq composite fell 57%. Translation: $1 invested in Berkshire Hathaway back then would now be worth $1.66, while a similar amount plunked down on the Nasdaq composite would now amount to 43¢.

"Many that are first shall be last; and the last shall be first" indeed. In the gospel according to Wall Street, it has been ever thus—up to a point. If we've learned anything from the recent bear rout, it's that what the market giveth, the market can taketh away, without warning. And nobody—not you, not us, not Alan Greenspan—can change that basic fact.

That doesn't mean we're powerless though. While we can't control the markets, we have absolute control over something much more important: our own actions. We're in charge when it comes to the things that really determine investing success: which investments we choose to own, the proportions in which we decide to hold them, when to buy, when to sell and—perhaps most important—how we respond to the euphoria that prevails when the market soars, as well as the pessimism that descends when stock prices fall.

That's the silver lining for many investors. "When you have so many sunny days, you think you can stop building the ark," says Vanguard Funds founder John Bogle. "But the market taught us that rainy days will come again." Adds Fritz Meyer, market strategist for Invesco Funds: "It's time to be an investor again."

14 LESSONS FROM THE MELTDOWN

1. Stock picking is hard.

For a while, it seemed like a breeze. All you had to do was buy and buy and let a rising tide lift your boat. During the frenzy of the bull market, even the initial public offerings of garage-based Internet start-ups seemed to be no-lose bets. In 1999 the average IPO was up 194%, reports Thomson Financial Securities Data. In 2000? The average offering lost 27%. In the first half of 2001? It was difficult for any company to come public at all.

The Internet heightened the illusion that investing is a cinch. One benefit of the great American rush into the markets these past few years (85 million of us now own individual stocks) was the amazing development of online-trading tools. But just because you can trade with the flick of a wrist doesn't mean you should. Stock picking—good stock picking—demands time, energy, vigilance and more than a little iron lining in one's gut. Says Jeremy Siegel, finance professor at the Wharton School: "It's always extraordinarily difficult to pick individual stocks."

If you don't have the patience, discipline and willingness to do your homework, then get some help. Whether you choose individual stocks or mutual funds, "the good news is, the Web makes it easier and cheaper to research and analyze," says Mark Riepe, investment research chief at Charles Schwab. The bad news, of course, is that all the data in the world isn't necessarily enough.

2. Get a plan and stick to it.

Without a road map and a clear destination, it was easy to get sidetracked by the blaring horns and gyrating neon—dotcom this, IPO that—delivered via intravenous feeds from CNBC and the Web. However, tailgating the latest trend rarely works. Indeed, a recent study by Financial Research Corp. found that fund investors sliced 20% off their returns over the past decade by chasing hot performers. The upshot: You need a plan, and not one that says buy high, sell low. "What are your goals? When do you need the money? How much risk can you take?" asks Ross Levin, a financial planner in Minneapolis. "When you have a plan, throughout the market's ups and downs, you're sitting back objectively and dispassionately instead of being emotional."

3. You can't buy past performance.

Past returns are no guarantee of future returns—is there an investor on earth who doesn't know this line by heart? But despite the disturbing 20% statistic quoted in Lesson 2, when it comes to buying stocks and funds, we act as if we've never heard this warning. Instead, we scan some newspaper's top-performers chart, pore over Morningstar's list of five-star funds or the Schwab Select List—anything we can do to identify investments with the biggest gains.

Unfortunately, we can't buy yesterday's gains. And while there is some marginal evidence in the case of funds, at least, that superior performance persists into the future, the effect is relatively small, doesn't last very long and is difficult to capitalize on after transaction costs and taxes.

The biggest danger, of course, is piling into stocks or funds that have generated humongous gains over a brief period. Short-term outsized gains are almost always unsustainable, which means investors who jump aboard such high fliers often end up strapping themselves in just in time to experience a white-knuckle ride down.

Tech and Internet stocks have taken the rap lately when it comes to chasing performance, but the truth is that investors will chase any investment that moves fast enough. Remember the 184 funds that reported 100%-plus returns in 1999? Naturally, investors lemminged in. Of those triple-digit funds, 11—11— delivered more than 0% in 2000. Many had huge losses. Take Warburg Pincus Japan Small Company fund. In 1999, its position in Japanese tech and telecom stocks paid off big with a 100% gain in the first half of the year, followed by another 114% surge over the next six months. Not surprisingly, investors rushed into the fund, driving assets from a minuscule $50 million at the beginning of the year to more than $1 billion by year-end. Unfortunately, folks who chased 1999's stellar gains anticipating an encore got less than they planned for: The fund nosedived in 2000, losing a staggering 71.8%. Ouch!

Considering how quickly sizzle can turn to fizzle in the market, you're taking a big risk if you jump aboard a stock or fund that's recently skyrocketed to stupendous short-term gains. And even if rigorous analysis leads you to believe that such an investment still has plenty of upside potential, you should consider buying it only as part of a diversified portfolio that can help cushion the blow if your high flier flames out.

4. Insist on quality.

Whether the stock is big or bite-size, go-go growth or steady value, there's one thing all your investments should have in common. They should be quality companies with good earnings, pristine balance sheets and topnotch management. Period.

Infatuation with the Web—and the explosion of Internet IPOs—led too many of us to stray from market leaders to early-stage start-ups with uncertain business models. Let's not do that again, shall we? "Real fundamentals do matter," says Erik Gustafson of Liberty Growth Stock. "Owning the great companies of the world—that's where individual investors should focus. Time has tested this philosophy."

5. Risk is a four-letter word.

At some point, risk became an attractive quality for a stock. "People were enthralled by the upside of equities," says value manager David Dreman. "Risk was not being in stocks. Risk was being parked in Old Economy stocks and bonds." The real risk, in other words, was the risk of missing out.

But many folks forgot the reasoning behind what's called the *risk premium*: Stocks reward you with the chance of getting back more because you stand a real chance of getting back less. The latter is exactly what happened for many companies in 2000 and 2001.

Handling risk is a matter of preparation. If you know how much you're willing to take—say, a 15% hit in addition to the hoped-for 15% gain—then a year like 2000 or the first quarter of 2001 won't frazzle you. "Your prime consideration is not the probability of returns or gains but the consequences of loss," says Bogle. "Most important, don't do anything when risk comes to roost. Even if the market fails, don't say, 'Now is the time to get out.' Say, 'I was ready for it, I can handle it.'"

One of the ironic things about investing is that just when we should be getting wary about the risk we're taking on, we start to feel invulnerable. At the beginning of 2000, for example, with the Nasdaq coming off an 85.6% annual return, investors were feeling positively bulletproof. But history tells us that the odds of a meltdown are highest after the market's had a huge run-up and companies are selling at bloated prices.

What accounts for this paradox? Why are we likely to invest more aggressively when alarm bells should be ringing in our heads? One reason, says Robert Shiller, a finance professor at Yale and author of *Irrational Exuberance*, is that we "just feel better about getting into the market when it's going up. Our self-confidence is enhanced." But there's another factor at work too. When we haven't experienced bear markets for a while—which was the case until recently—we tend to forget that they are a normal part of the investing cycle.

However, euphoria may not return for a long time. In the eight previous bear markets since 1961, it took almost three years on average for the S&P 500 (an index of 500 of the largest companies in America, as selected by a committee) to get back to its pre-bear peak.

Clearly, you want to factor in a healthy respect for the kinds of spills stocks can take. On other hand, you don't want to become so focused on avoiding short-term losses that you hunker down in bond and money-market funds, thereby limiting your ability to participate in the stock market's superior long-term gains. Such a strategy would be particularly foolish now, since stocks generate some of their biggest gains after they've suffered a severe set-back. In the six years after the 1973-74 bear market, for example, the S&P 500 gained an annualized 17.3%. Since the bulk of that return came early in that six-year run, investors who deserted stocks for the security of cash likely missed much of those gains.

6. Diversity rules.

"If you don't know what's going to happen in the market," Bogle says, "then diversify." Sound advice, yes, but also boring stuff to many people in the 1990s, when one chunk of the portfolio could double in months or sometimes weeks and the rest would just plod along or even shrink in value.

Maybe that's why folks listened to the likes of Bob Markman, the Type AAA fund impresario who called the benefits of diversification "an extraordinarily popular delusion." Markman was saying what many of us wanted to hear, and people who owned nothing but tech looked like geniuses. We all know what happened next. As Bogle puts it: "The leading stock groups become laggards, the laggards become leaders and the twain shall always meet." (Markman's Aggressive Allocation fund, by the way, finished 2000 down nearly 28% and fell another 43% through the beginning of April 2001.)

The disdain for spreading one's assets came down to one thing during the bull market: the mind-bending return of one sector. "Tech stocks made many people forget that other asset classes exist," says noted investment researcher Roger Ibbotson. A pity, really. Those who had bet too much on tech missed out on the resurgence among other types of investments. In 2000, bonds outperformed stocks for the first time since 1993, for instance. Real estate investment trust funds, which attracted only a tenth of the investor money that tech funds hauled in, returned 26% on average in 2000. Tech funds lost 33%.

7. Never lose sight of price.

Investors unlucky enough to have bought Dell at $59 or Home Depot at $70 back in March 2000 have learned the hard way that valuation—what we pay for a stock—does matter. Sure, those are solid companies, and even if you bought at those prices you'll probably make money in the long run. But it'll take a lot longer than if you had waited and scooped up Home Depot at $34 in October 2000 or Dell at $16.50 in December 2000.

We're not talking about market timing. No one can pick the precise moment when a particular stock or sector has hit its lows. Rather, this is about having discipline. MONEY's in-house market guru, editor-at-large Michael Sivy, suggests that you buy a stock when its PEG ratio (price/earnings ratio divided by expected earnings growth rate) is less than 1.5. Stocks that are growing significantly faster than the market average may deserve a higher PEG.

It's also valuable to compare the stock's P/E and growth rate with the market's. The S&P stocks have an average P/E of 23 on 2001 estimated earnings. And the typical S&P stock should see earnings decline in 2001 but rise 11% in 2002. Best bets: stocks growing faster than the index companies as a whole and trading at a P/E that's lower than the group P/E.

8. Never underestimate the impact of costs.

Obsessed as we are with returns, it's not surprising that we spend little time thinking about the cost side of investing. And even if we do manage to devote the occasional passing thought to expenses, they really don't seem like such a big deal. After all, you can buy and sell stocks online these days for $12 or less per trade. And if you pay an extra half a percentage point or so a year in operating expenses for a stock fund, what's the harm? That's nothing compared with annualized returns of 20% or more that many funds have earned in recent years.

But that kind of thinking betrays a misunderstanding of the true costs of investing and their long-term effect. Brokers' commissions are only one part of the cost of trading stocks. There's also the "spread," essentially a markup to compensate the broker for holding the stock in inventory or for buying and then reselling it to you. In large frequently traded stocks, the spread may be half a percentage point or less, but in small stocks it can easily swell to two, three percentage points or more. Then there are taxes, another cost that in some cases can slash upwards of 40% off your short-term gains. "In the short term, those costs seem to matter very little," says Bogle. "But over the long run, they have a dramatic effect on your return."

To get an idea of the effect that high operating expenses can have on mutual fund returns, we conducted a little experiment. Using Morningstar's Principia program, we screened for all large-cap stock funds that have been around at least 10 years and then ranked them by their annual operating expenses. Next, we divided the funds into four groups, or quartiles, with the first quartile containing the funds with the lowest expenses and the fourth quartile containing those with the highest expenses. We then compared the performance of the lowest- and highest-cost groups over the three, five and 10 years to the beginning of 2001. The results were amazing. The lowest-cost funds outperformed their expensive counterparts by 1.8 to 2.3 percentage points a year. If that margin doesn't seem like much, think of it this way: On a $50,000 investment, earning an annualized 10% instead of 8% for 10 years translates to an extra $21,741 going into your pocket before taxes.

Given how much high costs can erode returns, Bogle offers this advice: "Do your fishing in the low-cost pond." You can do just that by screening for low-cost funds at the Fund Selector on Morningstar's website (www.morningstar.com) or at MONEY's site (www.money.com/money/fundcenter). The Securities and Exchange Commission would also like investors to give more thought to expenses, which is why the SEC recently issued a report suggesting that funds divulge to shareholders in semiannual and annual reports the dollar amount they pay in expenses. It's hard to describe the report as scintillating reading, but it's worth perusing, if only to help you appreciate the importance of keeping investing costs down. You can find it on the commission's website at www.sec.gov/news/studies/feestudy.htm.

9. Buy and hold isn't a sure bet.

Many thought they had found the simple recipe for investing: Buy a "good" company no matter the price, hold tight, watch it grow; repeat. Recently, we learned otherwise.

Bill Reilly, a 68-year-old car dealer in Tarrytown, N.Y., held Cisco, Lucent and WorldCom in what he considered his blue-chip retirement account. That account lost 30%—or $80,000—in 2000, and both Cisco and Lucent plummeted again in 2001. "Even the greatest companies can become overvalued or can hit a growth snag," Reilly now realizes. "These were stocks I thought I could hold forever."

What's changed is the definition of forever. "Buy and hold doesn't mean buy and ignore," counsels Alan Skrainka, chief market strategist of brokerage Edward Jones. "If you bought the original Dow Jones industrial stocks and kept them, what you'd have today is a portfolio of buggy whip, ice and textile companies."

In many folks' minds, long term means 20 or 30 years—a true lifetime in business—but the horizon now looms much closer, especially in change-a-minute fields like technology. Consider Dell. Its fantastic 5,670% surge in value was crammed into a mere five-year period before the stock tanked in 2000 on fears of sales and earnings-growth slowdowns. Observes Siegel: "People who bought into Yahoo, Amazon and AOL thinking they could hold them forever learned that lesson the hard way."

10. It's okay to sit out a dance or two.

The bull-market pressure to jump in often overwhelmed all notions of look-before-you-leap investing. You were a sucker if you didn't get in on Qualcomm at $162 or Cisco at $80. That fear was evident in the surge of stock buying that followed every market dip during the past few years. "Even as the market started to stumble in 2000, people bought into the dips because it had always worked in the bubbly atmosphere of the past," says Dreman. "Then, suddenly, it didn't work." Qualcomm plummeted as low as $42.75. Cisco plunged to $13.18.

The larger lesson is that capital gains aren't the only kind of gains. When easy upticks vanished in 2000, dividends and interest income filled in the gaps. Stocks like Philip Morris yielded 4.9%. Treasury bonds generated more than 6%. Even CDs and money-market funds kicked out upwards of 6%. No, you can't get rich in a hurry on returns like that. But it sure beats getting poor in a hurry instead.

11. Bear-market bargain hunting is a good thing.

No one has ever lost big, over the long run, when they bought quality companies after significant crashes. That's why fund managers love big downturns, because they can load up on their favorite stocks at bargain prices. Investors should think exactly the same way. "These cycles are good things because they give you opportunities," says Bob Smith, manager of T. Rowe Price Growth.

Invesco strategist Fritz Meyer argues that the recent tech crash and the broader S&P 500 bear market have been good for investors because they have purged the market of untested companies with "flaky business plans" and flushed out speculators who drove up prices to unjustifiable highs.

Of course, it's tough to get into a buying mood amid bleak headlines of corporate layoffs and missed earnings estimates. But try to set emotions aside when contemplating your next move.

12. Tune out the noise.

There's no doubt that the information revolution has vastly increased the amount of data, news and analysis available to us today. A few clicks of the mouse and we can review the latest earnings releases, the most recent economic barometers—even check out arcane (and quite possibly useless) technical indicators like Bollinger Bands and the Bolton-Tremlay Indicator. We can then tune in one of the ubiquitous cable-TV financial shows to watch a parade of pundits argue endlessly over what this cornucopia of information means for stock prices.

But does this tsunami of news necessarily make us better investors? The research of Paul Andreassen, a psychologist at Harvard in the late '80s, suggests not. Andreassen studied the relationship between the news media and investing. In one experiment, Andreassen separated people into two groups; one bought and sold stocks based solely on recent price data and the other traded after being given the price information plus headlines that explained the price changes. Andreassen found that when stock prices were volatile, the group that had access to the news earned less than half as much per share traded as the group that received no news.

Why would no news be good news? Andreassen theorized that we tend to take news reports almost as predictions. When a jump in a stock's price is accompanied by news that seems to make sense of the movement, we take that as a sign that the trend will continue. Conversely, when news reports make sense of a price decline, we tend to take that as an indication that the negative trajectory will prevail. As a result, we're likely to buy, buy, buy when the news is good and stock prices are rising, and sell, sell, sell when pessimism prevails and prices decline. With thousands of investors reacting this way, stocks can be driven to unrealistically high—or low—levels.

The solution isn't to ignore the news but to avoid reacting to every tidbit of financial information that comes your way. Your first reaction to virtually any new development in the economy should be, "Don't just do something, stand there!" That's right, do nothing—at least until you can sort out what's going on. If the fundamentals seem to have taken a turn for the worse, you may want to join the hordes headed for the exit. But if the long-term case for the stock is intact, you may want to buy more shares.

13. Get by with a little less help from your friends.

Would you buy a stock if it were recommended by Chandler, Ross or Monica on *Friends*? How about a fund touted by Phoebe, the ditsy member of the sitcom team? Okay, maybe not Pheebs. But if you're like most investors, you probably do look to your circle of acquaintances and co-workers for investing tips. When MONEY polled a statistically representative sample of its subscribers in 2000, almost half of those surveyed said that they regularly or occasionally use relatives, friends and colleagues as a source of financial information.

But just because someone you know is touting an investment that he just made in his retirement account, does that mean the same investment ought to work just as well for you? Of course not. For one thing, the two of you may have completely different tolerances for risk. An investment that's suitable for a colleague who rides out market declines of 30% or more without so much as breaking a sweat may be wildly inappropriate if you're the type who reaches for the Maalox every time the Dow drops 100 points. There's also the issue of the price you're paying. Any tip you get from a friend is not likely to be news. It's probably wended its way through hundreds, if not thousands of other investors. By the time you invest, the price may have been bid up so high that any future appreciation is limited. (Think Amazon.com at $110 a share in December 1999.)

Besides, even though we tend to bestow credibility in financial matters upon friends and acquaintances who are successful in their careers, the truth is that expertise in one area of life doesn't automatically translate to expertise in investing. Recently, for example, Buffalo financial planner Anthony Ogorek was setting up a portfolio for a client who directed him to include a few stocks recommended by a relative, a biologist familiar with the latest trends in biotech. How have those stocks done so far? "One is down 87%, another is down 89%, and the third is off 92%," says Ogorek. "My sense is that my client's relative confused great companies with great stock picks. They're not the same thing." Finding terrific companies is only half the equation. The other, more important, half is finding them at reasonable prices.

However tempting a tip from a neighbor, friend or co-worker might sound, always do some research on your own or run it by a financial adviser. If you decide to buy the investment and it turns sour, at least you'll know you bought in on the basis of your own due diligence and judgment, not just the word of the guy who happens to live next door.

14. Give your expectations a reality check.

Think of a boffo market like the one we've seen the past few years as a kind of lovely, unexpected bonus. "Then your expectations are in line with reality," says Meir Statman, a professor of finance at Santa·Clara University, "and you're delightfully surprised by returns like those through 1999. Those who thought they were geniuses— well, now they'll realize they were just lucky."

From 1995 through 1999, the S&P 500 racked up an annualized gain of 28.6%, the highest by far of any five-year stretch in its history. For all those years of 20% returns in the past decade, there may well be times when the market doesn't do much. Some years we will even lose money. Get used to it, says Bogle: "Reversion to the mean is in fact Sir Isaac Newton's revenge on Wall Street."

But with things going so well for so long, it wasn't hard to convince ourselves that this extraordinary run would go on and on. A survey of individual investors by UBS PaineWebber in December 1999 found that for the next 10 years investors were expecting annualized gains of 19%—19%! Nearly twice stocks' annualized return of 11.3% over the past 75 years.

While the big bear market has certainly shaken those assumptions, it may not have broken them. "I still don't believe expectations have been lowered enough yet," says Ogorek. "Until the markets really break people's hearts and dash their spirits, I think any sanity will be temporary." (For MONEY columnist Jason's Zweig's take on how to look into the future, see "A Matter of Expectations" on page 17.)

The problem with overly optimistic expectations is that they can lead you to make lousy planning and investing decisions. Let's say you're trying to figure out how much you need to put away each month to have a $150,000 education fund for your Ivy League-bound toddler 15 years from now. If you believe that stocks can earn 20% year in and year out, you'd feel comfortable socking away about $160 a month. That's great if those 20%-a-year gains materialize. But if returns come in at their long-term average of roughly 11%, you'd fall about $80,000 short. Bye-bye, Harvard.

A Matter of Expectations BY MONEY COLUMNIST JASON ZWEIG

Well, how much should we really expect stocks to return in the future? Few questions are more important to investors—and few are harder to answer.

What proportion of your money you put into stocks and how prosperous a retirement you have hinge on how much you expect stocks to return over time and whether the future lives up to your expectations.

These days, as recent surveys of individual investors by Scudder Kemper and UBS PaineWebber show, most people seem to expect the stock market to return about 12% to 15% a year over time. Based on history, that sounds plausible enough. You know about those 11% returns since 1926. And according to data from Jeremy Siegel, who has tracked stock returns all the way back to the Jefferson Administration, U.S. stocks have averaged nearly a 9%-a-year return since 1802. How can we tell if expectations like these are reasonable?

Misusing the past. Unfortunately, 75 years—even two centuries—of data don't prove that stocks will average at least a 10% annual gain in the future. That's because the past is not merely that portion of the future that has already happened. Au contraire; if the present is drastically different from the past, warns Yale's Robert Shiller, then "history cannot be a reliable guide to the future." In the past, the stocks in Standard & Poor's 500-stock index sold for an average price of 25 times their dividend income and 15 times their net profits—meaning that investors back then got to buy at bargain prices. But now, even after the 2000-2001 bear market, the S&P 500 sells at 72 times dividend income and 23 times earnings—about as expensive as U.S. stocks have ever been. Common sense says that you're not likely to get high future earnings out of anything if you pay too high a price for it.

Still, many pundits claim that stocks will always outperform bonds because equity investing gives you a piece of a growing business, while bonds simply allow you to lend money at a fixed rate of interest. But what if the rate of interest on bonds is at least as high as the expected growth of the businesses? Then bonds could beat stocks for surprisingly long periods, as they did for the 20 years that ended in 1948 and again for the 17 years that ended in 1982. Some very smart investment thinkers, such as Yale's Shiller, Robert Arnott of pension fund manager First Quadrant in Pasadena and institutional investor Jeremy Grantham of Grantham Mayo Van Otterloo & Co. in Boston, believe we may be at the start of another period in which stocks will lag bonds—and may even lose money—for years.

Measuring the future. Before you panic, it's worth learning how the pros put their forecasts together. Grantham believes that average annual returns over the next decade will be -2%, while both John Bogle and Laurence Siegel, director of investment policy research at the Ford Foundation, expect annual returns to average 6% to 9%. They all agree that future returns depend on two factors. The first is the growth of corporate profits and dividends (including the repurchase of shares by the companies that issued them). Bogle calls these combined elements "the investment return." All these experts agree that the long-term investment return should reliably average between 5% and 6% annually before inflation.

The second factor, which Bogle calls "the speculative return," is the change in market valuation over time—a huge wild card. As investors become willing to pay more (or less) for stocks in the future than they are today, the market's price/earnings ratio will go up or down, raising or lowering future stock returns accordingly. Unfortunately, no one has a clue how to read the mood rings of tomorrow's investors. Jokes Laurence Siegel: "I decided not to put that in my forecast because I'm scared to." Bogle warns: "The speculative element is as unpredictable as the investment return is predictable."

But Grantham is willing to guess how investors' sentiment will change. He reckons that the S&P 500 will go from selling at 23 times earnings today to 17.5 a decade from now—"a friendly, optimistic assumption," he says, since it's above the long-term average P/E of less than 15. That single adjustment accounts for most of his forecast that stocks will lose nearly 2% a year after inflation for the next decade.

As the old saying goes, there are two kinds of forecasters: those who are wrong and those who know they are wrong. So you've got to take all these predictions about future stock returns with a grain of salt the size of Mount McKinley. However, while they may not be right, these forecasts aren't useless. Here's how they can help you think about your own future returns.

Hope for the best, but expect the worst. You won't suffer if stocks do better than you expected, but if they do worse, your dreams could be demolished. And the higher your expectations, the lower your chances of having them fulfilled. Do you think stocks will return, say, 25% a year in the future? Despite the 21% average returns of the past five years, a 25% long-run return is about as likely as a Pat Buchanan pep rally in Palm Beach. According to the researchers at Sanford C. Bernstein & Co., over the past half century only 10% of companies in the S&P 500 have increased their earnings at an average rate of at least 20% a year for five years running. Only 3% have raised earnings at least 20% annually for a decade. And none—zero, zippo, the big schneid—have sustained 20% earnings growth for 15 years or more. In the long run, it's just not possible for stocks to go up faster than the earnings of the companies they represent; the past few years' average returns of better than 20% cannot last.

Be realistic, and scale back your expectations. As G.K. Chesterton said, "Blessed is he who expecteth nothing, for he shall enjoy everything."

What's average? The stock market is not a bank CD; when you hear that stocks have returned an "average" of 11% a year, that doesn't mean they gained 11% every year. In fact, in all the years since 1926, stocks have returned 11% only one solitary time (in 1968), and they've gained between 10% and 12% in only three of those 75 years. The rest of the time, returns were all over the place, from a 43.3% loss in 1931 and a 26.5% drop in 1974 to a 52.6% gain in 1954 and a 54% surge in 1933. It's not surprising for a short-term result to differ from what you expect for the long run; in fact, it's normal. So brace yourself for surprises. And remember that a bad year like 2000, or even several sorry years, can't tell you anything about what you'll earn in the long run.

Bad news, good news. What if the bears do turn out to be right? If you've complemented your U.S. stocks with bonds, foreign stocks and, perhaps, specialized investments like real estate investment trusts, you'll always have something that goes up. But the best thing about a protracted down market is that stocks will go on sale, and stay on sale, for years. Unless you're retired, that may turn out to be the best investment news of your lifetime. Wall Street hasn't put stocks on the remainder rack since 1973-74, when the market lost roughly 40% and P/E ratios fell to half their long-term averages. If it takes you by surprise, a sudden sale is a disaster. But if you're prepared, you can shop while stocks drop, and muster the years of patience it could take for them to recover.

Plus, your efforts to get that unattainable 20% may lead you to some pretty dicey investments: risky IPOs, overpriced momentum stocks, dotcoms that are long on promise and short on performance. And given the propensity for such speculative vehicles to flame out, you might not only miss your 20% target, you could very easily wind up with less than the 11% average return, putting you even further behind.

You'll have a much better chance of reaching your goals if you set your sights on returns that are realistic—and build your portfolio from there. No one can foretell what that rate of return should be, of course. But the point isn't to predict the future. No one can do that. Rather, the idea is to base your decisions on expectations that are reasonable—returns that are achievable even if all the stars aren't aligned in your favor. That way, if results come in close to the levels you're expecting, you'll have no trouble sending junior to a top school.

And if returns come in much higher? Well, consider it a bonus that will allow you to retire in grand style.

VITAL SIGNS

So far, we've given you some ideas of what you can expect of the stock market in the long term. But what about assessing the economy—and stock market prospects—at a particular moment in time? What should you look at and what should you ignore?

It would be great if there were a simple way to determine whether a slowing economy will teeter into recession or whether rate cuts by the Federal Reserve will breathe new life into the economy. But short of having economists and psychics join forces to develop an economic version of one of those fortune-telling eightballs, we can't think of one.

Which brings us to the only real option investors have for trying to gain a sense of what might lie ahead: tracking a select group of economic indicators. The operative word here is select. As anyone who's watched CNBC or surfed the Web knows, you can quickly find yourself drowning in a flood of confusing economic minutiae. Our goal is to help you home in on a few easily accessible stats that provide insight into several areas of the economy and don't require a Ph.D. in economics to understand.

We'll go over four key gauges that we think fit that bill. (If you have a higher tolerance for this sort of thing, you'll find a more exhaustive—though not exhausting—list of indicators among the Investing 201 columns at www.money.com.) But first, a few caveats. No set of indicators is going to provide you with a connect-the-dots path to the future. Even major turning points tend to be clearest in hindsight. For example, the Business Cycle Dating Committee of the National Bureau of Economic Research didn't announce the starting date of the 1990 recession until April 25, 1991—a month after it had ended. And even when all economic signs seem to point in the same direction, it's not a given that the economy will follow. In economics, as in Florida elections, outcomes are often hard to predict.

One more thing: If the market is working correctly, stock prices should reflect investors' future expectations for the economy. In fact, stock prices often drop six months or so in advance of economic slowdowns and soar about six months before a recovery. (That said, the market isn't a perfect prognosticator. As economics Nobel Laureate Paul Samuelson once quipped, "The stock market has predicted nine of the last five recessions." That line is considered a laugh riot in economic circles.) So even if we were supremely confident about our reading of the economy, we'd be wary of using that knowledge to make big bets on specific investments.

Here are MONEY columnist Walter Updegrave's views on the four indicators you need to follow.

- **The employment report.**
Typically released the first Friday of each month, the Employment Situation Summary, as the Bureau of Labor Statistics calls it, provides a quick update on the job market. Growing employment leads to increases in consumer spending, which accounts for two-thirds of the U.S. economy. Thus most economists consider the report an advance peek at future economic growth.

The financial press usually zeroes in on the unemployment rate, which in April 2001 stood at 4.5%, near its all-time low of 3.9%. But that figure says more about where the economy has been than where it's headed. To get a glimpse of the future, check out the increase in "nonfarm payroll employment," or the number of new jobs created in the economy each month.

Basically, job growth is a harbinger of economic growth. Indeed, in early 2000, when investors were more concerned about the economy overheating than fizzling, strong job gains actually sent the market down by raising the specter of rising inflation. In the spring of 2001, however, investors were disturbed by the slowdown in job creation. In 1997 and 1998, for example, we added jobs at a frenetic pace of more than 250,000 a month on average. By the fourth quarter of 2000, an average of only 77,000 new jobs were being created each month, a drop of 70% from 1999's fourth quarter. And in March 2001, the job creation number actually turned negative.

That kind of decline doesn't guarantee a recession, but it certainly suggests much slower growth for the economy—and corporate profits. If job creation numbers actually go negative for several months running, that would definitely be a red flag, since sustained job losses typically occur only during recessions. You can find the employment figures on the BLS website at www.bls.gov/ceshome.htm.

- **Consumer confidence.**

Employment data can tell you about consumers' ability to spend but not about their willingness to spend. For that, economists and investing strategists turn to a variety of surveys that gauge the fickle phenomenon known as consumer sentiment. One of the most widely followed is the Conference Board's consumer confidence index, released on the last Tuesday of every month.

The idea behind the index is simple. "We're measuring changes in consumer attitudes about the economic situation," says Lynn Franco, director of the Conference Board's Consumer Research Center. "If there's a dramatic shift from spending to saving, it can apply the brakes to economic growth."

The board polls 5,000 different households each month, asking people how they feel about current and future business conditions, the job market and their own income prospects over the next six months. The board's number crunchers massage those responses into an index that measures confidence in the economy. A rising trend in the index suggests that consumers are becoming more upbeat—and more likely to open their wallets and propel the expansion forward. A downward trend indicates that consumers are more likely to pare back spending. In the early months of 2001, the trend was clearly negative, but it showed signs of stabilizing in April and May.

The consumer confidence index grabs most of the attention, but you get a better reading on what lies ahead from the board's expectations index. This gauge, which is derived from the overall confidence index, measures how well we think the economy and our personal finances will be doing six months down the road.

A downward trend in expectations suggests a slowdown in economic growth, but it is the steepness of the decline that can presage imminent recession. "Generally, the expectations index has to dip below 80 and stay there two months or so before we consider it a warning of recession," says Franco. You can get the current readings on the consumer confidence and expectation indexes by going to the Conference Board's Consumer Research Center website at www.conference-board.org/products/c-consumer.cfm.

- **Purchasing managers' index.**

After taking the pulse of consumers, the industrial sector of the economy is the next place to turn to for clues about the economy's future direction. For a timely assessment of our industrial might, most economists track something called the purchasing managers' index (PMI). Each month, the National Association of Purchasing Management surveys roughly 400 manufacturing executives who buy raw materials and oversee inventories, querying them about production, hiring and new orders at their firms. From their responses, NAPM computes an index of industrial activity for that month, releasing it on the first business day of the following month.

Most pundits focus on whether the index falls above or below 50, the break-even point for the manufacturing sector. For gauging the direction of the overall economy, however, the key index level isn't 50, but 42.7. If the index comes in above that number, the economy continues to grow; anything below 42.7 means the economy is contracting.

In early 2001, the news from the PMI was hardly cheerful. The index dropped as low as 42.1 in May. That reading left little doubt that the manufacturing sector was in trouble and that the economy was slowing.

By the way, this index seems to carry some weight with the gang at the Fed. After the weaker than expected December PMI figure was released at 10 a.m. on January 2, 2001, the Nasdaq slumped 7.2%. By early afternoon of the next day, the Fed had made its surprise move to cut the federal funds rate by half a percentage point, citing, among other reasons, a further weakening in economic production. You can get details of the PMI index by clicking on the NAPM Report on Business banner at the NAPM website (www.napm.org).

- **Leading economic indicators.**
If you don't have the time or the inclination to track a variety of gauges, consider tracking a bunch of benchmarks rolled into one. That's where the index of leading economic indicators, released monthly by the Conference Board, comes in. Developed during the Depression to predict changes in growth roughly three months ahead, the index reflects 10 separate components, including the length of the workweek, building permits, interest rates, the money supply and stock prices. While putting the index together may take some major calculating power, following it doesn't. Basically, when the leading indicators are rising, that's a sign the economy will continue to chug along in the near future. When the indicators stagnate or fall, that's a signal that growth is slowing.

The indicators have done a good job over the years at anticipating slowdowns, but their record at predicting recessions is more mixed, leading some economists to dub the index "the mis-leading economic indicators." For example, the oft-invoked rule of thumb that three consecutive monthly declines in the indicators means we're headed for recession has generated at least one false signal during six of the past eight expansions. You can find the latest leading indicator figures at the Business Cycle Indicators section of the Conference Board website at www.tcb-indicators.org.

Of course, in the fast-changing world of markets and the economy, all outlooks are subject to revision. So unless that fore-casting eightball actually becomes a reality, we suggest you keep one eye on our indicators, and the other on the Fed.

Chapter 2
BUILDING A
SMART PORTFOLIO

There is an old Wall Street adage about the impact of market fluctuations on investors: "When the tide goes out, you can see who is swimming naked." The point: investing behavior that seemed perfectly acceptable (and rewarding) in boom times can leave you overexposed should the tide ever turn. The leverage or portfolio concentration that boosted your returns so heroically on the way up can hurt you badly—or even wipe you out—on the way down.

As millions of investors discovered in the 2000-2001 bear market, the market tide always turns eventually, even if the reversal is temporary. One of the keys to being a smart investor is not to learn how to predict these important turning points—we can't help you there, and neither can anyone else—but to assemble the type of portfolio that can weather the storms when they occur. This most recent bear market has hurt almost all investors, but it has been particularly brutal for those who had too much of their money in tech stocks, and it has been financially fatal for some tech-besotted investors who bought stock on margin. For investors with balanced portfolios, the downturn has been highly unpleasant—and sometimes scary—but it has been manageable because they were prepared.

Designing a portfolio that is right for your goals means creating one that suits your tolerance for risk. That's where intelligent diversification comes in, and we'll show you how it can help take you where you want to go. The wisest investors allocate their assets in a manner that allows them to stick with their investment plan—and not liquidate their holdings—no matter how grim present conditions appear.

That doesn't mean, though, that a *bad* investment plan should not be scuttled at the first sign of trouble. If reading this chapter's discussion of risk and diversification makes you feel that—oops—you've been swimming without a bathing suit, don't wait for the lifeguard's whistle. Make the appropriate changes today.

UNDERSTANDING RISK

Investors who may not have known a great deal about risk before March of 2000 certainly know a lot more about it today. Many investors who piled headlong into technology stocks suffered tremendous losses in the crash. Some speculative folk who discovered Internet stocks very late in the game when prices were sky-high saw their portfolios shrink by 90% or more. Like you, they might have had dreams of sending their children to college, buying a larger home and enjoying a comfortable retirement. What are they going to do now?

Granted, it's always possible to start fresh and attempt to rebuild a nest egg from scratch—but wouldn't it be far better to avoid having to face that particular problem? That's why we favor a strategy of *prudent* risk-taking.

In the previous chapter, you encountered a respected market-watcher who thinks stocks will decline an average of 2% a year for the next decade. If he's right, we'll all be better with money in bonds and certificates of deposit. But what if he's wrong?

Well, we won't know until the decade is over. And that's the way it always is, which explains why smart investors neither try to maximize returns (by owning a portfolio consisting exclusively of fast-growing tiny tech stocks) nor avoid temporary losses at all costs (by holding nothing but CDs).

In investing, the rational choice is to avoid extreme positions and to diversify among several asset classes, including stocks, bonds and cash or cash equivalents (i.e., certificates of deposit). If it turns out that the next 30 years are like the past 30, adding bonds to your portfolio would mean building less wealth than you would get by going 100% into stocks. If it turns out, however, that the future isn't as kind to stocks—maybe that -2% annual return forecast is a tad optimistic—then you could come out way behind by making an all-or-nothing bet.

Why diversification pays.   Of course, it's impossible to know in advance what mix will give you the best trade-off of risk and return. So the best you can do is limit risk by diversifying the assets in your portfolio.

The idea of diversification—which goes by the equally euphonious name *asset allocation*—has been around for centuries. Check out Act 1 of *The Merchant of Venice* and you'll find Antonio, the 16th-century version of a global trader, explaining that his "ventures are not in one bottom trusted, nor to one place." Our Elizabethan English is a bit rusty, but we think that translates into "I don't put all my eggs into one boat."

In the booming 90s, some investors came to believe that diversification was as outdated as Shakespeare's dialogue. And, forsooth, anyone who threw all his money into a Standard & Poor's 500-stock index fund 10 years ago did better than the prudent soul who spread his dough among large and small company stocks, foreign shares and bonds.

On the other hand, buying only Japanese stocks seemed foolproof back when the seemingly invincible Nikkei index peaked at 38,957 in 1989. By April 2001, the Nikkei was 65% below that lofty level and the once-mighty Japanese economy, which had so threatened the industrial world, was a wreck.

How then are we to cope in a world where hot sectors turn frigid overnight? Where emerging market funds lure billions of investor dollars with a 73% return in 1993 and then lose roughly 7% annually for the next five years? A world where the only certainty is uncertainty?

Well, you can turn to a Ouija board. Or you can try something a bit more practical. "A diversified portfolio will not give you a grand slam in any given year," says Roger Gibson, a Pittsburgh investment adviser and author of *Asset Allocation: Balancing Financial Risk*. But, he explains, it should help you avoid a shutout.

Now, diversification seems intuitively obvious to some—and a colossal waste of opportunity to others. Rather than rely on intuition, though, here's a more detailed explanation of how diversification works in investing—and the academic theories behind it:

Benefiting from the zigzag effect.   The key premise underlying diversification is that all assets do not move in lockstep with one another, or to put it another way, some zig as others zag. To quantify this zigzag effect, market pros use a statistic called the *coefficient of correlation*.

We'll spare you the formula, but the basic idea is this: If two investments move precisely in tandem, they have a correlation of 1; if they move precisely in the opposite directions, their correlation is -1. A correlation of zero means their movements are unrelated.

Most, but not all, of the assets individual investors own are positively correlated, although the extent to which they move together varies substantially. Over the past 10 years, for example, the Standard & Poor's 500-stock index (large companies) had a correlation of 0.79 with small U. S. firms. The returns don't move in lockstep, but they do follow each other somewhat—not surprising since both track the fortunes of the U.S. economy. The less that two investments react in the same way to the same forces, the lower their correlations. The S&P 500's correlation with foreign stocks is only 0.53 and even lower with real estate investment trusts (0.44) and intermediate-term government bonds (0.36).

When volatility can help.   As scintillating as math freaks might find such statistics, correlation lay dormant on the investing front until the early Fifties, when Harry Markowitz came to a remarkable counterintuitive insight: Adding volatile assets with low correlations to your portfolio could actually lower the volatility of your holdings overall. The riskiness of a portfolio is less than the sum of the riskiness of its parts because of that zigzag effect. Markowitz then went on to prove that you could get the biggest gain with the least pain by blending assets that have low correlations to one another so that some parts of your portfolio chug along while other parts stagnate or get clobbered. Markowitz's work eventually won him a share of the Nobel Prize in 1990.

Building a diverse portfolio: science vs. seat-of-the-pants.   As a practical matter, then, how should you create a diversified portfolio? We see two approaches: the *quantitative* method and the *seat-of-the-pants-strategy*. To go the quant route, you'll have to consult with a financial adviser with optimization software, who will create a portfolio based on such factors as your time horizon (the number of years before you expect to dip into your investments, and the length of time you'll be drawing on them), the level of volatility you're comfortable with and the size of the returns you would like to earn.

If you're already in or near retirement, you can try T. Rowe Price's Retirement Income Manager Program on the Web at www.troweprice.com. T. Rowe Price generates 500 simulations, or patterns of returns, based solely on historical performance. These simulations are then used to come up with combinations of assets with a high "success rate"—that is, portfolios that will provide a target level of income without running out of money during the investor's lifetime. (You can also check out the asset allocation advice on the websites on page 31.)

For the seat-of-the-pants approach, begin by setting a stocks/bonds mix appropriate for your time horizon. If you're investing for a goal that's less than three years away, you can pretty much forget stocks (and stock funds). Why? Because you might not have enough time to bounce back from short-term losses in the stock market. If you're looking at a three-to-five-year horizon, you might go 20% or so in stocks; 50% or so is reasonable for five to 10 years; and 70% or more makes sense for longer-term investing. You can vary these percentages depending on how much volatility you can stand. Even if you do nothing beyond a simple stocks/bond combo, you can get some of the risk-reducing benefits of diversification. For the 20 years through September 30, 1999, for example, a mix of 60% large-cap stocks and 40% intermediate-term bonds would have earned a 14% annual return, giving you 85% of an all-stock portfolio's gains while reducing volatility by 35%. (See "A Plan for Every Stage" on page 30 for more detailed asset allocation suggestions.)

Feel free to branch out into other asset classes, but don't act as if you're at an all-you-can-eat buffet and load up on everything from Finnish bonds to platinum futures. Simple is better. A portfolio that includes both large- and small-cap stocks, as well as bonds and foreign shares, should do just fine.

Whatever mix you choose, make sure that the blend you end up with passes the smell test. Are the investments themselves sensible? Are the proportions reasonable? Given their relatively low correlations, a combination of tech stocks and emerging markets funds (which invest in less develpoed markets around the world) might seem like a low-risk route to high returns—in theory. But do you really want your future riding on such a wacko combo? We wouldn't. After all, the reason for diversifying

Divvy It Up

These allocations are derived from the Fidelity website (www.401k.com). Like many one-size-fits-all models, they're conservative. Consider holding cash in another account, for instance, to make better use of your plan's tax deferral. To help you make allocation choices, decide which profile most nearly matches your own.

- **Aggressive growth**   For daring investors with plenty of time—say, 15 years or more—and the nerve to ride out dramatic dips. You aren't counting on borrowing from your plan to purchase a home, and you've got a stash of cash in an emergency fund. Extra small-cap and international exposure adds a kicker. There's no cash inside the 401(k) to hold the portfolio back—or to cushion a fall.

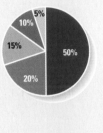

- **Growth**   You still have a way to go until retirement, and you are willing to take some risk. However, you don't want to go all out. Perhaps you've got a couple of kids and some debt besides your mortgage, so you'll want a buffer here. The big, broadly diversified stock stake has good growth potential. The 25% bond stake lends significant stability, so you could forgo that 5% dash of cash.

- **Balanced**   Maybe you are near or in retirement but are still gunning for growth to the extent you can reasonably do so. Or perhaps you are only in your late thirties but can afford to play it safer because you expect real estate income to help support you in retirement. Only half of the portfolio is in stocks, but a bit of smaller-cap and foreign exposure add flair. The bonds and cash provide a sober contrast.

- **Conservative**   Either you're terrified of taking on much risk (and you can set aside enough so that you don't have to), or you have saved enough to live off of now. There's still room for growth here, with 20% in stocks, because you'll be living a long and happy retirement. But volatile small-cap or international names aren't part of the plan. And 30% in cash is thick padding against rocky markets.

STOCKS ▮ Large-cap ▮ Mid- and small-cap ▮ International   BONDS ▮ Investment-grade ▮ High-yield   CASH ▮

in the first place is to lower risk, not create a new set of uncertainties that could turn your portfolio into a comedy of errors.

AVOID DIVERSIFICATION PITFALLS

Diversification sounds easier than it actually is. In a mutual-fund-picking contest, a famous financial planner once selected the Schwab 1000 fund, an index fund of the 1,000 largest U.S. stocks; Vanguard Index Value, an index fund that owns the cheapest stocks in the S&P 500; and Wilshire Target Large Company Growth, a third index fund that holds the fastest-growing members of the S&P 500.

These three funds are all stalwarts, but owning them together makes no sense—as the planner now readily concedes. That's because, at the time, 324 of the 364 stocks in the Vanguard fund and 214 of the 227 in the Wilshire fund were included in the Schwab 1000. There was a huge overlap, which was not what a normally intelligent investor would seek. But if a big-time expert can make a mistake like this, you know the rest of us can too. It's a good reminder that we all need new and better ways to think about diversifying our portfolios. That's especially urgent because diversification is just about the only tenet of modern finance that has proved to be unassailably true.

But fund investors tend to make two serious errors when they try to diversify. First, they forget that their funds need to complement all their investments. Second, they fail to check, when buying a new fund, how much it overlaps with those funds they already own. (For a tool that will help, check out the Portfolio X-Rays feature at Morningstar.com.

For diversification to work its magic, you need to consider all the sources of risk and return in your total portfolio. And your portfolio does not consist only of investments in funds, stocks, bonds and cash. If you're like most people, the single biggest investment in your portfolio is you. That's because your career is an asset—and your total labor income constitutes the return on that asset.

Let's say you work in Silicon Valley and a large portion of your earning power is dependent on the health of the technology industry. (In mid-2001, the industry wasn't looking very healthy and tens of thousands of technology workers were being laid off.) In a broad industry downturn, you might take a pay cut or lose your job. In addition, the value of your home might fall. That's just when you'd want your investments to be there for you—but if you were paid partly with options on your company's stock, and you allocated much of your 401(k) into company stock, and you even bought some technology mutual funds to boot, then your investments will be down at the same time you are.

Alas, many employees of technology companies had almost all their money invested in tech stocks when the market peaked in March 2000. Then, their portfolios imploded. One reason they were overinvested in tech was that they thought their knowledge of the industry would give them an investing edge. That seems logical, but it is a potentially dangerous way to behave. Suppose that you worked in the steel industry in 1989 and decided to bet the ranch on that sector. Well, Bethlehem Steel, once one of the largest companies in America, was $28.50 back then. Today it is $3.44. There have been no stock splits. Some rival steelmakers have fared even worse.

BUILDING A PORTFOLIO THAT NEVER GOES OUT OF FASHION

Different approaches to picking stocks—what analysts refer to as investing styles—go in and out of favor much like clothing, but with one important difference. While outdated items in a wardrobe such as Nehru jackets and white patent-leather go-go boots are usually relegated to the trash bin of history (or Goodwill boxes), out-of-favor investing styles regularly make a comeback.

In taking a look at the elements of style—investing style, that is—our aim isn't to make you a slave to whatever investing fashion happens to be dominating Wall Street. We want you to understand how different investing styles work so that you'll be able to build a portfolio that can thrive regardless of what's "in" at the moment.

Size matters.   When it comes to matters of style, stock analysts look at two key characteristics. The first is size—the total market value of a company's outstanding shares. The second major distinction is between growth stocks—those with rapidly expanding earnings—and value shares, unpopular issues that sell at depressed prices.

Let's tackle size first. Most mutual fund managers and other pros specialize in either large-company stocks, which have market values of about $10 billion or more, or small-company shares with market capitalizations of roughly $1.5 billion or less. (Yes, some managers focus on the stocks that fall between those extremes—midcaps—but when it comes to investing style, the most important division is between large and small.)

Both sizes act in distinctive ways and have advantages and drawbacks. Large-cap stocks are known for their financial strength and relative stability. Sure, their share prices fall when the market heads south, but they tend to hold up better than their runtier counterparts. No surprise. Large companies are more likely to have a broad range of products and services that can help them weather economic storms.

But buying the big bruisers also has its disadvantages. Large stocks are followed on a nanosecond-to-nanosecond basis by Wall Street analysts. That incessant scrutiny makes it difficult to unearth opportunities that can lead to market-beating gains. Pint-size firms, by contrast, are far less likely to attract a crowd, which gives you a greater chance of finding an undiscovered company that can generate extraordinary returns.

And little stocks can rack up big gains. From 1975 through 1980, small-fry shares went on a rampage, gaining an annualized 39.8%, more than double large companies' 17.5% annual returns. To get such gains, however, small-cap investors sometimes have to weather gut-wrenching downturns. During the market's four-month slide in the summer and fall of 1990, for example, small stocks plummeted 29.1%, almost twice as much as the big guys' 15% decline. One reason small-caps get whacked harder is that their profits dry up faster than those of large companies when economic growth peters out. But there's also a less obvious reason. "When people are nervous about the market, they gravitate toward large shares, which have more liq-uidity," says Ned Davis Research analyst Sam Burns. As investors unload small shares to buy big ones, small stocks take a hit.

Growth vs. value.   After making their cut on size, investing pros usually stake a claim in either the growth or the value camp. Those who go for growth like to find companies whose profits are increasing faster than earnings for the overall market, usually a 15%-or-higher annual pace. Chipmaker Intel, for example, was a favorite of growth investors in recent years because it had managed to increase earnings at a better than 26% annual rate. Growth stocks typically perform best late in an economic expan-sion, when investors are more willing to cough up premium prices for companies that can deliver earnings increases in the face of a slowing economy.

While buying stocks with accelerating profits may seem like a no-brainer path to outsize returns, this approach does have a downside. Seeing growth stocks' rosy profit projections, investors often bid up their share prices to inflated, even absurd, levels. (Cisco Systems at $82 in April 2000, for example.) That's why growth shares' price/earnings ratios (which measure how much investors are willing to pay for a dollar of a company's earnings) may be as much as two to three times higher than the P/E for the overall market. If these companies fall even a bit short of investors' lofty expectations, they can get hammered. For example, when Intel announced in September 2000 that its third-quarter revenues would increase at a slower rate than expected, investors began dumping the stock, pushing down its price by 20% within hours. (For a more detailed explanation of P/E and other stock val-uation measures, see the box on page 48.)

Value investors, on the other hand, are like people who sift through piles of kitsch at a flea market hoping to find misplaced antiques. They're looking for companies selling for less than the true value of their earning power or assets. In 2000, for example, Preston Athey, manager of the T. Rowe Price Small-Cap Value fund, owned shares of Culp Inc., a company that makes fabric for furniture and mattresses. Its appeal? "I'm getting a solid company with good management whose tangible assets are worth at least $7 a share." said Athey. "And I'm paying just over $3 a share."

In effect, value stocks are the exact opposite of growth stocks: They usually sell at below-market P/E ratios—which means investors have little respect for their profit potential—and below average price-to-book value ratios, a sign that investors don't put a very high value on their assets either. And unlike growth stocks, which tend to fare best late in an economic expansion, value stocks usually do better in the early stages of an economic recovery, when it's easier to rack up profits.

Since value stocks are already selling at relatively low prices, they tend to hold up better than growth stocks during market downturns, although that's not always the case. In the two-month sell-off triggered by the Asian financial crisis in the summer of 1998, mutual funds that focus on large value-oriented stocks lost 16.6% of their value, which is pretty darn close to the 17.2% drop in large-cap growth funds. One reason for value's relatively poor showing was that many of these funds were loaded up with beaten-down financial stocks whose shares managed to get beaten down even more as shocks from the Asian crisis reverberated through financial institutions worldwide.

My style's better than yours. So which size and style provides the best gains? Well, several academic studies suggest that over long periods the little guys outperform the behemoths and value beats growth. Lately, however, some market observers have questioned whether investors should expect one style to dominate long term.

Take small stocks. Statistics from Chicago investment research firm Ibbotson Associates show that over the 74-year period from 1926 through 1999, small shares gained 12.6% annually vs. 11.3% a year for large-company stocks. If you look behind those figures, however, it's unclear whether investors would have actually been able to achieve those small-stock gains. For one thing, many small stocks are so thinly traded that buying more than a couple hundred shares can push up their prices by 20% or more, raising the price of all but the first handful of shares. So those small stocks' outsize returns may be available to only a few investors.

Small stocks' lofty returns can also be eroded by their higher trading costs, which can be three or more times the cost of trading large stocks. In any case, if there is a small-stock advantage, it hasn't been enough to propel the Davids of the investment world over the Goliaths over the past two decades, as the chart on page 36 shows.

As a practical matter, it probably makes more sense to think of investing styles in terms of how they act over shorter time

Goliath Beats David

Conventional wisdom says that small stocks beat large ones over the long run. While that's certainly been true for some periods, over the past two decades the big bruisers have been the big winners.

Note: Small-stock returns are based on the Russell 2000 index; large-stock returns are based on the Russell 1000 index.

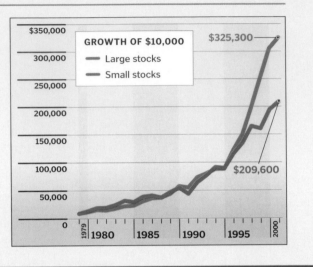

GROWTH OF $10,000
— Large stocks
— Small stocks

$325,300

$209,600

periods—and that's like a seesaw, with large stocks staying on top anywhere from three to six years and then switching positions with small stocks. (See the chart on the opposite page.) The same up-and-down pattern applies to value vs. growth. In the five years through August 31, 2000, the action was mostly been in large stocks (which gained an annualized 22.4% vs. 13.5% for small shares) and growth shares (which returned 27.3% vs. 17.6% for value). In the ensuing nine months, however, the trend reversed, with small stocks beating large ones (-7.7% to -18.4%) and value trouncing growth (4.8% to -36.9%).

This ebb and flow of styles is partly due to the ways that different styles respond to underlying economic forces. But it may also have a lot to do with human nature. We see growth shares, say, starting to move upward, and we all scramble aboard the growth bandwagon until prices have been bid up so high it's virtually impossible for these companies to meet our unrealistic expectations. When they inevitably disappoint, the herd moves to value—and the process starts again.

Staying in styles. This recurring seesaw pattern may seem like an invitation to jump back and forth between styles, catching each on the upswing. Ah, but the trends that look so clear-cut in charts of past performance aren't so easy to project into the future. "I can say with 100% confidence that one style will out-

The Style Seesaw

Although growth stocks have outgained value shares recently, the two styles actually behave like a seesaw, with value out-performing growth for several years and then growth taking the lead.

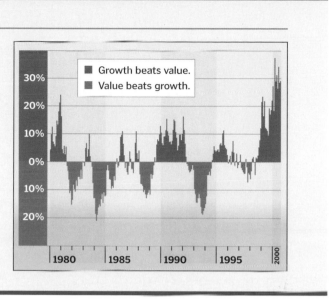

Notes: The chart shows percentage difference in returns between the Russell 3000 growth and the Russell 3000 value indexes over rolling 12-month periods.

perform over some period of time," says Brad Lawson of Frank Russell Co., a firm that creates indexes of stocks based on their style. "But I have very little confidence that I or anyone else can determine in advance when those periods will be."

So rather than shifting your money around, Lawson recommends having all styles represented in your portfolio. We wholeheartedly agree and would add that you should hold them in approximately the same proportion as their market values. That would mean putting about 10% to 15% of your stock portfolio in small-cap stocks and 85% to 90% in mid- and large-caps, and then dividing those stakes roughly equally between growth and value.

This spread-it-around strategy will smooth out the ups and downs in your portfolio's value as gains in the leading style offset losses or sluggish performance in the style that's lagging. And it will ensure that you always have some money in whatever style is in style—unless leisure suits make a comeback, in which case all bets are off.

KEEPING YOUR PORTFOLIO ON TRACK

Once you've determined how your assets should be allocated, how often should you analyze your investment performance? Some people track their investment results every day, while others follow the ups and downs of their stocks on an hourly basis. That's far too often for the average individual investor.

But checking in only every five years or so doesn't cut it either, in our opinion. We think the typical investor should reassess his holdings every year, and usually at the same time each year so the ritual becomes a habit. Below we'll discuss the essential aspects of that annual check-up. (Of course, if a segment of your portfolio is crashing, or soaring, you don't have to wait a year to take action.)

Analyze performance.   Sometimes, despite our incredibly diligent research efforts, a stock or fund we bought with high hopes of spectacular performance doesn't quite measure up—or maybe even flops outright. Nothing to be ashamed of there. Even the mighty Warren Buffett doesn't bat a thousand. So it's important to scrutinize each of your investments to assess its performance for the past year and over the longer term.

Don't concern yourself so much with an investment's percentage gain or loss. What really matters is how your holdings have performed relative to their peers or an appropriate benchmark. If you own shares of a drug company such as Merck, for example, you want to go to a website such as Market Guide (www.marketguide.com) and compare its performance with that of other pharmaceutical firms. In the case of a mutual fund, see how your fund stacks up against others that buy similar stocks. You can do that by getting a free "Quicktake Report" on your fund at the website run by Chicago fund research firm Morningstar (www.morningstar.com). To get an idea of how misleading raw performance numbers alone can be, let's take a look at two funds: Artisan Small Cap and Gabelli Westwood Equity Retirement. At first glance, Artisan would seem to have been the better performer, gaining 20.8% over the 12 months through September 30, 2000, vs. 16.7% for Gabelli Westwood. But if you looked at the Morningstar Quicktake Reports for both funds during that period, a different picture would have emerged. Though impressive at first glance, Artisan's 20.8% return ranked in the bottom 15% of small-cap growth funds. So 85% of small-cap growth funds earned a higher return over that 12-month period. The report also showed that over the previous five years, the fund underperformed 90% of all small-cap growth funds. By contrast, Gabelli Westwood's 16.7% return put it in the top 10% of its peers—that is, funds that invest in large value stocks. And over the past five years, Gabelli Westwood ranked in the top 10% of funds in its category.

We're not suggesting that you automatically dump an investment because it's lagged its peers. But if we owned a fund that seriously trailed its peers for one year and hadn't shown signs of a turnaround within another year or so, we'd be inclined to dump it. With stocks, things can change much more quickly, so if a company hadn't shown signs of improving its performance within a year, definitely consider giving it the boot.

It's also a good idea to see what kind of return you've earned on your entire portfolio over the past year. If you haven't added or withdrawn any money during the past year, calculating your percentage gain for the year is simple: Divide the value of your portfolio at the end of the year by its value at the beginning of the year, subtract one and multiply the result by 100. More likely, though, you've invested money or pulled some out. That complicates the calculation, since different amounts of money have been invested for different periods of time.

Not to worry. Just go to the Rate of Return calculator in the Tools section of money.com (www.money.com), plug in the beginning and ending values of your portfolios, plus the amounts of additions and withdrawals and their dates, and voila! Up pops your portfolio's return for the year. Performing this exercise each year can tell you whether you're on track toward goals such as building a decent retirement nest egg or whether you need to adjust your saving and/or investing strategy.

Trim your tax bill.　If you find that a few of your stocks or funds have dropped significantly in value, you may be able to get the Internal Revenue Service to share some of your pain. How? Simple. Sell one or more of the losers in your portfolio and use the realized loss to reduce the taxes on gains you've taken in other investments. (See Chapter 10 for a variety of tax strategies that show you how to do this most efficiently.)

Reassess your plan.　If you try to go about your investing in a systematic way—and since you're reading this book we assume that's the case—then you've got a "grand plan" or overall strategy that helps determine everything from your choice of investments to your asset allocation, the proportion in which you hold those investments. But economic situations and financial goals can change—and if they do, your plan might need overhauling too.

Out of Whack

The pie charts below show how big gains in one asset—in this case stocks—can throw your portfolio's asset allocation way out of kilter. To avoid such swings, rebalance your holdings each year.

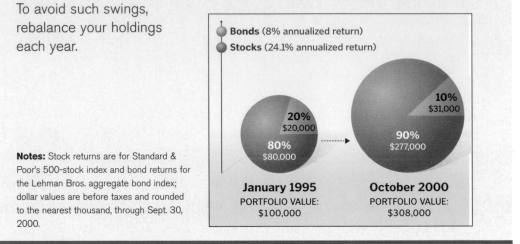

Bonds (8% annualized return)

Stocks (24.1% annualized return)

20%
$20,000

80%
$80,000

10%
$31,000

90%
$277,000

January 1995
PORTFOLIO VALUE:
$100,000

October 2000
PORTFOLIO VALUE:
$308,000

Notes: Stock returns are for Standard & Poor's 500-stock index and bond returns for the Lehman Bros. aggregate bond index; dollar values are before taxes and rounded to the nearest thousand, through Sept. 30, 2000.

For example, investing 80% of Junior's college fund in stocks and 20% in bonds made perfect sense when she was a toddler. But now that Junior is a junior and looking forward to starting college in two years, you'll want to cut that stock stake way back. Otherwise, a severe setback in the market could zap the value of her college fund, possibly forcing your prodigy to transfer from Princeton to Podunk U.

Similarly, if a growing salary has pushed you into a higher tax bracket, you'll probably want to rethink what types of stocks and bonds you buy. In the case of bonds, high-tax-bracket investors typically get higher after-tax returns from tax-exempt municipal bonds than from taxable Treasuries or corporates. As for stocks, you may want to consider growth stocks and tax-efficient stock funds, both of which minimize taxable distributions.

Rebalance your portfolio. Since stocks have beaten bonds by a margin of more than three to one in recent years, your portfolio may be more heavily weighted toward stocks than you think. As the chart above shows, if you had invested 80% of your money in stocks and 20% in bonds in 1995 and let your gains ride, by October of 2000 your portfolio would have morphed into a volatile mix of 90% stocks and 10% bonds.

In addition to ensuring that your allocations stay on target, annual rebalancing dramatically cuts your risk and, over the long term, may add another half a percent a year to your return. Why? Because when you rebalance, you are typically selling your better performers and buying your out-of-favor laggards. While that may be difficult psychologically, it's a key tenet of investment success: You are selling high and buying low. Bingham Osborn & Scarborough compared results for two portfolios, each worth $100,000 as of January 1, 1998, and all allocated identically: 25% stashed in Vanguard Total Bond Market index, 25% in Janus Fund, 25% in Dodge & Cox Stock and 25% in Artisan International. New contributions—$10,000 a year to each account—followed the same allocation. As of March 31, 2001, portfolio No. 1, which was rebalanced at the end of each year, would have been worth $189,760; portfolio No. 2, which was not rebalanced, would have been worth $183,884.

So to keep your portfolio on track, you should rebalance your holdings every year, bringing them back to their proper proportions. That's a simple task with a 401(k) or other tax-deferred account. Just sell some assets that have grown in value and invest in laggards. But do you move your money all at once or do you make gradual adjustments? Most participants make changes by directing new money into their desired allocations, but this method takes too long.

• **Tax-deferred accounts:** Advisers recommend moving existing retirement assets to make an immediate change. Of course, that's difficult for die-hard tech investors, who may fear that they'll be selling at the bottom of the market. But the fact is, they are not likely to make all their money back. Consider the math: A tech fund that's down 50% will have to double in value to get back to square one. And that doesn't reflect the cost of missing out on other, more profitable investments. A compromise strategy, suggests financial adviser David Bugen of Chatham, N.J., is to move a portion of your money every month for six months until your allocations are in line. That way, if the tech sector recovers, you'll still capture some gains.

• **Taxable accounts:** You must be more careful about rebalancing taxable portfolios since selling may trigger taxes. If your allocations aren't too far out of whack, bring them back in line by directing the new money you invest into the areas of your portfolio that have lagged. If this process would take a year or longer, more drastic action is needed.

First, see how close to your intended mix you can get by redirecting the proceeds from any sales you've made to rid your portfolio of underperformers. For example, if your portfolio is light on value stocks, plow the sale proceeds of any growth stocks you've unloaded into value shares. If that's not an option, then sell some winners and put the gains into lagging asset classes. Yes, you may owe taxes, but you can minimize the bite by, say, selling shares with the highest cost (to reduce your gain) or by unloading shares that you've held more than a year so you qualify for the lower capital-gains tax rates.

Chapter 3
HOW TO MAKE
STOCKS PAY OFF

O ne of the essentials of smart investing is to have appropriate expectations. If you expect the stock market to reward you with returns of 20% per year for the next several decades, you will either be very disappointed or you will take big risks to meet that very optimistic target.

But no matter how aggressive you may feel, it's never wise to equate stock investing with playing the lottery. Yes, putting a good chunk of money into Microsoft, Cisco, EMC or even Qualcomm at the right time could have landed you on Easy Street. As indeed it did, for some investors. But many people lost fortunes or even went bankrupt because, instead of buying the right companies early, they put large sums into the wrong companies too late. The upshot: High-risk investing strategies can be rewarding, but when they don't pay off, watch out.

So how well can you realistically hope to do as a stock picker? We think individual investors can match the historic return of the S&P 500 (of almost 12% annually) by putting together a diversified portfolio built around a large core of blue-chip growth stocks. Those are the shares of companies with sales and market capitalization of at least $5 billion, strong balance sheets and projected earnings and dividend growth that will support a total return averaging at least 12% a year. (See the table beginning on page 45 for a list of 100 such stocks—the Sivy 100— developed by

MONEY's Wall Street guru Michael Sivy.) There's nothing shabby about 12% annual returns. If that's what you average, you'll double your money every six years—and multiply it 16-fold over the next 25 years.

These 100 household names do not constitute a buy list. Instead, the Sivy 100 is a list of good companies that may—at a certain point in time—be selling at attractive prices. Michael Sivy's columns at www.money.com flag stocks like these when they look undervalued. But you can also do this on your own, as we'll describe in detail.

As you know, for every stock that delivers turbocharged returns like some of the highfliers on the Sivy 100, there are hundreds or thousands that simply dry up and blow away. So rather than risk plowing all your money into the next high-tech train wreck, you may want to use growth stocks to anchor your portfolio and then look around for other equities—like value or income stocks—that have different performance profiles to balance your holdings. The first part of this chapter provides advice and insights from Michael Sivy to help you master the fundamentals of selecting growth, value and income stocks. Growth and value stocks were discussed in Chapter 2, but here we'll show you how to select good examples from each camp. And don't neglect income stocks, which can offer respectable growth and solid overall returns to people of any age. We also encourage you to check out the glossary of investment terms and valuation measures on page 48. Knowing the lingo and how to use these measures to evaluate equities will improve your stock-picking skills.

GROWTH STOCKS

Stock prices follow earnings. In fact, over a long stretch of time, rising corporate profits are the only force that can keep share prices moving higher. Investors may pay up for the earnings of a popular company, which boosts the price/earnings ratio. But while rising P/Es can lift stocks for a few years, there's a limit to how high they can go.

That's why growth investing, or seeking out companies with above-average earnings growth, should be a key component of your investment strategy. It's also the simplest approach to the stock market. Here's why: Historically the S&P 500 has returned around 12% a year. So by picking a company with earnings growing faster

Sivy's 100 Stocks for Long-Term Investors

Investing in companies that are growing faster than the market average is the simplest and safest way to reach your financial goals. These 100 big, financially solid stocks all offer double-digit annual returns, based on projected earnings growth and dividends. Even without P/E increases, these stocks should match or outpace the S&P 500, which has returned an average of about 12% annually over the past 75 years. You increase your odds of beating the market if you can pick up these stocks when they're unusually cheap. Stocks with a PEG ratio (price/earnings ratio divided by expected earnings growth rate) of 1.5 or less are often the best buys, while those with PEG ratios of two or more may be overpriced. Of course, it's also important to see where a stock has traded over the past year and to compare its P/E with its multiples in the past. For more updated statistics on the Sivy 100, including yearly trading ranges, go to www.money.com/sivy.

STOCK	PRICE	P/E RATIO	PROJECTED EARNINGS GROWTH RATE	PEG RATIO
Abbott Laboratories (ABT)	$50.63	27	12.5%	2.1
Aetna (AET)	26.01	N.A.	12.3	N.A.
AFLAC (AFL)	32.91	24	15.6	1.6
Air Products & Chemicals (APD)	46.50	19	10.5	1.8
Albertson's (ABS)	29.13	16	11.7	1.3
Alcoa (AA)	39.28	19	13.4	1.4
American Home Products (AHP)	60.84	28	14.3	1.9
American Express (AXP)	39.78	19	13.5	1.4
American Intl. Group (AIG)	80.75	28	14.1	2.0
Anheuser-Busch (BUD)	42.30	22	10.4	2.1
Applied Materials (AMAT)	51.15	46	24.0	1.9
AT&T (T)	20.52	103	8.5	12.1
Automatic Data Processing (ADP)	51.52	34	15.7	2.1
Bank of America (BAC)	57.68	12	9.4	1.3
Baxter International (BAX)	49.80	28	13.9	2.0
Bellsouth (BLS)	39.42	17	10.5	1.6
Best Buy (BBY)	58.29	27	20.9	1.3
Boeing (BA)	63.56	17	17.0	1.0
Bristol-Myers Squibb (BMY)	56.28	23	12.8	1.8
Burlington Northern (BNI)	28.69	12	8.8	1.3
Cisco Systems (CSCO)	17.95	44	25.5	1.7
Citigroup (C)	48.60	16	13.9	1.1
Coca-Cola (KO)	45.02	28	12.4	2.3

(continued)

STOCK	PRICE	P/E RATIO	PROJECTED EARNINGS GROWTH RATE	PEG RATIO
Colgate-Palmolive (CL)	$57.70	30	12.8%	2.4
Comcast (CMCSK)	40.85	N.A.	14.1	N.A.
Compaq Computer (CPQ)	14.45	27	14.3	1.9
Conagra Foods (CAG)	20.55	14	9.5	1.5
Corning (GLW)	15.97	18	23.1	0.8
Costco Wholesale (COST)	40.39	32	14.3	2.2
Deere & Co. (DE)	38.72	27	11.8	2.3
Dell Computer (DELL)	25.50	35	19.8	1.8
Delta Air Lines (DAL)	42.76	43	11.2	3.8
Disney (Walt) (DIS)	29.87	36	14.1	2.6
Dow Chemical (DOW)	34.35	30	9.7	3.1
Duke Energy (DUK)	39.53	16	11.8	1.3
Electronic Data Systems (EDS)	59.39	22	15.0	1.5
Emerson Electric (EMR)	65.05	19	12.5	1.5
Enron (ENE)	47.91	27	16.9	1.6
ExxonMobil (XOM)	88.84	18	8.9	2.0
Federated Dept. Stores (FD)	41.21	10	12.1	0.8
FedEx (FDX)	37.42	17	12.2	1.4
Gannett (GCI)	61.64	17	11.4	1.5
Gap (The) (GPS)	30.76	30	18.0	1.7
Gateway (GTW)	15.84	51	15.8	3.2
General Electric (GE)	48.85	33	16.2	2.1
Gillette (G)	28.28	28	10.0	2.8
Halliburton (HAL)	43.40	34	22.5	1.5
Heinz (H.J.) (HNZ)	42.30	17	8.3	2.0
Hershey Foods (HSY)	59.99	22	9.4	2.3
Hewlett-Packard (HWP)	26.78	25	12.7	2.0
Home Depot (HD)	49.52	40	20.8	1.9
Illinois Tool Works (ITW)	65.62	22	13.9	1.6
Intl. Business Machines (IBM)	115.50	24	13.2	1.8
Intel (INTC)	27.95	51	18.3	2.8
Johnson & Johnson (JNJ)	51.02	26	13.1	1.0
JP Morgan Chase (JPM)	43.44	14	12.2	1.1
Kimberly-Clark (KMB)	58.85	17	11.4	1.5
Lilly (Eli) (LLY)	83.07	29	12.0	2.5
Limited (The) (LTD)	15.56	17	14.3	1.2
Lowe's Companies (LOW)	72.93	30	20.6	1.4
Lucent Technologies (LU)	6.69	N.A.	16.1	N.A.
MBNA (KRB)	34.13	18	20.4	0.9
McDonald's (MCD)	29.97	20	11.5	1.7

STOCK	PRICE	P/E RATIO	PROJECTED EARNINGS GROWTH RATE	PEG RATIO
Merck (MRK)	$73.90	23	11.9%	1.9
Merrill Lynch (MER)	60.85	17	15.0	1.1
Microsoft (MSFT)	68.91	38	16.9	2.3
Minnesota Mining (MMM)	120.44	25	11.7	2.1
Motorola (MOT)	13.80	N.A.	16.9	N.A.
Newell Rubbermaid (NWL)	25.89	17	12.6	1.4
Nike 'B' (NKE)	41.44	19	14.2	1.4
Nortel Networks (NT)	10.70	N.A.	25.2	N.A.
Oracle (ORCL)	14.87	35	22.6	1.5
Pfizer (PFE)	43.19	33	20.7	1.6
Philip Morris (MO)	47.04	12	13.2	0.9
Procter & Gamble (PG)	64.78	21	10.8	1.9
Raytheon (RTN)	29.64	18	10.9	1.7
Safeway (SWY)	49.99	19	16.0	1.2
Sara Lee (SLE)	19.40	14	8.4	1.7
SBC Communications (SBC)	41.55	18	12.0	1.5
Schering-Plough (SGP)	40.55	25	13.1	1.9
Schlumberger (SLB)	57.01	30	25.1	1.2
Schwab (Charles) (SCH)	16.15	36	20.2	1.8
Southern Company (SO)	22.49	13	5.7	2.3
Sprint (FON)	19.96	18	9.1	1.9
Staples (SPLS)	14.26	21	19.9	1.1
Sun Microsystems (SUNW)	15.72	37	21.1	1.7
Sysco (SYY)	28.61	33	13.4	2.4
Target (TGT)	36.60	24	15.0	1.6
Texaco (TX)	71.66	15	9.3	1.6
Textron (TXT)	57.33	13	13.6	0.9
Tyco International (TYC)	55.53	20	20.9	1.0
United Technologies (UTX)	76.99	19	14.2	1.3
UnitedHealth Group (UNH)	58.04	22	17.3	1.3
Verizon Communications (VZ)	53.51	17	10.5	1.6
Viacom 'B' (VIA.B)	53.94	207	18.2	11.4
Wal-Mart Stores (WMT)	49.51	32	14.4	2.2
Walgreen (WAG)	41.01	47	17.8	2.6
Washington Mutual (WM)	36.46	12	12.5	0.9
Wells Fargo (WFC)	43.74	16	12.8	1.2
WorldCom (WCOM)	16.12	14	16.7	0.8

Notes: P/E based on estimates for next fiscal year. Projected earnings growth based on average annual estimates for the next 5 years. Data as of June 12, 2001.
N.A.: Not available.

Stock Valuation Measures

Here are some of the key fundamental tools to measure the health of your stocks. You can find measures like these at virtually any online investing site, including MSN MoneyCentral (www.moneycentral.com) and Yahoo! Finance (finance.yahoo.com). Use these tools to evaluate a company that you hear described as a good investment. Taken together with the latest news on a company, measures like these can give a rough idea of whether a stock is cheap, fairly priced or overpriced compared to others in its class.

Price/earnings ratio (P/E): Current stock price divided by annual earnings per share, usually using projected earnings for the next 12 months (forward P/E) but sometimes for the preceding 12 months (trailing P/E) as well. Growth stocks trade at relatively high P/E ratios because investors are willing to pay more for the prospect of higher earnings. Value stocks trade at relatively low P/E ratios because they are seen to have problems that lower their earnings potential. A value investor bets that whatever ails these companies will end, and that—given enough time—the stock price will rise to reflect the company's true value.

Debt-to-equity ratio: A company's debt divided by shareholder's equity (or the value of its assets after all liabilities have been subtracted out). This ratio is often used as a measure of a company's health; the higher it is, the more vulnerable a company's earnings may be to industry changes and swings in the economy.

Price-to-book value ratio: A stock's price divided by its so-called book value, expressed on a per-share basis. The book value is calculated by adding up the worth of everything the company owns and then subtracting its debt and other liabilities. As with all ratios, this one is most useful when looked at in the context of a particular industry and a company's own history.

than that—usually at a 15%-or-higher annual pace—the stock will eventually outpace the market, provided its earnings come through as expected and the stock was fairly priced when you bought it.

What's a fair price for a growth stock?   P/E ratios and price/cash-flow ratios are the most common measures of how expensive a stock is. A lot of factors influence P/Es, including interest rates, the company's track record and the industry it's in. But one reliable tool is to compare a company's P/E to its project-

Price-to-sales ratio: Determined by dividing current stock price by revenue per share, this measure is often used to evaluate companies in rapidly growing industries with low earnings. (Revenue per share is determined by dividing revenue for the past 12 months by the number of shares outstanding.)

PEG and PEGY ratio: The PEG, or price/earnings/growth, ratio is calculated by taking the P/E ratio based on forward earnings and dividing by the projected growth rate. Stocks with a PEG ratio of less than one (meaning that they are trading at less than their projected growth rate) are generally said to be cheap, while a PEG ratio of 1.6 or higher indicates a stock that may be overpriced. For stocks that pay a substantial dividend, the PEGY ratio—which is the P/E divided by the growth rate plus the dividend yield—may be an even better measure than PEG alone.

Profit margins: Earnings (net income) divided by revenues. Good margins for a software company might be 25%, while 2% is considered fabulous for a grocery chain. So when gauging a company's profit margin, be sure to compare it with that of other companies in the same industry.

Return on equity (ROE): Net income divided by shareholder's equity, or, literally, how much a company is earning on its money. This ratio can be used to show how a company's earnings measure up to those of the competition, as well as how they compare with past performance. A rising ROE is a good sign.

Market capitalization: This is the current stock market value of a company, which is calculated as the share price multiplied by the number of shares outstanding. *Large-cap company* (generally more than $10 billion in market cap); *midcap* ($1.5 billion to $10 billion): *small-cap* (less than $1.5 billion).

Yield: The percentage rate of return paid on a stock in the form of annual dividends or the effective rate of interest paid on a bond or note.

ed earnings growth. Ideally, you don't want to buy at a P/E that's much more than the growth rate, and in a normal stock market, there are plenty of such bargains. But over the past five years, they have become harder and harder to find.

Today, most high-quality companies with double-digit earnings growth have P/Es that are at least 1.5 times their growth rate. For example, shares of a company with 14% earnings growth would trade at a P/E of 21 or higher. If you're interested in the most popular growth stocks, you may have to grit your teeth and pay even more—P/Es that are double the growth rates, for instance. But you have to draw the line somewhere. Our advice: Hold off on buying stocks that are trading at P/Es more than 2.5 times twice their growth rates, no matter how good the companies are. As we pointed out earlier, when a company with a P/E that high stumbles, its shares drop like a rock.

Some of your best bargains will be found at the opposite end of the spectrum, with companies that have earnings growth around 12%. With those stocks you may want to add in the dividend yield to get a *total return* (based on earnings growth and the dividend yield) estimate. For instance, a stock with 11% growth and a 3% yield might really be able to return a total of 14%. Getting a stock like that for a P/E below 20 could be a great deal.

For some stocks—particularly industrial companies—cash flow provides another reliable benchmark for value. You can find the amount of cash a company generates each year listed on the Web or in brokerage reports (some firms also report a similar measure, EBITDA, which is *earnings before interest, taxes, depreciation and amortization*). When a stock is selling at less than 10 times cash flow per share, it may well be a compelling value.

Whichever spot on the growth spectrum you favor, remember that the key to long-term profits is consistency. Companies with above-average growth that you can buy and hold indefinitely are the most valuable additions to your portfolio. Since commissions and other fees—not to mention taxes—are a significant drag on returns for individual investors, the less often you buy and sell, the less you have to think about expenses. In addition, if you don't trade much, you won't have to worry about mistakes in your timing.

It's also important for investors (those with horizons of ten years or more who are willing to assume a reasonable amount of risk) to create a portfolio with some balance. If you like individual stocks, we recommend that you keep 35% to 50% of your money in blue-chip growth stocks, such as those in the Sivy 100.

Seven questions to ask before buying a growth stock.   In theory, no company should be able to show earnings increases that are way above average for very long. Whenever a market offers opportunities that can lead to rapid growth, those high profits attract more and more competitors. As these firms try to undercut each other, profit margins—and growth rates—deteriorate.

Nonetheless, companies from Pfizer to Home Depot to Wal-Mart manage to remain stars for years. They can do this in one of two ways—either by maintaining a leading position in a fast-growing industry or by gaining market share and operating more efficiently in an average industry. In either case, the companies need some sort of competitive advantage—proprietary technology, patents or even an innovative management system—that's hard to duplicate.

Since growing companies go after the most profitable markets first and eventually face tough competition, even the most dynamic businesses slow down sooner or later. So here are Michael Sivy's seven questions to help determine if a stock still has plenty of growth ahead of it.

1. Does the company have a unique product or service? Growth companies have to earn above-average profits. To do that for any length of time, a company must offer an innovative product or service that isn't readily available elsewhere. For example, The Gap's stock soared in the late 1990s, but began slipping in 1999 because there were no barriers to prevent other companies from successfully copying the retailer's casual apparel style.

2. Does the firm have recurring revenues? Truly sustainable earnings growth comes from steadily rising revenues, not from cost cutting, financial restructuring or lower taxes. Microsoft, for instance, has long been able to sell revised versions of its operating system every few years.

3. Is the company early in its growth curve? Since nearly all growth stocks eventually plateau, make sure you're getting in early. Be careful if everyone is familiar with the company, knows about its success and assumes it will grow forever. Dell attracted an almost fanatical following of investors who believed that the company's direct-selling strategy would make it a great stock forever. In 2000 and 2001, however, sales growth slowed, profit margins contracted and the stock got creamed.

4. Is the company at the forefront of its industry? Even when an industry is booming, there's no guarantee that all companies in it will continue to prosper. Take IBM, which for decades led many major technological advances and was the must-own tech stock. But by the mid-1980s, the company fell behind in cutting-edge technology. IBM relied far too heavily on old-line mainframe computers and failed to adapt successfully to the PC era—and its stock began a decade-long slide. (Since the mid-1990s, however, the company has made a terrific comeback under the leadership of Lou Gerstner.)

5. Is the return on equity higher than 15%? Some companies are able to show high earnings growth only because they borrow to finance expansion. But eventually, they can't afford to borrow any more. Sustainable growth is best funded with the earnings that a company retains after it pays dividends. Those retained earnings are added to shareholders' equity—and it's the profits earned on such additional equity that provide most of a company's long-term earnings growth. These potential profits can be gauged with a measure known as return on equity, or ROE. As a rule, a company needs an ROE above 15% to sustain a growth rate above 12%.

6. Is the company's debt low—or at least stable? The best growth companies have little or no debt. Those with debt less than 20% of long-term capital (equity plus long-term debt) shouldn't have any trouble financing their growth.

7. Do you believe the share price can double in five years? A stock that meets all these tests should be able to double in price over five years. Stocks with earnings growth of 15% or more can reach that target if their P/Es stay constant and earnings come through as expected. Stocks with slower growth will need some increase in their P/Es, while stocks with much faster growth can afford to have their P/Es erode a bit. Whichever type of stock you favor, make sure that the growth and P/E numbers you're counting on aren't wildly out of line, based on the company's industry and its own history.

VALUE STOCKS

All investors search for stocks that they think are good values— after all, no one wants to overpay. But when stock pickers talk about value investing they mean something more specific. These bargain hunters are looking for stocks that are so cheap their share prices can rise substantially if investors start viewing them more positively. That upward revaluation can occur because of favorable changes in a company's prospects, or even just because of a change in investor sentiment.

You generally can divide value stocks into two categories— turnarounds and stocks with below-average P/Es. The former are companies suffering from depressed earnings because of business problems. If the companies have strong franchises and healthy balance sheets, they will be able to weather bad times, and earnings should eventually come back. But to invest successfully in turnarounds, you need to understand the specific nature of those problems—whether, for example, they are unique to the company, or the result of external circumstances. And you need to decide whether management's plan for turning around the company is credible.

A good example is Toys "R" Us, which was languishing at $9.75 in January 2000. It was languishing for good reason. It had infuriated customers by failing to promptly deliver holiday gifts that were ordered online. Furthermore, its stores looked dreary and its employees were renowned for their lack of competence. No wonder the toy giant was losing market share to Wal-Mart.

To get back into the game, Toys "R" Us brought in John Eyler as CEO, an industry veteran who earned high marks when he ran FAO Schwarz. Eyler renovated stores, motivated employees and got the retailer moving in the right direction. In May of 2001, Toys "R" Us shares hit $31.

Profiting from low-P/E stocks is easier because there are benchmarks to guide you. Today, for example, the average P/E for all publicly traded companies is around 16 and that for the S&P 500 is 23. So any stock with a P/E below 20 could possibly qualify as undervalued.

One low P/E stock that bears watching today is Bear Stearns, an investment bank that in June 2001 traded for just nine times its estimated earnings for the year. The company is highly liquid with little debt. By every pricing measurement—P/E ratio, price/sales, price/book—it's far cheaper than its peers. And it is one of the last remaining independents in a consolidating industry.

But stocks can trudge along with low P/Es for long stretches of time, so it's best to look for a company that also has moderate earnings growth. It's a combination sometimes called GARP (*growth at a reasonable price*). GARP stocks should have most of the same characteristics as growth stocks, including a strong balance sheet and a record of steady earnings growth (probably in the 9% to 13% range).

The simplest way to tell when GARP stocks are cheap is to compare their P/Es to their earnings growth rates (that's called the PEG ratio, or P/E to growth). In this market, stocks with P/Es lower than their growth rates are very cheap. It's also helpful to add a stock's dividend to its earnings growth rate to get a gauge of potential total return and use that number to figure the PEG ratio (it's called the PEGY ratio when dividends are included). In 2000, the projected future earnings growth for auto-parts maker and defense supplier TRW, for instance, was 9% to 10% with a dividend yield of 3.1%. That 12% to 13% potential total return is quite attractive, considering that the P/E is less than 10.

Few depressed stocks stay down forever. And once a value stock rises, you have to decide whether to continue holding it. Since there won't be much room for further P/E increases, the stock is only worth hanging on to if it offers a total return of at least 14%—or slightly above the market's long-term historical average. Otherwise, it's smarter to cash out and use your profits to buy another unappreciated gem.

INCOME STOCKS

"Show me the money" is the cry of conservative income investors who want a steady stream of cash from their investments and count on the dividends to buoy the stock's price if the market takes a spill. These investors don't want to bet on future explosive earnings growth or higher valuations. Instead, they want safe, reliable cash payouts that rise faster than inflation. Two good examples of relatively high-dividend income stocks: utilities and real estate investment trusts (REITs).

Today, though, most investors don't give dividends a second look. After all, many of the great stocks of our time, like Dell and Microsoft, don't even pay dividends. And between 1990 and 1999, the aggregate dividend yield on the Standard & Poor's 500-stock index fell from 3.7% a year to as low as 1.1%. Why? The simplest explanation is that companies just didn't have to offer dividends to get investors to buy their stock. What's an extra 1.1% when the market is posting double-digit gains year after year?

However, in a less euphoric market, dividends take on a more important role. And that makes a lot of sense. Indeed, nearly half of the market's 11.4% average annual gain between 1926 and 1999 came from reinvested dividends.

Selecting stocks for income. We all want a stock that will double overnight. But there's something to be said for including income investments in any portfolio. And remember, shares of companies that pay dividends have an important advantage over many of the other income alternatives: Bond payouts don't increase over time, but dividends do rise for most income stocks.

Historically, blue-chip stock yields have averaged around 4%. And most of the time they've ranged between 2.8% and 5.4%, with a few exceptional periods. We were in one of those periods during the second quarter of 2001, with the yield on the S&P 500 not much above 1%. Nonetheless, even in that market it was possible to find stocks with yields of 3% or more.

You shouldn't focus only on yield, however, and ignore everything else. The dividend growth rate is equally important. A stock raising its dividend 6% a year will double its payout over 12 years and quadruple over 24. If you hold long enough, even a stock with a modest yield could end up paying out far more than you could earn with a bond.

To evaluate an income stock, you should consider the current yield and the likely dividend growth. Since dividends usually increase more or less in line with earnings, you can gauge a stock's long-term potential simply by adding the growth rate to the current yield. If a stock has a 3.5% yield and 6% annual earnings growth, for instance, its long-term return is likely to average about 9.5%.

You can compare that total return estimate to the yield available on bonds. If you figure that high-quality bonds pay as much as 7% or 8%, income stocks will need potential total returns even higher to be top choices. Many good utilities—including electric, gas and water companies—clear that hurdle.

The big risk to any income investment is an upsurge in inflation. You should therefore award extra points to any income investment that incorporates an inflation hedge. Oil stocks and mining shares, for instance, would benefit from any increase in raw materials prices and some of them pay fairly high yields. Similarly, real estate investment trusts profit from rising property prices and some REITs pay yields of 7% or so. That's a whole lot more than you'll earn in a money-market fund.

THE APPEAL OF SECTOR INVESTING

Growth, value and income isn't the only way to slice the stock market pie. When assessing the diversity of your stock holdings, you should also take into account the sectors represented in your portfolio. Some investors take a purely sector approach to portfolio building.

In theory, sector investing makes very good sense. Who would not want to invest in the most promising portions of the economy and ignore those with the dimmest prospects? Clearly, an investor who loaded up on tech stocks early in the 1990s would be smiling today, even after the recent tech debacle. But what about someone who discovered the wonders of tech only weeks before the entire sector went tilt? That's a very different story.

Before adopting a sector investing strategy, recognize the different ways in which this ostensibly sensible approach could backfire.

• **You're simply wrong about the sector.** Many gold stocks were rising smartly in the first half of 2001—but for the preceding 10 years they had been stinkers. Apparently, no one told them about the great bull market. Newmont Mining, one of the sector's "leaders" (if that is the right word), stood at $43.16 in January 1990. In October 2000, it hit $12.75. Such a loss would be considered a dreadful investment in almost any era, but, in the context of the historic bull market, it was unspeakably awful.

• **You're right about the trend, but you overpay.** Perhaps the greatest flaw sector investors have is waiting until a trend becomes obvious to virtually everyone and then jumping aboard. When everyone acknowledges how great a development is, you can bet that stocks in the sector won't be bargain-priced. And valuation remains crucial, no matter how entrenched the trend. Those famous tech darlings may eclipse their 2000 highs someday, but it will probably take quite a while.

• **You get whipsawed.** If you jump into a sector after it has had a huge rise in a relatively brief time, you run the risk of enduring a correction right after you join in the fun. So much for fun. Many investors who suddenly find themselves 15% to 20% in the hole may sell and promise never to chase a hot group again. This doesn't mean they necessarily overpaid, however, so taking that loss could be a mistake. You have to expect this kind of volatility in a fast-moving group, which is why it is often best to wait for a pullback before buying. (Or you could wait to buy a leading sector when it is out of favor.)

We certainly don't mean to dissuade you from making sector analysis part of your investment approach. Anyone contemplating the purchase of drug stocks, after all, should be aware that the companies are operating with a tailwind. The population is getting older every year, and as people age they take more pills. That doesn't make every drug company a buy, but it sure can't hurt.

But let's take a closer look at three other vital sectors: technology, energy and financials.

Technology

It was easy to be dazzled in 1999 and 2000. The brilliant promise of new technologies and the blazing ascendance of tech stocks were everywhere. It felt like a new era. Then, of course, investors saw Internet companies implode and tech stocks tumble. In 13 months, about $5 trillion of investor wealth was vaporized. Talk about prices fluctuating.

How should investors approach a sector that clearly suffers from bipolar disorder? Carefully, to be sure. We think today's tech investors should have patience and recognize that the instant-gratification market is gone. The rocketlike surges of the recent past may never be repeated. But for investors with long-term needs to finance, like college or retirement, tech stocks will remain an important investment opportunity.

That's because we are indeed in a new era—just one not as revolutionary as stock valuations once seemed to imply. Technology revolutions—and evolutions—can and do take place without repealing the business cycle. While the valuations of onetime darlings like Amazon.com and Cisco got way ahead of themselves, tech mania has helped pave the way for future gains in corporate America. The pressure on companies to develop and adapt to new technologies has made them far more nimble. The furious pace of innovation has spawned new markets, such as the small but rapidly growing e-commerce sector, and enhanced productivity in ways that will affect bottom lines for far longer than the life span of, say, Pcts.com.

Wealth, worries—and good news.   Much of the tinder for the tech bonfire of the past five years came from abundant low-cost financing and massive capital spending on tech equipment by telecom and Internet ventures. Now a lot of that fuel has gone up in smoke. (For lessons you can learn from a telecom stock gone awry, take a look at the Lucent profile on page 60.) In 2001's first quarter, for example, the market for high-tech initial public offerings consisted of two companies raising a total of $175 million, according to Thomson Financial Securities Data. Compare that with the 91 IPOs that rounded up $10.5 billion in the same period in 2000.

With demand for tech products—and tech stocks—thus reduced, the investing calculus has changed. Some of the market dynamics and valuation yardsticks that we've grown to rely on need to be re-examined. Take momentum investing, the popular sport of chasing rising earnings and share prices. It was an extremely profitable strategy in the '90s. Try it now and it may lead you off a cliff.

What tech investors want to know is: Is it safe yet? Steven Leuthold, head of investment research firm the Leuthold Group, thinks the answer is yes. Leuthold, who has been so pessimistic for so long that he's been called a perma-bear, says "the tech sector is back to what we think is normal valuation." In 1999, his firm's analysis of over 300 tech stocks put the median price/earnings ratio at 115. By April 2001, that median P/E was 32—lower than the median of 33 since 1962.

Another good sign: Although tech companies don't receive the same benefit from an interest rate cut as Old Economy stocks, partly because they tend not to borrow as much in the capital markets, lower rates do make it easier for customers to finance tech purchases. "Tech spending depends on Old Economy cash flows for a lot of its vibrancy," notes Ned Riley, chief investment strategist for State Street Global Advisors. "Eventually, information-technology spending and capital spending on productivity enhancements respond to cuts in interest rates."

But a full tech recovery may take considerable time, so we need to approach tech investing with a different mind-set. In the '90s, simply buying tech—any tech—worked. Now identifying winners is going to become much harder, says Ed Yardeni, chief investment strategist of Deutsche Bank Securities. "The 1990s were an aberration because a few tech companies managed to obtain nearly monopolistic positions," he explains. "It's going to be harder to make profits because it's going to become increasingly competitive."

These days, a tech investor must carefully analyze any potential purchase. Tech stocks face very different issues and risks. Consider, for instance, the long-term impact of slumping PC sales on Dell, Intel and Microsoft. Microsoft remains a near monopoly, and every PC sold will continue to have the Windows operating system. Intel's products will continue to be the industry standard, but since consumers rarely notice performance differences between brands of microprocessors (how many people still demand that their PC have "Intel Inside"?), there's the threat of inroads by other competitors. Dell is in many ways the most vulnerable. Yet with only 12% market share worldwide, Dell has room to grow even if the PC market doesn't—if it can execute.

Just don't be lulled into complacency by any company's glorious past. The future is all that matters.

Energy

Utilities used to be so square. Sure, they paid stable dividends and held their own during stormy stock markets. But compared with tech stocks, utilities were dull. Not anymore. Electric, gas and nuclear power firms are on fire, fueled by deregulation, the industry's rampant merger spree, soaring consumer demand and the freedom to move into higher-growth businesses. "Utilities always wanted to be growth companies, they just were not allowed," says Andrew Levi of Credit Suisse First Boston.

The Dow Jones Utility Average rose 38.8% in the 17 months ending May 31, 2001 vs. -4.3% for the S&P 500. And some utility stocks have posted tech-stock returns. Calpine and Dynegy—two of a group, with AES and Enron, that fund managers have gamely dubbed the Fab Four—soared 208% and 304%, respectively, during that same period. But there are still buys out there. Electric companies, on average, trade at about 12 times estimated 2001 earnings vs. about 23 for the S&P 500.

We think you should focus on companies, such as Enron, that are thriving as they change from monopolies to market players. Enron is in the lucrative, high-growth wholesale energy trading and marketing business. Before deregulation, power companies had little incentive to compete and innovate. They sold energy in local regions, charged regulated rates and were legally required to pass along operating-cost savings to customers. Today, with deregulation breaking out all over—there are only eight states without active deregulation efforts—companies are selling their products on the open market, providing unprecedented opportunities to boost revenues and profits. For some consumers this may mean higher energy bills, but it also offers a ripe investing opportunity.

Lessons from Lucent's Cliff Dive

Anyone contemplating the purchase of a stock has to think about the potential downside. Any owner of a stock has to be very wary if the fundamentals begin to deteriorate. Always ask: What could go wrong? In the case of Lucent Technologies, the answer was "just about everything."

Marcelle Hobbs is no rube when it comes to playing the market. The 52-year-old real estate agent pays attention to valuation, studies quarterly reports and keeps tabs on what the experts are saying about her stocks. Yet in 2000, when deciding what to do about her stake in Lucent, Hobbs threw discipline to the wind and held on despite what she knew to be warning signs.

Reading Lucent's quarterly reports, Hobbs spotted that cash flow from operations (the money that actually winds up in corporate coffers) had turned negative—an unexpected hint of weakness at a time when the company's reported earnings were still booming. "With any other stock, I probably wouldn't have been so forgiving," Hobbs says. "But Lucent had such a good reputation and had done well for me in the past." Her faith would prove costly. Her 500 shares, once valued at $40,000, are now worth about $3,000.

Hobbs is hardly the only smart investor who rode the nation's largest telecom-equipment maker down from its 1999 high of $82.31 to a recent low of $5.50. Some of Wall Street's biggest names bungled the call on Lucent—ace investors like UBS Warburg's Ed Kerschner, Fidelity Magellan's Bob Stansky and Firsthand Funds' Kevin Landis.

So too did MONEY. We recommended Lucent twice in 2000; the second time was in March, shortly after the company stunned Wall Street by falling far short of analysts' quarterly earnings expectations. Then-CEO Richard McGinn assured us that the company's growth rate would soon revive, and we, like so many other Lucent admirers, were too willing to believe.

What first looked to us like a one-quarter glitch turned out to be the start of a disastrous trend. Lucent fell short of earnings expectations again in the second, third and fourth quarters. And this financial failure was matched by technological failure. Unable to produce the next generation of optical-networking gear, Lucent was trounced by archrival Nortel Networks in this fast-growing telephony market.

Lately, the news out of Lucent has only gotten worse. McGinn was fired in October 2000. The company was obliged to restate its fourth-quarter earnings in both November and December 2000. The Securities and Exchange Commission is now investigating Lucent's accounting, and the firm's credit rating was slashed to junk status in June 2001. The fallout for investors has been brutal: $250 billion in shareholder value has been wiped out—astonishing for a once-beloved name that until 2000 was America's most widely held stock.

Of course, stock picking is an imperfect science, so the occasional disaster is inevitable even for stars like Stansky. But the Lucent debacle stands out because there were so many advance warnings that the company was headed for trouble. And you didn't need a background in accounting or engineering to detect these clues. Says Brad Rexroad of the Center for Financial Research and Analysis, an early Lucent naysayer: "Not since Cendant had I seen a company with this many red flags."

Here, then, are five key lessons that every investor should learn from Lucent's implosion. They'll make you a savvier investor and should help you sidestep future stock market blowups.

- **Don't treat quarterly reports like junk mail.** We know all that minuscule print can induce eye strain and that the stilted language can sound as oblique as Alan Greenspan's testimony to Congress. So if you don't have the patience to scour reports cover to cover, at least check out two numbers—receivables and cash flow from operations—and compare them with the company's revenues and earnings.

That's what Lehman Bros.' Steven Levy did. Before becoming an analyst, Levy worked for six years at Lucent's ex-parent AT&T, yet it wasn't his engineering background or any inside knowledge that fueled his skepticism about Lucent. "All the clues were in the balance sheet," says Levy, who sounded the alarm as early as 1999. Back then, receivables—sales for which a company has yet to receive payment—were growing at double the rate of Lucent's revenues. (Receivables can be found in the consolidated balance sheet section of every quarterly or annual report.) That was worrisome because rising receivables are often a sign of financial distress among customers or of salespeople using every trick in the book to reach their quotas, even if that means sacrificing future results.

Lucent's cash-flow situation was even more troubling. Typically, there's a strong correlation between a company's cash flow and its earnings. But because the latter figure is so easily manipulated, cash flow should always be used as a reality check. In 1999, Lucent lost $276 million on a cash-flow basis, even though earnings surged 360% to $4.8 billion. As Levy puts it, "The warning signs were there if you knew where to look." Now you do.

- **Follow the money.** If a company's customers are hit by financial problems, it's a pretty safe bet that they won't be buying as much as they did when times were sunnier. Sounds obvious, but most Lucent shareholders failed to connect the dots. It was well known that AT&T, which had spun out Lucent in 1996, had remained its biggest customer. Yet few investors foresaw trouble for Lucent in the spring of 2000 when it was widely reported that AT&T's corporate and consumer long-distance businesses had slowed dramatically.

Around the same time, competitive local exchange carriers (upstart phone companies known as CLECs), which were also major customers of Lucent's, started to have problems too. The junk bond market, which had helped to bankroll the CLECs, sank into a deep funk. Unprofitable and unable to raise more capital, two major CLECs declared bankruptcy. Seen in this context, it should have come as no surprise when, in December 2000, Lucent blamed its waning fortunes on a "decline in sales to one large customer" (read: AT&T) and on "an overall softening" in sales to CLECs.

● **Never fall in love with your stocks.** Many of Lucent's shareholders simply couldn't accept that a stock market hottie could turn into a dog almost overnight. "It's just so hard to believe that it hasn't rebounded," says Monica Huddleston, a retired operations director for Southwest Bell. She, like many other individual investors, still owned Lucent by the time the company reported its third consecutive earnings disappointment in October 2000. The stock's spectacular long-term gains had clearly engendered intense loyalty among regular investors, many of whom were also hesitant to trigger capital-gains taxes by cashing out—less of a concern for most fund managers.

Indeed, professional investors were much quicker to pull the plug. "When the objective evidence is headed in the wrong direction, you just have to be ruthless about the stock," says Bob Rhodes of the STI Classic Capital Appreciation fund. Between January and August 2000 the number of large-cap growth funds owning Lucent dived from 212 to 135, and in the past two years the percentage of Lucent shares held by institutional investors has fallen from 48% to 32%.

Lucent has always had far more retail shareholders than most tech companies, and Lehman's Levy says that's one reason the stock held up well for so long. As late as July 2000 the stock had slipped just 12% for the year. While the pros were kissing Lucent good-bye, infatuated amateurs refused to let the love affair end.

● **There are some things you'll never know.** "The moral to the Lucent story," says Tom Lauria, a telecom analyst at ING Barings, "is that investors have much more limited information about companies than many of them would like to believe." For example, one important detail unknown to most investors was that Lucent's bookkeeping systems were remarkably dysfunctional. The result, says Lauria, was that even McGinn had poor data on the health of his own company. That might help to explain why the CEO's rosy earnings forecasts later proved so unreliable.

Trouble is, only a Lucent insider could have known about the bookkeeping problem. So how did Lauria know? Before joining ING last year, he worked as an investor relations manager at Lucent.

The point here is not that stock picking is a hopeless crapshoot, but that there are unknowns about every company. That's why investors should be skeptical of bullish growth promises and why they must never lose sight of how much they're paying for a stock. Which brings us to the final lesson.

• **Valuation matters.** As bad as Lucent's business has been, the stock would never have taken such a beating had it not been so richly priced. Lucent began 2000 with a P/E of 70 vs. 32 for the S&P 500. And when stocks are priced for perfection, they tend to get perfectly hammered if things don't go according to plan.

Compare Lucent's experience to Ford Motor's. Hit by a massive tire recall, a slew of wrongful-death lawsuits and a slowdown in earnings, Ford could scarcely have had a more hellish year. But because it was already a cheap stock with a single-digit P/E, Ford's share price didn't get crushed by all this bad news. While Lucent was going over a cliff, Ford's stock gained 15% between March 2000 and March 2001. The comparison is even more stark over the four years through March 2001, with Ford jumping 130% vs. a 19% loss for Lucent. Keep that in mind the next time someone claims you can't pay too much for growth.

Financials

While tech stocks were blowing up in the second half of 2000, the financial sector was sizzling. Merrill Lynch leaped 26%, MBNA 28%, Fannie Mae 39% and Lehman Bros. 59%. Investors were betting that Alan Greenspan would cut interest rates—historically a huge boon to the financial services sector. In 2001, that wager was won: Between January and May 2001, the Federal Reserve chief cut rates five times, and by mid-2001 they were lower than at any time since 1994.

Why the euphoria for financials? Well, over the past 20 years, brokerage stocks have beaten the S&P 500 by an average of 25% in the six months following a rate cut, according to a study by Instinet. The cuts were especially welcome, since in the first quarter of 2001 the financial sector was beginning to show signs of wear and tear as the economy slowed. Now that rates have dropped, many investors expect financial firms to get their groove back.

Trouble is, after the sector's recent run-up, financial stocks aren't strikingly cheap. As Jeff Morris of Invesco Financial Services fund warns, you can't just "buy any name in the group and do well."

For investors with a long time horizon, there are added reasons to consider financials. Aging baby boomers, with their increasing needs for retirement planning and insurance, are likely to flood the industry with money for decades to come. And thanks to the 1999 repeal of the Glass-Steagall Act, the boundaries between banking, brokerage and insurance are disappearing. That gives the best companies more ways to wring money out of existing customers. "Long term, the financial industry is benefiting from deregulation and demographics," says Jim Schmidt of John Hancock Financial Industries fund. "The main risk people are grappling with is the economy."

Indeed, the way you play the financial sector depends largely on your view of where the economy and the stock market are headed. If you're bullish, it makes sense to bet on brokerage stocks and asset managers like Goldman Sachs or a financial conglomerate like Citigroup, a brokerage house and bank rolled into one. If you're not convinced the worst is over, stick with defensive plays like property and casualty insurers, savings and loans, consumer-finance companies and mortgage lenders. For this play, you may want to consider a company like Household International, the leading consumer-finance company, which provides credit cards, car loans and other loans for middle-income customers in the U.S., Canada and the U.K. Another defensive play: Fannie Mae, a government-backed company that buys mortgages from lenders and resells them as bundles of fixed-income securities.

THE STOCK EXPERT FEW PEOPLE KNOW

Some investors believe that they keep growth and value in balance by buying inexpensive stocks that have solid growth characteristics. Two champions of this style with outstanding track records are Warren Buffett and Lou Simpson.

Lou who? That's the response many investors had to Buffett's 2000 announcement that Louis A. Simpson is the man who will manage Berkshire Hathaway's investment gazillions if, one day, Berkshire's Cherry Coke-fueled chairman cannot. Even the legions of Berkshire loyalists who have heard Simpson's name bandied about over the years know very little about the very private and very accomplished man tapped to become the next "Oracle of Omaha."

Among the investing cognoscenti, however, this man's name is legend. Michael Horowitz, a principal at money-management firm EnTrust Capital, sums up the sentiment of many top investors: "Lou Simpson, to me, is one of the deans of investing."

Simpson, 64, already plays an important role at Berkshire. Officially, he manages $2 billion-plus in equities for Berkshire subsidiary Geico, the auto insurer, but "I think he's been key in the last few years in bringing new ideas to Mr. Buffett and Mr. Munger [the vice chairman of Berkshire Hathaway] in terms of asset allocation," says David Braverman, an equity analyst with Standard & Poor's. Who is this mystery man, and how might he shape the Berkshire of the future? How can you benefit from his investing style?

Simpson is a highly confident, self-disciplined, intellectual loner, a man with a rare intuitive sense for evaluating businesses and people. But he is not a Buffett clone. While Simpson shares core values with the master, he seems willing to move faster than Buffett. Moreover, his penchant for investing in telephone and cable companies, combined with his venture-capital experience, may make him more comfortable with technology stocks than the notoriously tech-averse Buffett.

Just how good is he?   In Berkshire's annual report for 1995, the last year that Simpson's returns were reported separately, Buffett proudly noted that "between 1980 and 1995, the equities under Lou's management returned an average of 22.8% annually vs. 15.7% for the S&P 500."

Simpson runs Plaza Investment Managers, the investment arm of Maryland-based Geico, out of the small, exclusive community of Rancho Santa Fe, Calif. He didn't come into the Berkshire fold at Geico until he was in his mid-forties, after he handled investments at Stein Roe & Farnham and Shareholders Management. Unfortunately, he picked the wrong moment to join Shareholders Management— and the experience changed his investing style forever.

When Simpson joined, the firm's Enterprise Fund, under maverick investor Fred Carr, was red hot. But it took a terrific fall in the late Sixties. "It was a painful, searing experience for Lou," says former Stein Roe colleague Richard Peterson. "Before then, Lou was a pure growth investor—a shoot-for-the-moon guy. I think he learned the importance of going into really good situations that are relatively low risk—that you need growth, but also low valuation."

Lou's rules.   Simpson laid out his basic investing guidelines in an old Geico annual report: Think independently; choose high-return businesses that are run for the shareholders; pay only a reasonable price, even for an excellent business; invest for the long term; and do not diversify excessively.

Glenn Greenberg, co-head of money manager Chieftain Capital and a former Simpson employee, elaborates: "He tries to find businesses with few competitors, pricing that's not volatile, steady demand for the product and low capital needs so that most of the earnings can be reinvested in the business or paid out to shareholders or used for acquisitions." Adds fund manager L. Roy Papp, who worked with Simpson at Stein Roe: "Lou is very definitely a growth-stock buyer—but it could be modest growth, and surely growth at a reasonable price."

Here are three other key elements of Simpson's style.

- **Strong management.** Simpson spends a lot of time getting a feel for an organization's culture and the motivation and skills of its CEO. Simpson wants management that "has done things to show they're good people," such as share repurchases, and "not giving away the house in terms of stock options," says a major Berkshire shareholder.

- **Strong cash flow.** When Simpson turns to the financials, he takes a hard look at a company's free cash flow—defined as the cash generated by the company's operations minus the money it needs to maintain the business. It's a good indicator of how much money the company has available to boost shareholder returns. Specifically, Simpson assesses free cash-flow "yield"— that is, cash flow per share divided by the stock price. "In essence, he looks for companies that have a free cash-flow yield significantly higher than prevailing interest rates," says a money manager who knows Simpson well. "If he thinks the prevailing rate is 7%, then he wants at least 10%."

- **Concentration.** At times in the past, Simpson has kept as much as 60% of his assets in his best four ideas. Things haven't changed much: The most recent detailed data available for Geico (as of Dec. 31, 1999) show a seven-stock portfolio: Jones Apparel, First Data, Freddie Mac, Shaw Communications, U.S. Bancorp (which has since been acquired by Firstar), Nike and Great Lakes Chemical. Less detailed filings indicate that he did some buying in 2000, paying $611 million for Dun & Bradstreet, GATX and several unnamed stocks. He also unloaded Nike.

So how does Simpson apply his rules? Look at Jones Apparel. Jones doesn't need to make big cash outlays; it has strong management and good brands. Clothing is a notoriously fad-driven

Lou Simpson's Stocks

The stocks in Geico's portfolio are a motley bunch: a data-service company here, a chemical company there, a cable play for good measure. There's the unlikely sight of $47.6 billion market-cap giant Freddie Mac next to relative shrimp $1.5 billion Great Lakes Chemical. The stocks do have some things in common, such as price/earnings ratios usually below the S&P 500's 23. And eight of the ten have outperformed the S&P so far in 2001.

Lou's Rules
Simpson looks for companies with...

- **Stable pricing**
- **Steady demand**
- **Few competitors**
- **Shareholder-friendly management**
- **Strong free cash flow**
- **Clean accounting**
- **Low capital needs**

COMPANY (TICKER)	MARKET VALUE (BILLIONS)	P/E	PRICE/ CASH-FLOW RATIO	2000 RETURN	COMMENT
Dun & Bradstreet (DNB)	$2.2	16.2	12.1	3.8%	The reorganized company, with new leadership, has a Web strategy for its valuable business database.
First Data (FDC)	26.4	27.1	17.4	27.7	The second largest independent data-service company is making inroads in e-commerce.
Freddie Mac (FRE)	47.6	16.8	3.6	-0.3	The government-sponsored residential mortgage lender has a valuable stream of interest income.
Gap (The) (GPS)	26.5	30.8	19.9	20.9	The apparel retailer has been beset by troubles, but Simpson foresees a turnaround.
GATX (GMT)	1.9	15.7	5.0	-21.4	This lessor of commercial aircraft and railroad equipment also offers supply-chain management.
Great Lakes Chemical (GLK)	1.5	15.4	7.7	-19.1	This specialty chemicals company is benefiting from new management and a restructuring program.
Jones Apparel (JNY)	5.1	13.9	11.5	28.5	The world's largest manufacturer of women's apparel and footwear is extending its strong brands.
Moody's (MCO)	5.4	26.0	29.8	33.3	The credit rating analysis firm, spun out of Dun & Bradstreet, is poised to enjoy global growth.
Shaw Comm. (SJR)	5.4	N.A.	25.5	2.4	This cable-TV/telecom company is No. 2 in Canada and has very strong management.
U.S. Bancorp (USB)	43.4	13.0	13.5	-1.9	This regional bank, with a struggling retail operation, will benefit from merger partner Firstar's strong retail unit.
S&P 500	N.A.	23.4	15.5	-7.7	

Notes: Data as of June 25, 2001. Price/earnings ratio based on current fiscal year earnings estimates. N.A.: Not applicable. **Sources:** Baseline, Standard & Poor's, First Call, Dow Jones.

business, but Jones focuses on more basic styles. While the absolute growth prospects are "not great," compared with the likes of, say, Cisco, Chieftain's Greenberg notes that "after you analyze the quality of the business, you have to look at what price you're paying." In late 2000, you could have bought Jones for about 14 times its free cash flow; for Cisco, you would pay 71.3 times its cash flow (that was before its cash flow began to disappear). In sum, you've got reasonable valuation, strong brands and good cash flow—a classic Simpson scenario.

SPECIALTY INSTRUMENTS

Investors looking to play in an even more sophisticated market playground may want to think in terms of preferred stock or convertibles. However, the first order of business is to understand the nomenclature, which can be confusing. Preferred stocks are actually very much like bonds, while convertible bonds perform more like stocks.

Preferred stock

Among income investments, one of the best deals often goes unrecognized. We're talking about preferred shares. The reason they can be such a good deal has to do with the way corporate balance sheets are put together. All corporations are financed with equity, represented by common stock. Most also borrow money, usually by selling bonds. The bonds have first claim on the company's assets, so they're the safest investment. But any increase in the company's value goes to the equity.

Preferred stock is a third category, falling between common stock and bonds. Preferreds have a stronger claim on company assets than common shares do, making them a safer investment. And like bonds, preferreds have a fixed payout, with yields on many high-quality issues running more than 8%. In addition, they're far more convenient than bonds, particularly for individual investors with limited funds. Most preferreds trade for around $25 a share, so you can buy a 100-share round lot for $2,500. It's generally thought that you need at least $75,000 to buy individual bonds efficiently.

Preferreds do have a couple of drawbacks. Unlike common stock, they barely benefit from increases in the company's value. Second, preferreds often can be called—that is, redeemed—within a few years. If you pay more than face value for a preferred, and it's called, you'll be stuck with a loss. Many preferreds are callable within four years of the date they're issued.

To lessen your call risk, you can buy recently issued preferreds. You also can look for unusual issues with greater protection. Some Merrill Lynch issues, for instance, aren't callable for up to eight years. Or, you can buy preferreds selling for less than face value—it's not so bad to be called at $25 if you only paid $22.

Not all companies issue preferred stock. And since there are so many variables to consider, there may only be a handful worth buying at any particular time. So you'd be smart to buy them through a knowledgeable broker, which probably means someone at a giant, full-service brokerage with a large staff of analysts. But even though top preferreds are hard to track down, they're worth the hunt. One or two well-chosen issues can be the perfect income additions for a broadly diversified portfolio.

Convertible securities

If you can't choose between the growth of stocks and the income of bonds, convertibles may be your answer. There's a theory that when you cross two breeds of animal, the offspring can be more robust than either parent. Biologists call that hybrid vigor—and what holds true for dogs and horses also applies to investments. Convertibles combine the traits of both stocks and bonds, and under the right conditions, they can outperform each of their parents.

Convertibles are bonds or preferred shares that can be exchanged for a specified amount of common stock at the owner's option. Like bonds, convertibles typically yield more than the common shares. But they also benefit from any substantial rise in the stock price.

It's easy to see why convertibles often outperform straight bonds. Capital gains on bonds are limited, but the stock market usually rises substantially over a long stretch of time. And though convertibles have a tough time keeping up with stocks in booming markets, their yields can put them out in front in sideways markets. And in a falling market, convertibles' yields offer downside protection.

That yield support explains the most characteristic feature of convertibles. They share more in stock gains than they do in losses. A convert might move up 70% as much as the common when it's rising, but fall only 30% as much. The exact ratios depend on the security's price and yield.

Convertibles almost always trade at a premium over the value of the common stock for which they can be exchanged. The rule of thumb is that the convertible is a better buy if it offers a yield advantage that would pay off that premium in four years. For example, if a convertible offers a 4% yield and the common pays 1%, the three-point difference over four years would cover a premium of up to 12%.

Sometimes companies have the right to call a convertible. When that happens, you are essentially forced to convert it or sell it back to the company—in either case, the value may be less than what you paid. Companies don't always call these issues at the first opportunity, but it's important to know the call terms.

Obviously, investing in individual convertibles requires a lot of research. And although some information is available in newspapers, magazines and on the Web, you'll probably need more details. That could mean subscribing to an expensive investment research service or sifting through original SEC documents.

The easier alternative is to use a broker who specializes in convertible issues and works at a major firm that does proprietary research. Or better yet, find a mutual fund with a good track record and below-average expenses. This is one case where it's worthwhile to pay for professional management.

THE ART OF SELLING

Clearly, it takes a lot of skill to be an astute buyer of stocks, but buying is a snap compared to selling. Deciding when to dump your holdings is the toughest question you face as an investor. And chances are you don't get the answer right as often as you would like. Individual investors routinely "sell winners too early and ride losers too long," wrote researchers Hersh M. Shefrin and Meir Statman in a 1985 *Journal of Finance* article. They concluded that investors often succumb to fears of loss and regret when making sell decisions. People who don't want to make paper losses "real" hold on to poor performers, and those who don't want to regret a missed opportunity for profits sell winners.

It's easy to understand why. The great bull market that lasted into 2000 elevated buy-and-hold from strategy to religion. The great tech inferno that ensued, however, reminded all market participants that, for many stocks, the ideal holding period may not be forever. Clearly, there are times when the most devout buy-

and-hold practitioner should consider selling: Perhaps a couple of your stocks have posted extraordinary gains and now represent a big chunk of your holdings. Maybe you're near a goal—college tuition, retirement, a second home—and you need to trim risk. Or you're wondering if this year's losers can rebound. Or you're just doing an annual, semiannual or monthly portfolio review.

Whatever your reason for pondering a sale, don't look at a stock's price and ask simply whether you should unload it. Instead, take time to pose questions and search for answers about the stock's prospects. Below we discuss four familiar scenarios.

1. I've got an enormous winner.   Does it still offer me what it did a year ago? Is it too big a piece of my portfolio? This is the kind of sell dilemma we would all like to face, but it doesn't have a one-size-fits-all answer. William Nygren, manager of the Oakmark Select fund, says you should always have in mind a target price you feel reflects the potential you saw when you bought the stock. Some managers swear by these sell targets: They hit one and get out. But that often leaves money on the table, and individuals—remember—tend to cut loose their winners too quickly. Nygren sees the target "not so much as an absolute sell signal but as a benchmark when periodically reevaluating your investment rationale." If earnings come in better than expected, he says, "or if similar companies sell for more than expected in the private market, raise your target."

If you have a stock that's risen, say, eightfold, it probably represents more of your holdings than prudence dictates. Most benefits of asset allocation can be gained with fewer than 15 stocks, and you likely don't have time to keep tabs on many more. So you should consider setting a limit of 3% to 10%.

Or you could employ a strategy familiar to anyone who plays blackjack. Cut your position in half. That way, you lock in a profit and get to keep playing with house money.

Remember, though, that when you sell a winner, you're going to give up a big chunk of your gain in taxes (unless you're trading in a tax-deferred account). If you invest what's left in a new stock that you sell after three years, it must beat your old one by about 10% annually just to get you to where you would have been had you simply delayed the sale of the old stock.

2. My stock is plunging.   Is it temporary? Should I buy more? Or is there a long-lasting problem? Research suggests that the biggest mistake people make is hanging on to losers. But panic is an investor's enemy, and buying on dips to average down is a time-tested investing method. What do you do?

Growth fund manager John McStay generally sells a stock if it declines 20%. If the market is falling, he'll cut his losers more slack, but in a strong market, even a 10% decline may prompt him to bail.

Because you, unlike fund managers, don't have to deliver short-term performance, a rigid sell rule may not be a necessity. But be careful not to commit the sin of pride that McStay's dump rule is designed to avoid. That leads us to a second strategy: If a stock drops 15% or more in a flat or rising market, reevaluate.

3. My stock is going nowhere.   Should I be doing something better with my money? The question of how long to wait for a stock to soar is especially relevant to investors who may not have cash to invest in new ideas. Many stock sales by money managers are prompted by their desire to buy something else.

If you conclude you don't have a better idea, consider spreading the money tied up in your going-nowhere stock among your existing best ideas, if that won't overly concentrate your portfolio. Or just sit tight. An idea will come.

4. My stock has done okay.   But some of the fundamentals have changed. Which ones are noise, and which ones tell me something? Investors pay too much attention to news events that have little to do with a company's value, says Richard Howard, manager of $913 million T. Rowe Price Capital Appreciation fund. In particular, he thinks the significance of political events and changes in company management tend to get overblown. Likewise, Howard says, investors wrongly concentrate on price-to-earnings ratios. "Prices are not fundamentals. They reflect fundamentals."

The key is to discriminate between meaningful developments and temporary distractions. Here are two fundamental shifts that you absolutely must heed: changes in a company's core business and a falloff in its market position.

If a company has changed its focus or made a major acquisition that looks questionable, it isn't really the stock you bought. Is there still a reason for you to own it? Even a well-run company can see its franchise threatened, says Tom Marsico, manager of the Marsico Focus fund and the Marsico Growth and Income fund. "When I buy stocks, I'm looking for ones that I never have to sell," he says. "But I'd be wrong to hold on just for the sake of holding on."

Chapter 4
THE MECHANICS OF SMART STOCK INVESTING

Having good stock selection strategies can take you only so far. You also need to execute those strategies well, to make the right trade with the right broker at the best price.

In this chapter, we'll discuss the key elements of smart trading, everything from choosing a broker to placing special trading orders to buying on margin (don't do it before finishing this chapter, please). The smartest investors use every available tool to maximize their returns and increase their peace of mind. Sometimes, as you'll see, one of those tools might even be a full-service broker.

By trading more effectively and avoiding small but ultimately costly mistakes, you can improve your investment returns year after year.

CHOOSING A BROKER

When you're looking for a broker, you have four choices. From the most to the least expensive, they are: full-service brokers, discount brokers, deep discounters and online brokers. What differentiates them is the advice they give and how much they charge. Full-service brokers will call with stock ideas, and offer reports from their research department. They'll keep an eye on your picks and let you know when they think changes are necessary. Discounters do less of this. Deep discounters do nothing of the kind. And while there's typically plenty of research available on the best online brokerage sites, it's up to you to dig for it.

Smart investors choose different kinds of brokers for different purposes. For instance, if you've done your research yourself, we don't see any reason to pay a hefty commission—discounters and online brokers probably are fine. We also believe that full-service brokers should get paid for their stock ideas. That seems only fair. (If you need a compelling reason to stick with your broker or find a real pro to work with, read MONEY columnist Joseph Nocera's "My Broker, My Friend: Why I'm Sticking with My Old Economy Full-Service Firm" on page 75.)

The nice thing about the way the brokerage world is shaping up is that you probably can do both of those things in one account at one firm. Merrill Lynch and many other full-service brokers offer an online component—and charge you lower commissions when you use it. And discounters like Schwab and Fidelity have both started offering a fuller range of services in recent years, while retaining their low-cost structure.

If you decide to sign on with a full-service broker, you should make sure that person has nothing to hide. To get a report on any broker, contact the National Association of Securities Dealers (800-289-9999; www.nasdr.com). To get our take on the best online brokers, see our rankings in Chapter 11.

MAKING THE TRADE

Once you pick a broker, you're open for business to trade. Or are you? Stock traders employ a cryptic language. And if you engage in trading individual stocks before becoming familiar with the esoteric lingo, you can easily blow a good deal without even knowing it. That's because studying trading terminology is a great way to learn how the stock market operates. And ultimately, understanding the jargon can help you get the best price for your shares.

Trading basics.   Whether dealing with a broker face to face, over the phone or trading online, most individual investors buy or sell stocks using a *market order*. This type of order assures you

My Broker, My Friend:
Why I'm Sticking with My Old Economy
Full-Service Firm BY MONEY COLUMNIST JOSEPH NOCERA

My broker works for one of those big, lumbering old-line firms, the kind that employs literally thousands of brokers across the country. The firm operates on the classic, pre-Internet Wall Street model. It offers lots of "proprietary" stock research to its customers. It distributes its "products" through its vast brokerage network. It expects its brokers to generate its clientele. And it makes much of its money by charging that clientele commission rates on stock trades that can seem, in this age of $8 trades, a little short of usurious. It's the kind of firm, in other words, that the Internet—and the rise of online trading—is supposed to be destroying. (It's also the kind of firm that gets all hot and bothered when one of its brokers is interviewed, which is why my broker asked me not to use her name.) To read the business press these days, my broker is a dinosaur.

And yet one of the things my broker told me over dinner was that she had stopped taking on new clients. "I just have so much business right now, I can't in good conscience add clients," she said with a happy smile. I was startled by this news, but I shouldn't have been. For it turns out that despite the rise of E-Trade and other online discounters, they are still utterly dwarfed by the big boys from the Old Economy. E-Trade's customer assets, for instance, total around $44 billion. That sounds impressive, until you realize that Merrill Lynch's assets under management are over $1.7 trillion—and growing. The truth is, the full-service broker is not nearly as close to extinction as he or she is usually made out to be. Indeed, according to Charles Schwab & Co., some 35% of America's financial assets reside with full-service brokerages, while their online competitors have only 4%.

But why? Why do so many of us stick with full-service, full-commission brokers? Why do we turn our backs on the cheap commissions, the obvious convenience, the plethora of research and the elimination of the greatest flaw in the old brokerage house model—the broker's built-in conflict of interest—that online trading offers? And why am I, of all people, among them? After all, I've written a fair amount about the brave new world of Internet stock trading. I know how little Ameritrade charges compared with how much my full-service broker charges. What's more, I have fairly strong opinions about which stocks I want to own at any given moment—indeed, over the past few years especially, much of the business I've done with my broker has consisted of my calling her and placing a buy or sell order, something I could do far more cheaply with an online broker. On the face of it, I should be the perfect E-Trade customer. Yet I've never been tempted to break from my broker. So I ask again: Why?

The silent majority

The folks at Schwab, who have built a hugely successful business prying investors away from full-service brokers, have seen people like me before. They even have a name for us: "validators." That is, we're a class of people who know our own mind when it comes to stocks and money but want somebody—somebody in a professional capacity, somebody we have faith in—to "validate" our financial decisions. It turns out that there are a lot of us out there: According to Schwab, some 23 million investor households act in this fashion, about twice the number of the next largest category, "delegators," which is Schwab-speak for people who want others to make their financial decisions for them. (By contrast, the segment that Schwab calls "self-directed"—that is, the type who naturally gravitate to do-it-yourself investing—adds up to only 2.6 million households. If you're wondering why Schwab is moving away from its discounting roots and preparing to make advice part of its business model, the answer lies in those numbers.)

The crucial point here is that Schwab sees my loyalty to my broker as mainly an issue of my behavioral patterns. And up to a point, I don't disagree. Since I trade only a few times a year—and since I believe in holding stocks for years at a time—cut-rate commissions mean less to me than they would to someone who trades more than I do. And yes, now that I think about it, I do like having my trading decisions "validated" by someone else. When my broker disagrees with a trade I want to make—and sometimes she does—I find myself talking it through with her. As I've come to learn, that's an enormously useful exercise.

This latter example, though, speaks to what I think is the real issue here: It's her behavior, far more than mine, that is the crucial ingredient. I've heard all the stories about brokers who churn, or who constantly call their customers to push whatever the firm is pushing that day, or who promote some in-house mutual fund that comes with an unconscionable load. My broker doesn't do any of those things—and, so far as I know, never has. Although she does, obviously, suggest stocks to me, she does so only when I'm looking for something to buy—and even then I never feel as though I'm being pressured to make a trade just for the sake of generating a commission. On the contrary. "A lot of what I do with my clients is persuade them not to sell," she told me over dinner. "I have one client who bought some Microsoft shortly after it went public," she continued. "At least once a year, he starts talking about selling some, and I have to persuade him not to. His Microsoft shares are now worth several million dollars." Later, as we were finishing our wine, I asked her how she could possibly make much money on a client like me. She laughed. "I don't," she said.

What clients really want

The crux of the matter is that, while she does work for a big Old Economy firm, I simply don't worry about where her allegiance is. Although she certainly wants the firm to do well, it is clear that my interests—and those of all her clients—come first. Indeed, one of the things that strikes me about the way she does business is that she seems to operate as if she's an independent financial adviser who just happens to have an office at a big firm. She largely ignores the firm's research. (She and I agree that most sell-side stock research is worthless.) She has her own group of stocks that she follows closely. For some of her clients she manages a portfolio—a little like a mutual fund manager—and makes her money by growing those assets.

I suppose the obvious question my rapturous description of my broker raises is whether she is too good to be true—an anomaly who doesn't really fit into the brokerage business. But I would argue that there are more like her than you think. Yes, there are still unethical brokers, but thanks to the online competition, they're the real dying breed. More and more, the people in the full-service end of the business are having to follow the lead of my broker. They've come to understand what my broker has always understood: that their interests and the interests of their clients have to be utterly aligned. And that what clients really want is not so much somebody who gives them stock tips—hell, if they want stock tips they can always head for the chat rooms—but someone with whom they can have a real relationship. Someone whose advice they can trust. This is my broker's competitive advantage.

Sure, the Internet is a powerful force, but when it comes to our money, having a relationship with someone we trust still matters a lot. Indeed, it may matter more than ever before, now that investing itself has become an increasingly important aspect of creating a good life for ourselves and our children. The brokers who can create that kind of relationship, like my broker, are not going to have to worry about how much they charge in commissions. They are giving us what we hunger for—and for which we will gladly pay what they charge. For most of us, the stakes are too high to go it alone. Sorry, E-Trade.

---

of two things: You'll get the prevailing price for a stock, and you'll actually complete the purchase or sale.

But there's also a downside to market orders: You have no control over what price you will get. In the few minutes or less it takes for your order to filter its way to an exchange or a computerized trading system, the price could go up or down, in some cases by a significant amount. When the doyenne of domesticity Martha Stewart went public in October 2000, for example, her company's stock soared to $49.50 a share after opening at $37.25. Sanity later set in, and the stock closed just under $36. Hey, we love Martha. But if we paid nearly 50 bucks for a stock that just hours later sold for $12 less, we'd feel sillier than if we'd mixed our Wedgwood dinner plates with Tupperware serving bowls.

Setting limits.   You can set a ceiling on the purchase price that you'll pay or a floor on the sales price you'll accept by using a *limit order*. For example, if you had entered a limit order for Martha's stock at, say, $38 on its opening day, your trade would not have been executed during the big spike in the price. You would likely have acquired it at a price of $38 or less.

When you're dealing with volatile stocks or situations that can trigger big swings in price, limit orders can prevent you from paying more than you would like for a stock or selling it for less than you want. However, these orders also have their limits, so to speak. If the stock stays above your limit on a buy order or below it on a sell order—or if other limit orders gobble up all the shares available at the limit price—the trade isn't executed.

There's another reason to consider a limit order: It can sometimes give you a shot at a slightly better than market price. To attempt that, you need to understand how stocks are priced. There are two quotes on each stock: the *bid* (the price at which a marketmaker or another investor will buy the stock from you) and the *ask* or *offer* (the price at which someone will sell the stock to you). The difference between these two quotes, which typically ranges from one cent to 25 cents, is known as the *bid/ask spread*. When you place a market order, your trade is executed at the NBBO—*national best bid or offer*. So if shares of Florida Rock, a company that produces ready-mix concrete, were bid at $37 and offered at $37.25, a market order to buy 100 shares would be executed at the offer price of $37.25.

But you might be able to get a better price by placing a buy-limit order inside the bid/ask spread, say at $37.13. (Pros call this *driving the inside*.) You're essentially hoping that an impatient seller will accept your price, saving you the difference between your limit order and the posted offer.

To pull off such a trade, you've got to know the current bid/ask quotes on the stock. Fortunately, that information is available free at many websites. In addition, some of these sites also show the *bid and ask size*, that is, the number of shares available at the quoted bid and ask. Some brokers, including Fidelity and E-Trade, offer active customers an even deeper level of data known as Nasdaq Level II quotes. These quotes show the bids and offers from a variety of marketmakers in the stock, plus the bid and ask size for each quote. If you're buying or selling a stock that trades frequently—such as Microsoft or GE—the effort might not be worth it because the spread is almost always extremely narrow. But if you're trading in large quantities or dealing in relatively illiquid stocks with a big spreads, this ploy is worth considering.

Pulling out the stops.   Another type of order you should know about is a *stop order*. Let's say in November 1999, you paid $25 a share for 100 shares of Pinnacle Holdings, a Sarasota, Fla. company that provides space on wireless-communication towers and that recently traded for $40.50 a share. You're thrilled with your paper profit and you would like to hang on to at least some of your gain if the stock goes down. You can, sort of, by entering a sell-stop order (also called a *stop-loss order*) at, say, 15% or so below the current price of the stock, or at $34 in this case. If Pinnacle drops to $34, the stop triggers a sell order to unload the stock, and you keep a $9, or 36%, profit.

But stop orders have two potential pitfalls. First, you may end up selling when you don't really want to. On December 30, 1999, for example, Pinnacle shares plunged from $40 to just under $30, only to rebound to more than $42 the very next day. If you had set a stop order at $34, you would have been "stopped out" of this stock. "And you'd probably feel pretty stupid the next day when the stock was above $40," says Andrew Brooks, head of equity trading at T. Rowe Price.

The other problem is you can't assume the trade will be executed at the stop price. When a stock hits your stop price, it triggers a market order. If the market is in freefall, the price can sink a few bucks or even much more below the stop price before your stock is finally sold.

You can protect yourself against the possibility of selling well below the stop price by placing a stop and limit order rolled into one—a *stop-limit order*. So if you set the stop price at $35 and the limit at, say, $32, a limit order would be entered when the stock hit a price of $35 and a sale would take place only at $32 or higher. Though less common, some investors use stops and stop-limit orders to buy stocks, usually when they believe a stock rates a "buy" after climbing to a certain target price. As with a regular limit order, though, there's no guarantee that your trade will be executed.

The downside of trading.   At this point you're probably itching to unleash a flood of market, stop and stop-limit orders on a cou-

The More You Trade the Less You Earn

When University of California–Davis finance professors Terrance Odean and Brad Barber calculated returns for 66,465 investors, they found that transaction costs and lousy stock picking seriously eroded investors' returns.

Specifically, between February 1991 and January 1997, the most active traders earned five percentage points a year less than average traders and seven percentage points less annually than buy-and-hold investors.

Note: Turnover measures how much of an investor's portfolio he or she replaces each year. **Source:** *Trading Is Hazardous to Your Wealth* by Terrance Odean and Brad Barber.

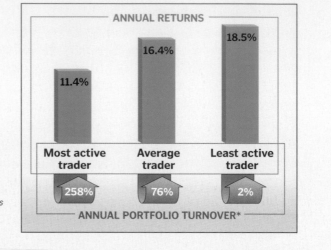

ANNUAL RETURNS

11.4% — Most active trader — 258%

16.4% — Average trader — 76%

18.5% — Least active trader — 2%

ANNUAL PORTFOLIO TURNOVER*

ple dozen stocks. But before you make a move, there's one last thing you ought to know: The more you trade, the lower the returns you'll likely earn.

That, at least, is the conclusion University of California-Davis finance professor Terrance Odean came to after studying the performance of the discount-brokerage accounts of 66,465 households. As the chart above shows, the most active traders earned an annualized five percentage points less than average traders and seven points less than the least active traders. Why do active traders stink up the joint? Odean points to two reasons: "transaction costs in the form of commissions and bid/ask spreads, and poor stock selection. Basically the stocks that people bought tend to perform worse than the ones they sold."

BUYING ON MARGIN

The most hyperkinetic traders are also those who are most likely to buy on margin. For a great trader, margin investing can be a blessing. But for anyone who guesses wrong about the market or a particular stock, it can be a terrible curse.

Margin debt has long tempted investors, and three quarters of a century ago it helped spur the great bull market of the 1920s. Back then, an investor needed to put down only $100 to acquire $1,000 worth of General Electric stock. Margin requirements have since been raised and, today, a person must put down at least $500 to make that $1,000 investment in GE. But the temptation remains as great as ever.

The Internet makes trading on margin easier than in the past. During Nasdaq's wild 1998-2000 ride, many investors used margin debt to turbocharge their stock returns. But when the market turned down, thousands of investors discovered to their horror that margin could increase losses as well as gains. Margin debt—make no mistake—can be harmful if you use it recklessly or without knowing all the rules, and even a small amount of margin can greatly increase your stress level if the market turns against you.

All it takes to open a margin account is a $2,000 balance and a click of the mouse. There's usually a questionnaire in place of a credit check. And there's no human broker to raise a judgmental eyebrow. No wonder margin debt soared in recent years.

And it seems there's no bottom to the well of available cash. Despite the rise in borrowing, the Fed has been unwilling to alter the margin requirements set in 1974, which allow investors to borrow up to 50% of the purchase price of a stock. Though brokerages are free to raise their own requirements, many of them are reluctant to cut into the easy profits they make from the 7% to 10% lending rates.

The attraction of margin trading is devilishly simple. Say you've got $10,000 to invest in XYZ Corp. Borrowing an equal amount from your broker, you buy $20,000 of the stock. Now say XYZ shoots up 50%. Suddenly, you have $30,000 in shares. When you pay back the $10,000 you borrowed, plus interest on the loan, you wind up with nearly $10,000 in gains. Had you traded on your savings alone, your gains would amount to only $5,000.

But say XYZ tanks by 50%. The $20,000 investment drops to $10,000. After paying back your $10,000 loan (plus interest), your initial investment is decimated. Had you declined to borrow money in the first place, you would have salvaged $5,000.

Trading on margin is risky not just for you but for the brokerages too. If your bet goes sour, so might their loan. When a sinking stock approaches the level where selling it wouldn't raise enough money to repay your loan, brokers can issue what's known as a *margin call*. Here's how it works: In an investment made on margin, a drop in the stock's value eats into your contribution first. When the stock price falls so far that the amount you had to put up is less than 25% to 35% of the current value of the investment, the broker can order you to sell the stock at a loss to repay the loan (even if you still think the stock will go up) or deposit more cash into your account immediately. If you don't, the broker can liquidate your other stocks to cover the loan without even bothering to tell you.

That's what happened to Lael Desmond. He had about $50,000 and an equal amount on margin in his Ameritrade account, all riding on Internet stocks like Yahoo!, Excite and AOL. Then 27, Desmond had recently quit a $40,000-a-year job in chemical sales, hoping his investments would yield enough money for his medical school tuition. Desmond's thin grasp on how margin loans worked didn't stop him from using them. "My understanding at the time was that it was like a loan at a bank," he says. "You pay interest on the amount you borrow."

He got a brutally swift education in 1999. After a market drop, Desmond received a letter demanding a prompt infusion of about $9,000. When he called the brokerage, the demand had risen to $13,000. He scrambled to collect cash advances from five credit cards to make the payment. A swoon in the market soon upped the amount he owed to $21,000. He rushed to the bank and wired the money, just making Ameritrade's three-day deadline. When he called later that day to check up, he learned his entire portfolio had been liquidated at nine that morning.

Desmond took his dispute to arbitration and won, but the victory was bittersweet. After lawyer's fees, he wound up with $25,000, about half his original investment. Had his stocks been left untouched, he figures his portfolio would have been worth about $300,000 eventually. Then again, if he had remained on margin through the tech crash, he would have been wiped out.

CAN STOCK SPLITS MAKE YOU MONEY?

In investing, can one plus one equal more than two? Can you really profit from stocks splits?

Not too long ago, you certainly could. Remember when stocks used to soar whenever they announced a split? Was that merely yet another sign of market froth or was it an indication that the market had finally got religion about the virtue of splits?

Before You Buy on Margin

It has to be said: Trading stocks with money that isn't yours is not investing—it's speculating. But if you're thinking of giving it a try anyway, keep these essentials in mind.

- **Learn all your broker's rules before you take a loan.** Even if you've traded on margin before, each firm has its own maintenance requirements, restricted margin stocks and margin call rules.

- **Be prepared for the consequences of a margin call.** Your broker has the right to sell your stocks to cover its loan if you can't come up with extra cash fast enough.

- **Only borrow amounts you can afford to lose**—or be able to cover easily with cash from other accounts.

- **Keep your holdings diversified.** If you concentrate all your margined stocks in one sector—especially a volatile one—then the stocks are likely to rise or fall in tandem. If they all fall at once, there's an increased chance you'll get hit with a margin call.

In one sense, it's hard to imagine that a split should affect a stock's value. In a typical "two-for-one" split, a company gives you a second share for each one you own but cuts the price in half. In theory, that leaves you exactly where you started—but, in practice, the announcement of an upcoming split has often been enough to make a stock jump, particularly in 1999 and 2000. Hyped by a potent mix of their own press releases, the resulting frenzy in online chat rooms and day-traders whose pagers beeped on news of the latest splits, companies like CMGI and JDS Uniphase split their shares three times in just a year; Sycamore Networks even split only a few weeks after it went public. But then the dotcom bubble burst in the spring of 2000, and most of the overheated stocks that had split went splat.

Although we've said farewell to that latest get-rich-quick delusion, a real puzzle remains: Why do investors like stock splits, anyway? Imagine that someone asked you for a dime, then handed you back two nickels and said, "Don't you feel richer now?" You'd probably think he was insulting your intelligence. Yet that's exactly what happens when a company splits its stock.

Let's say you start with 100 shares of Whangdoodle Corp. trading at $100 apiece, and the stock splits two for one; now you have 200 shares, each worth $50, leaving you no better off than before. And the split has zero effect on Whangdoodle's earnings or assets. "A split is an empty transaction," says David Ikenberry, a finance professor at Rice University.

Well, not quite empty. In a fascinating research paper, Ikenberry studied more than 12,000 stock splits back to 1930. In every period, stocks that split outperformed those that didn't. Over the most recent decade that Ikenberry analyzed—1988 through 1997—companies that split returned an annual average of 23.3% vs. 18% for Standard & Poor's 500-stock index. Considering the essential emptiness of stock splits, Ikenberry's long-term findings are amazing. What's going on here?

Let's do the split.   Vanderbilt University historian Peter Rousseau says stock splits date back at least to the Boston Stock Exchange in the 1850s. In those days most people could afford to buy only one share at a time, since stocks traded at a percentage of their so-called par value—which typically ranged from $100 to $1,000 (after 150 years of inflation, that would be as much as $20,000 today). For instance, Salisbury Mills split 10 for one in 1857, carving its $1,000 stock into 10 slices at $100 each. These early splits, argues Rousseau, made it easier for America's pioneering manufacturers to raise capital from small investors.

But nowadays, almost every investor can afford more than a single share at a time, and there's no rational reason why a company would rather have, say, 20 million shares priced at $25 instead of 10 million shares at $50. Either way, its stock has a total market value of $500 million. So why do companies split their shares?

One reason, says Ikenberry, is that splitting has come to be regarded as a sign of good corporate health: "A split is a way for managers to say, 'We have confidence that bad news is not around the corner.'" Indeed, he notes, earnings at the typical splitting company have risen an impressive 20% and the stock an average of 50% in the preceding year.

Finance professors James Angel of Georgetown University and Michael Brennan of UCLA offer another insight. Stockbrokers make much of their money by pocketing the "spread" between what buyers are willing to pay for a stock and what sellers are willing to accept. A typical spread runs roughly from 13 cents to 25 cents a share. If you trade 100 shares of a $50 stock, your broker might pocket a quick, risk-free $25 in spread. But if that stock split two for one, and the spread stayed constant (as it often does), then your broker would double his take, since he'd get to skim the same spread off twice as many shares.

Why one plus one equals three.   Of course, the main reason firms split their shares is that investors want them to. It's bewildering that we can't outthink Yogi Berra—who, when asked whether he wanted his pizza cut into four or eight slices, replied, "Four. I don't think I can eat eight." Why is it so hard for us to realize that it's the size of the entire investment pie, not how many slices it's cut into, that really matters?

It's partly because our own minds play tricks on us. Many investors view a two-for-one split as if it were a windfall—congratulating themselves on having twice as many shares as before, while failing to see that their total stake is worth the same as ever. Casino gamblers use the same kind of "mental accounting" by viewing their winnings as the "house's money," not their own.

There's another mind game going on here too. Let's say you originally bought 100 shares at $10 apiece and the stock then runs up to $50 and splits two for one. Since you've already ridden the stock up to $50 once, it's easy to imagine you'll get there again. Now you're engaged in what psychologists call "anchoring": fixating on a previous high-water mark as a way to measure your likelihood of future success. In reality, of course, there's no guarantee that your stock will ever hit $50 again.

Another oddity of splits is that they can create the illusion that a stock has become cheap all over again. A $50 stock may lack bargain-basement appeal. But if it splits two for one, it can suddenly strike you as undervalued, since $25 is a much lower price. After stocks rise, it takes much larger price declines to make them look cheap again. Scientists even have a name for this; it's called Weber's Law, after a German physiologist who noted that people have difficulty perceiving small changes to large quantities.

Betting against Buffett.   Can you make money off something as dopey as stock splits? Yes and no. As Rice professor Ikenberry's numbers show, stocks that split have beaten the market by roughly five percentage points a year for decades. Unfortunately, explains Ikenberry, you could have captured those returns only by buying shares in every single one of the thousands of stocks that have ever split and holding them for one year. But nobody

Divide and conquer?

Companies that split their shares have long beaten those that don't. Splitting stocks trounced the broader market by an average of 7.1 percentage points a year from 1961 through 1987 and by 5.4 points annually from 1988 through 1997. Yet making money this way remains problematic.

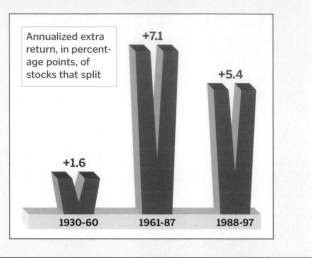

Annualized extra return, in percentage points, of stocks that split

+1.6   +7.1   +5.4

1930-60   1961-87   1988-97

Notes: Chart shows average annualized outperformance of splitting stocks, vs. a customized market benchmark.
Source: Prof. David Ikenberry.

invests that way, so Ikenberry also tested what you'd have earned with a more active split-trading strategy. That cut the outperformance nearly in half, meaning that you'd be left with only modest profits after paying taxes and commissions.

Ikenberry also hastens to add that his research stops in 1998, before serial splitters like Amazon, CMGI and DoubleClick came crashing down; updated through today, Ikenberry's numbers would lose still more of their gloss. In the end, Ikenberry advises against buying stocks solely on the basis of splits. However, he does have two suggestions. First, if you're already thinking of buying a stock, and it splits, you can take that as a fairly strong signal that the stock may be a good buy. And, he adds, if you're considering two similar stocks, and one of them splits, that's probably the one to go with.

Still, while it makes sense to use splits as one of the factors you look at before buying a stock, it's worth remembering that Warren Buffett has never split Berkshire Hathaway's shares (which now cost about $68,000 each). Buffett has explained that he doesn't want to attract "inferior" buyers who'd "downgrade the quality" of his current shareholders. That's his polite way of saying that people who buy stocks on the basis of splits alone are bozos.

Chapter 5
WHAT ALL BOND INVESTORS NEED TO KNOW

"Gentlemen prefer bonds," said Andrew Mellon early in the 20th century, but few people echoed that sentiment during the late 1990s. Besides, Mellon was already immensely rich when he made that statement, and he wasn't worried about saving enough for retirement and paying for his kids' education. Today, investors interested in growth have learned to look elsewhere. After all, everyone knows that stocks have returned more than twice as much per year as bonds over the past 75 years (11.3% vs. 5.5%). So who needs bonds? Smart investors, that's who. True, bonds don't regularly deliver gang-buster gains, but they do have considerable virtues.

That was very apparent in 2000, when long-term Treasuries were the big bond stars, with a very unbondlike 17.5% average gain. Long-term Treasuries beat the return of the S&P 500 by 26.6 percentage points. Bonds' supremacy continued through the first four months of 2001, with the average U.S. government bond fund outperforming the Wilshire 5000 stock index by 8.51 percentage points (2.1% vs. -6.50%).

But you shouldn't buy bonds simply because they've done well lately. Bonds deserve a permanent place in the portfolios of almost all investors. As it happens, though, millions of investors know far more about stocks than they do about bonds. We'll try to change that in this chapter as we answer some of the most frequently asked questions about bond investing.

Q. Why would any long-term investor be interested in an asset class that has a much lower long-term return than stocks?

A. For one reason, because bonds are much less volatile. That's why combining bonds with stocks produces a more stable portfolio. Portfolios that include stocks and bonds can give much of the upside of equities while limiting risk—a definite plus in today's volatile market. As noted earlier, for the 20 years through September 30, 1999, a mix of 60% large-cap stocks and 40% intermediate-term bonds would have captured 85% of an all-stock portfolio's gains while reducing volatility by 35%.

Bonds are also capable of beating stocks' performance when interest rates drop or when the stock market hits the skids or goes nowhere in particular. For instance, from 1969 to 1982, the 7.8% average annual return of medium-term U.S. bonds surpassed the 6.7% gain of U.S. stocks. Are you surprised, then, that back in 1982 many investors were selling stocks to buy bonds? And guess what: 1982 also began the biggest bull market in history. Just as you would have been wrong to put all your money in bonds in 1982, when stocks were stone cold, you might have been wrong in 2000 to put all your money in stocks when they were red hot.

Still not convinced? Well, consider these two examples: In 1973 and 1974, when stocks fell 37.2%, bonds went up 10.6%. And in the dreadful month of October 1987, stocks lost 21.5% of their value, but medium-term bonds rose 3%. As you can see, when stocks went south, bonds headed north—providing a cushion when investors needed it.

If you're an aggressive investor, you might be reluctant to commit much of your portfolio to bonds, but bear this in mind: 20% is probably the lowest you should go to get the full benefit of bonds.

Q. Are there any other compelling reasons to own bonds?

A. Absolutely. Bonds pay interest regularly, which makes them a good choice for investors—such as retirees—who want a steady stream of income.

Bonds can also provide a level of security that stocks could never hope to match. Next to cash, U.S. Treasuries are the safest, most liquid investments on the planet. Short-term bonds are a good place to

Taxable or Tax-Exempt?

To find out whether you're better off in tax-exempt municipal bonds (munis) or in taxable bonds or bond funds, fill out the worksheet below, or use the muni bond calculator at www.money.com.

		EXAMPLE	YOUR FIGURES
1	Enter yield on muni bond or fund	5.1%	
2	Enter your marginal federal tax rate[1]	31%	
3	Subtract line 2 from 100% (100%-31%=69%)	69%	
4	Divide line 1 by line 3 (5.1%÷69%=7.4%)	7.4%	
5	Enter yield on taxable bond or fund.	6.5%	
6	If line 5 is larger than line 4, you're better off in taxables. Otherwise, munis are the better bet.	Munis!	

Note: [1]If the bond or fund is also exempt from state and local taxes, multiply your combined state and local tax rate by 1 minus your marginal federal tax rate (example: 6% x 69%) and then add the result (4.1%) to your federal rate (31% + 4.1%). Enter this figure (35.1%) on line 2 and continue with steps 3, 4 and 5.

park an emergency fund or money you'll need relatively soon—say, to buy a house or pay college tuition in a few years.

Bonds provide a more subtle form of protection, as well. "Many investors," says Harvard economist John Campbell, "are unaware that their financial portfolio is dwarfed by the value of their human capital," by which he means their current and future job income. Most people's labor earnings are dependent on the health of the U.S. economy, since even a mild slowdown can retard salary growth and put people out of work. A recession, clearly, makes matters even worse. Unless you're minister, a mortician or a prison guard, your job income is probably tied to the stock market more closely than you think. Therefore, says Campbell, "if your labor earnings move with the aggregate stock market, you should take less risk in your financial portfolio."

Finally, bonds can help keep the taxman at bay. Certain bonds, such as municipal bonds, provide tax-free income. Although these bonds usually pay lower yields than comparable taxable bonds, investors in high brackets (generally 28% and above) can often earn higher after-tax returns from tax-free bonds. For instance, according to the fund firm T. Rowe Price, an investor in the 31%

Types of Bonds

U.S. Treasuries are the safest bonds of all because the interest and principal payments are guaranteed by the "full faith and credit"—that is, the taxing power—of the U.S. government. Interest is exempt from state and local taxes, but not from federal tax. Because of their almost total lack of default risk, Treasuries carry some of the lowest yields around.

Treasuries come in several flavors:

- **Treasury bills**, or T-bills, have the shortest maturities—13 weeks, 26 weeks and one year. You buy them at a discount to their $10,000 face value and receive the full $10,000 at maturity. The difference reflects the interest you earn.
- **Treasury notes** mature in two to 10 years. Interest is paid semiannually at a fixed rate. Minimum investment: $1,000.
- **Treasury bonds** have the longest maturities—10 to 30 years. They pay interest semiannually, and are sold in denominations of $1,000.
- **Zero-coupon bonds**, also known as "strips" or "zeros," are Treasury-based securities that are sold by brokers at a deep discount and redeemed at full face value when they mature in six months to 30 years. Although you don't actually receive your interest until the bond matures, you must pay taxes each year on the "phantom interest" that you earn. For that reason, they are best held in tax-deferred accounts. Because they pay no coupon, zeros can be highly volatile in price.
- **Inflation-indexed Treasuries (TIPs)**. Issued in 10- and 30-year maturities (plus some five-year bonds issued earlier that are still trading on the secondary market), these pay a real rate of interest on a principal amount that rises and falls with the CPI. You don't collect the inflation adjustment to your principal until the bond matures or you sell it, but

tax bracket would have earned returns equivalent to an annualized 10.3% in munis for the 10 years ended September 30, 1999 vs. 8.5% in corporates and 7.9% in Treasuries. To figure out whether you should be in munis or taxables, calculate the muni's taxable equivalent yield using the worksheet on page 89.

Q. How exactly do bonds work?

A. You need to know the answer before you invest in bonds, otherwise you could get burned in ways you never imagined. For a listing of types of bonds, see the box above.

When you buy a bond, you're essentially lending money to a bond issuer (a corporation, municipality or the federal govern-

you owe federal income tax on that phantom amount each year—in addition to tax on the interest you receive currently. Inflation bonds are best held in tax-deferred accounts.

Mortgage-backed bonds represent an ownership stake in a package of mortgage loans issued or guaranteed by government agencies such as the Government National Mortgage Association (Ginnie Mae), Federal National Mortgage Association (Fannie Mae) and Freddie Mac. Interest is taxable and is paid monthly, along with a partial repayment of the principal. Except for Ginnie Maes, these bonds are not backed by the full faith and credit of the U.S. government. They generally yield up to 1% more than Treasuries of comparable maturities. Minimum investment: typically $25,000.

Corporate bonds pay taxable interest. Most are issued in denominations of $1,000 and have maturities ranging from a few weeks to 100 years. Because their value depends on the creditworthiness of the company offering them, corporates carry higher risks and, therefore, higher yields than super-safe Treasuries. Top-quality corporates are known as *investment-grade bonds*. Corporates with lower credit quality are called *high-yield*, or *junk*, *bonds*. Junk bonds typically have higher yields than other corporates.

Municipal bonds, or *munis*, are America's favorite tax shelter. They are issued by state and local governments and agencies, usually in denominations of $5,000 and up, and mature in one to 40 years. Interest is exempt from federal taxes and, if you live in the state issuing the bond, state and possibly local taxes as well. Note, though, that Illinois, Kansas, Iowa, Oklahoma and Wisconsin tax interest on their own municipal bonds. No matter where you live, any capital gain you realize when you sell a municipal bond is fully taxable. (For a fuller description of municipal bonds, see the box on page 92.)

ment) in return for the issuer's promise to pay a fixed rate of interest (called the *coupon rate*) and to repay the principal or face value amount of the bond (typically $1,000) at the end of the bond's term (usually one to 30 years). While the coupon rate remains fixed, the bond almost always sells for more or less than its face amount. So a bond's *current yield*—the annual coupon payment divided by the current price—fluctuates daily. To know whether a bond's return is competitive, ask your bond dealer or broker for its *yield to maturity*. This is the return you'll earn based on the bond's coupon rate and current price if you hold the bond to maturity.

Generally, *long-term bonds* (those with 10- to 30-year maturities) have higher yields than *intermediate-term* (four to 10 years)

Bonding with Munis

If you think that municipal bonds are purchased only by the rich or by conservative investors who, good grief, remind you of your father, think again. Tax-exempt issues can be very attractive.

Even investors in the 28% tax bracket come out ahead with muni bonds. Here are some specifics. At first glance, a 5.32% yield on a 10-year Treasury, for instance, looks a lot better than the 4.74% yield on a 10-year insured muni. But you know what they say about looks. In reality, that 4.74% is equivalent to a taxable yield of 6.58% for investors in the 28% bracket, and 6.87% for those in the 31% bracket. The muni payoff becomes even juicier if you live in a high-tax state, since residents usually don't pay state income taxes on muni income, and in many large cities your yield will also be free from local levies. (The muni-bond calculator on page 89 can help you figure out taxable-equivalent yields.)

For most investors, mutual funds are the best way to buy munis. For an initial ante of $3,000 or less, you can find a solid bond fund that provides instant diversification, low fees and professional management.

When shopping for a bond fund, focus on these three questions: How long? How good? How much?

"How long?" refers to the average maturity of the bond that a fund owns. The longer the maturity, the more the fund will suffer when rates rise. Intermediate-term issues with maturities of 10 years are your best bet. "You get 95% of the yield of longer maturities but with just 65% of the market risk," says Chris Ryon, who runs three Vanguard muni funds.

issues, which, in turn, carry higher yields than *short-term* (one to four years) bonds. Under certain economic conditions, the Treasury curve can "invert," in which case this relationship would be temporarily reversed. When this happens, as it did in 2000, it often presages a slowing economy.

Similarly, because of the risk involved, the weaker the financial health of the issuer, the higher the rate investors demand. *Junk bonds*—or to use the euphemism preferred by issuers, *"high-yield" bonds*—typically pay two to $2^1/_2$ percentage points more than Treasury bonds, while high-quality corporate bonds usually yield one-half of a percentage point or so more than Treasuries. Those margins change with market conditions.

Municipal bonds work pretty much the same way. But since the income they pay is free of federal (and sometimes state and local) tax, their yields are lower than taxable bonds'.

"How good?" is a matter of ratings. Stick with funds that own investment-grade issues, that is, those rated at least BBB by Standard & Poor's.

The answer to the question "How much?" should be zero—that is, you should not pay a sales load for a bond fund. If you live in a state with high income taxes, you can duck local levies by going with a fund that buys only munis issued in your own state.

Although it's theoretically more cost-effective to buy individual muni bonds, it can get tricky. Complicating the issue is that investors have more muni bond choices than ever before. Of course, many of the 1.5 million outstanding issues are of topnotch quality—almost half the new issues are insured, for example, and therefore rated triple A. But there is also a plethora of new, unrated health-care, hospital and industrial-development bonds. Their yields are attractive, but historically these bonds default at quadruple the rate of the overall muni market. "These days, issuers are using muni bonds for aquariums, racetracks, housing in the middle of the desert, anything to gin up economic development," says bond expert Joe Mysak.

The result: Lacking reliable price information, too many investors have simply chased the highest available yields and wound up holding dubious bonds. "You get these little old ladies canvassed by telephone in California, offered 8% bonds that are too good to be true," says bond pro Zane Mann.

How can you avoid getting snared? Buy a fund or buy highly-rated individual bonds at reasonable prices (check www.investinginbonds.com for comparable price quotes).

Q. Do investors face any risks when buying bonds?

A. Bonds *are* relatively safe, but, despite their wimpish image, they can easily cause losses for investors. Although the interest payments you'll get from owning a bond are "fixed," your return is anything but. One pitfall you've got to be on guard against is *credit risk*, also known as *default risk*—that is, the chance that the issuer won't pay interest when it's due or won't repay the principal when the bond matures. This isn't a concern if you invest in Treasury securities; thus far, Uncle Sam has always made good on his promises to repay.

The danger of defaults is also relatively low for investment-grade corporates. A recent Standard & Poor's study of more than 7,300 bonds it has rated since 1981 found that just 2.1% of investment-grade corporates defaulted within 15 years of being issued. Default rates are generally far lower than 2.1% for high-

Bonds on the Web

The Internet is beginning to fill the bond information gap. There are some very useful bond sites now, and many of the leading online brokerages, including Schwab and E-Trade, have begun rolling out bond trading areas that promise to give individual investors timely information and, consequently, fairer prices. Here are four sites you should bookmark:

- **Standard & Poor's** (www.standardandpoors.com)
  Bond ratings and S&P's rating system

- **Bureau of the Public Debt**
  (www.publicdebt.treas.gov/sec/sec.htm)
  How to tap the Treasury Direct program

- **Investing in Bonds.com** (www.investinginbonds.com)
  Investing tips and recent prices and yields for specific corporate and muni issues

- **Bonds Online** (www.bondsonline.com)
  Full of basic info and a comprehensive glossary

quality muni bonds. By contrast, 23% of junk bonds had defaulted within 15 years. To gauge credit risk, check out the ratings assigned by firms such as Standard & Poor's (see the "Bonds on the Web" box above).

Even when the odds of default are low, you have to take the possibility seriously. Remember those "Whoops" bonds that caused so much misery? When the Washington Public Power Supply System (WPPSS) bonds defaulted in 1982—the largest municipal bond failure in U.S. history—many investors who had a high percentage of their assets in those bonds saw their retirement dreams dashed. You can do two things to avoid such a devastating loss. First, don't invest too much of your nest egg in the bonds of any single issuer. Second, sacrifice a little yield (usually about a quarter of a percentage point) and buy only insured municipal bonds.

Another type of risk is far more likely to wreak havoc with your bond holdings—*interest-rate risk*. To get a handle on this hazard, think of a see-saw. When interest rates go up, bond prices go down, and vice versa. The longer the bond's maturity, the more its price rises or falls in response to a change in interest rates.

But maturity gives you only a general idea of how a bond reacts to fluctuating interest rates. *Duration*, a technical measure that's too complicated and boring to go into here, provides a more accurate gauge. The higher a bond's duration (a figure that you can get from your broker), the more sensitive it is to interest rates. The price of a bond with a duration of seven years, for example, will decline a bit less than 7% if interest rates rise by one percentage point and rise a bit more than 7% if rates drop by the same amount.

Sometimes the risk of owning a bond isn't that you'll lose money but that you'll lose the bond. Warning: Some bonds have a call provision that allows the issuer to repay the principal on specified dates before maturity. If you own a *callable bond* with a coupon rate of 8% when new bonds are paying 6%, you can pretty much bet that the issuer will redeem it, leaving you to rein-vest your money at lower rates. Before you buy a callable bond, ask the broker for its *yield to call* for each call date. This will tell you the return you'll earn if the issuer repays the bond early.

Q. So what's a smart way to invest in bonds?

A. If you're looking to bonds for income or to dampen the jumpi-ness of a stock portfolio, you're probably better off in short- to intermediate-term issues. Over the past 20 years, intermediate-term Treasuries provided almost 90% of long-term Treasuries' return with only half as much volatility.

You may also want to spread your money around by invest-ing in a variety of bonds with different maturities. You could do this by buying several bond funds or by buying a half-dozen or so individual bonds (if you have at least $75,000 to invest) to build a laddered bond portfolio, where each rung consists of a different maturity bond, from one year right up to 10 years. When the one-year matures, you reinvest the money in a new 10-year issue. In this way, you always have more money to rein-vest every year, and you are somewhat protected from interest rate shifts because you have locked in a range of yields.

If you want to go big-gain hunting, long-term issues are the place to be. Here you're betting that interest rates will fall. Remember, though, you can lose big if rates seesaw against you.

Q. Should I buy individual bonds or bond funds?

A. Conventional wisdom says bond funds are bad because, in almost every case, you have no assurance of getting your money back. If you buy a bond fund and interest rates rise, your net asset value will fall. But if you buy an actual bond and hold it to maturity, you get your money back (barring the unlikely event of a default), no matter how much rates skyrocket.

As it so often is, the conventional wisdom is wrong. Individual bonds are better than bond funds only if you have a sizable sum to invest—say, a minimum of $75,000—to get the diversification you need. For the rest of us, bond funds with low expenses beat individual bonds hands down.

The reason: the power of compounding. True enough, any rise in interest rates will temporarily depress the fund's value, as investors learned to their shock in 1994, when a jump in rates knocked the average bond fund for a 4% loss. But in the long run, higher rates means a fund's income can be reinvested at greater yields.

Let's say you invest $1,000 in a 30-year Treasury bond at 6%. Between now and 2031, you'll get $30 in interest every six months. Now, let's say interest rates rise one percentage point. If you put each of your bond's interest payments into an investment yielding the new rate of 7%, you'd actually earn 6.54% annually over the life of your 6% bond.

Here's where being a small investor is a big problem: The interest payments on your bond are only $30 apiece, and no one will sell you a bond for a lousy 30 bucks. Instead, you'll have to put your little nubbins of interest into the bank or a money fund, and they're likely to earn far less than the rate on new bonds. And thus you fail to harness the full power of compounding.

But a good fund manager will sweep together all the interest payments and reinvest them in bulk purchases of new, higher-yielding bonds. For this management service, funds charge annual expense that average 1% or so of your account value.

Buy bonds on your own, and you sidestep the management fee. With the exception of Treasuries, however, most bonds don't trade every day, so it's hard to gauge their value. And although access to bond prices has improved a bit, bonds are still in the dark ages compared with stocks. Bond dealers are more than happy to exploit this situation. Treasuries aside, when you buy bonds in small amounts—and less than $1 million is small in the bond world—price variations of 2% to 6% among dealers for the same bond are all too common.

Buying Treasuries shouldn't be a problem, especially if you buy directly from the government through its Treasury Direct program. With corporates, the difficulty of getting a decent price, plus the need to diversify because of credit and call risk, argues in favor of a bond fund. As for munis, if you shop carefully—get price quotes from three brokers and check out recent prices (see the box listing bond websites on page 94)—you should get your bonds at a good price. And if you stay with the highest-rated issues and buy the bonds of four or five states, your risk of being decimated by a default is relatively low.

Q. Okay, you've finally convinced me. How should I buy bonds?
A. A good place to start is by buying the Vanguard Total Bond Market fund, which owns short- and long-term corporates and Treasuries. If you want something racier, add some high-yield bonds. High default rates (that's why they're called junk) hurt the prices of lower-rated bonds in 2000, pushing yields up to alluring levels, an average of 14.5%. Mighty tempting. "The last time the Fed eased and you had yields this high a decade ago, the following year you ended up with about a 35% return," says Ed Larsen, chief equity officer of AIM Funds. No less an investor than Warren Buffett has been dabbling in junk, recently scooping up several hundred million dollars in the junk paper of commercial lender Finova Group. (In June 2001, Buffett's Berkshire Hathaway and Lencadia National struck a deal to buy most of Finova.)

If you have less cash to invest than Mr. Buffett, you might consider Invesco High Yield (800-525-8085), run by Jerry Paul, which boasts a 8.6% annualized return over the past 10 years. Nothing junky about that, eh?

WHERE TO STASH YOUR CASH

You can lessen your exposure to stocks by using vehicles other than bonds, of course. The recent market swoon has convinced many investors that cash is no longer trash.

Back when your stocks and funds were generating double-digit gains, who cared if your spare cash was in the bank earning 1.5%? You probably care now, what with Standard & Poor's 500-stock index in bear market territory and many investors building up their cash reserves.

If you stash your cash more thoughtfully, you can squeeze out those key extra points of return. But first, you must figure out what kind of cash you're holding. Maybe you're waiting to jump back into stocks once the moment is right. Maybe you need to set aside $10,000 for next year's college tuition. Maybe your aggressive long-term portfolio needs a larger no- or low-risk component. Maybe you're worried about inflation. Each situation demands its own strategy.

Liquidity with lots of interest.   For cash you might need on short notice, go with a money-market mutual fund, not a bank money-market account. The difference? More than two percentage points as of mid-March 2001: The average bank money market was yielding 2.7%, while the typical fund was paying 5%.

There's another difference: The bank account is FDIC insured, while the money fund comes with no guarantee that you won't lose your principal. That might lead squeamish investors to stick with a money fund that invests only in U.S. Government securities. Don't, says Peter Crane, managing editor of iMoneyNet, which publishes *Money Fund Report*. It's highly unlikely that any money fund will "break the buck" (dip below the $1 share price at which investors buy in) because SEC regulations ensure that these funds invest in the safest instruments around. Yes, an issuer may default on its debt—as California's Pacific Gas & Electric did in March 2001, thanks to the state's energy crisis—but any major fund company left holding worthless notes will make it up to shareholders. The likes of Fidelity or Vanguard have insurance policies to cover defaults, as well as reputations to protect. "When it comes to safety," counsels Crane, "bigger is better."

The big fund companies also tend to keep fund expenses below the 0.5% norm, and low expenses are the only guarantee that a fund's yield will remain competitive. You can find the highest-yielding money funds listed in newspapers, on the Internet or in each month's issue of MONEY. But look carefully at these deals, because some companies temporarily waive fees to draw customers. Check the fund prospectus, and call to ask if a fee increase is imminent. Of course, some money funds do waive fees indefinitely; Strong Investors Money Fund is a leaders-list regular because of fee waivers.

Discount brokerages like Schwab and E-Trade offer decent money-market rates, but if you're working with a traditional firm, make sure your spare cash does not go into a money-market fund with high expenses that subsidize a commission to the broker.

If you live in a high-tax state such as California or New York, you might want a muni fund exempt from federal and state taxes. (Go to www.investinginbonds.com to calculate your best route.) But high demand has cut the average tax-free money-market yield to 2.3%, so even investors in the highest brackets may not come out ahead vs. taxable funds.

Short-term nest egg. What about the Christmas shopping fund? Next year's college bill? If you're not going to touch the money for a while, lock it up in a six-month or one-year CD.

As of mid-March 2001, you could lock in rates as high as 5.5% on a one-year CD. Smaller regional banks trying to drum up business often offer some great deals, and E-Trade Bank (www.etradebank.com) is tough to beat. Comparison shop by visiting www.money.com to access Bankrate.com's CD-shopping tools. A note of caution: Avoid "callable" CDs, which the bank can redeem before maturity; always look for that word in the bank's literature—if it's there, think twice before signing up.

Portfolio cushion. If you're saving for longer than a year or two, don't tie up cash in a CD. Venture instead into a short-term bond fund. Yields are higher, though they come with some risk. But Vanguard bond guru Ken Volpert says short-term funds these days "are not at all a risky business." If you're investing for several years or more, that's plenty of time to ride out any rough spots.

To limit risk, go with a diversified combo of government and corporate bond funds. Avoid the all-government funds: Even short-term bonds can be risky and hard to sell in a pinch, so be wary of funds with the words high yield or prime rate in the name.

Avoid sales charges too. Even a relatively low 2% load would take a huge bite out of your profits, given that a leader like Vanguard Short-Term Bond Index returned an annualized 6.8% over the past five years (through mid-March 2001). For the same reason, annual expenses can make or break you. That's why the Vanguard index fund, with a slim 0.21% expense ratio, places in the top 10% of short-termers over the past five years. With its similar index format and 0.3% expense ratio, TIAA-CREF Short-Term Bond promises to be a long-term leader too. And its $250 minimum (vs. Vanguard's $3,000) makes it accessible to just about every investor.

If you're willing to pay more and take on extra credit risk, check out Strong Short-Term Bond fund. Its 0.86% expense ratio is average for the group, but manager Bradley Tank has earned one of the best records in the class since taking over the fund in 1990.

Cash Alternatives

These sure beat your average savings account, but there are still pluses and minuses to consider.

Vehicle	Pros	Cons	Where to go
Money-market funds	Top yields with safety and liquidity	Yields may be heading south.	Strong: www.strongfunds.com, 800-368-1030 TIAA-CREF: www.tiaa-cref.org, 800-223-1200 Vanguard: www.vanguard.com, 800-871-3879
Short-term bond funds	Best return prospects, with liquidity too	You could actually lose money.	
CDs	High guaranteed interest rate	Penalties for early withdrawal	Compare at www.bankrate.com and www.imoneynet.com.
I-bonds	Tax-deferred growth, inflation adjustments	Must hold for six months; penalty if cashed within five years	Buy at your bank or online at www.savingsbonds.gov.

Inflation fighter. Looking out five years or more? Then inflation's power to devour really becomes a factor—notwithstanding that inflation has been low of late. With inflation-adjusted savings bonds, or I-bonds, your principal is safe and your rate is guaranteed to keep up with inflation (which historically averages about 3% annually). I-bonds don't provide current income; you don't get a payout until you cash in a bond. But that makes them a marvelous tax-deferred savings vehicle: You can earn interest for up to 30 years and owe no taxes until you redeem the bond. (And if you use the proceeds to pay college tuition, you won't owe taxes at all.)

You may buy $30,000 in I-bonds each year, and up to $1,000 a pop online (www.savingsbonds.gov). While their yields fluctuate with inflation, they're based on a fixed rate that's set at purchase. In June 2001, the rate was 3.0%, for an inflation-adjusted yield of 5.92%. The government resets the fixed rate every May 1 and November 1.

Chapter 6
SMART MUTUAL
FUND STRATEGIES

For a time, it seemed as if the allure of mutual funds had faded. Almost everyone we met suddenly seemed to be a stock-picker, whether they were a sixth grader or an octogenarian, or somewhere in between. And, certainly, the market did reward many aggressive stock-pickers—for a while.

Then they opened the trap door. Investors were reminded that individual stocks can fall far faster than diversified mutual funds. Since then, we've met some people who have scurried back to funds, swearing that they'll never buy another stock as long as they live.

That strikes us as an extreme reaction. We don't think most investors should shun either stocks or funds. Funds offer diversification, professional management and, in some cases, a low-cost way to participate in the market (especially if you use index funds). Funds also provide a more prudent way to buy hard-to-research investments such as small or foreign companies and bonds. But selecting the right funds from the 12,000 crying out for your business is not easy.

To help you sort through the universe of stellar funds, the editors at MONEY compiled one comprehensive list—the MONEY 100—to focus on. (You can find an updated list of the MONEY 100—with complete performance data and advice on using the list to build a portfolio—at www.money.com.)

So, what kind of funds do we like? We prize funds with consistent performance, sound strategies, low expenses and managers who inspire trust, because these are the factors we believe are most likely to lead to success. We encourage investors to pay particular attention to expenses since annual fees alone can range from 0.06% to more than 2.55% of assets. We also stress the importance of independent ratings, especially those that compare similar types of funds. You can find a lot of information (including ratings) at Morningstar.com, a major fund rating organization, and in a mutual fund's prospectus.

One thing we don't recommend when searching for funds is trying is predict the next hot sector or style. That's been a losing approach for many investors, who invariably pile into a hot area of the market only to see the sizzling sector turn ice cold. That's precisely what happened to many investors in Internet funds.

On page 110, we've listed 11 funds that seem to have permanent residency on the MONEY 100. All 11 are run by veteran money managers with impressive track records.

COPING WITH CHOICE

When you put together a mutual fund portfolio or buy mutual funds to diversify your existing stock holdings, remember to seek balance. As we've discussed earlier, a healthy portfolio weighs risk against rewards. To accomplish this, use your asset allocation model to decide what category of funds you want to investigate.

However, with mutual funds multiplying faster than rabbits on Viagra, it's easy to end up too confused to function. When Mae West said, "Too much of a good thing is wonderful," the good thing she was thinking of certainly was not mutual funds. Morningstar divides funds into about 50 categories, which include domestic, international and specialty stock funds; hybrid funds and general, specialty, government and municipal bond funds. (See "Types of Funds" on page 104.)

So here's the question: Do you stand the slightest chance of picking a suitable fund before the proliferation of choices drives you insane?

The answer is, yes you can. Mutual funds were invented to help simplify our financial lives—and you can still use them to reclaim your right to easier, more understandable investing.

So let's get down to business. You've probably heard the basic law of diversification expressed like this: Don't put all your eggs in one basket. That's one of the few universal truths about investing. But we'd like to add a corollary for today's fund-intoxicated world: Don't put an egg in every basket either. Even if you're exclusively investing in mutual funds, almost no one needs to own more than five or six funds.

BUILDING A DIVERSIFIED FUND PORTFOLIO

The basic building blocks of a diversified portfolio are cash, bonds and U.S. and foreign stocks. You can build a portfolio of mutual funds holding these investments by choosing actively managed mutual funds or buying index funds for the stock and bond portions of your portfolio.

Plenty of people will tell you to own at least a dozen stock funds to "cover all your bases," but that's hogwash. Finance professors have shown that if you taped the stock market pages from the newspaper to the wall and threw darts at them, you'd need to throw no more than 40 darts to get about 95% of the diversification you'd get if you owned every single one of the thousands of stocks in the listing. Since the typical U.S. fund owns more than 100 stocks, what on earth is the point of owning a dozen or more funds?

When picking stock funds, consider your tolerance for risk. For the most part, that boils down to two things: the size of the companies in which the fund invests and whether you prefer growth or value stocks. Over the past century. value investing and growth investing have taken turns as Wall Street's favorites, with each typically dominating for periods of three to six years. In the late '90s, growth was the clear winner. By 2001, value funds were ascendant. "Value tends to underperform some 30% to 40% of the time," says Jeremy Siegel, finance professor at the University of Pennsylvania's Wharton School. "But over the long term, the evidence shows that value and growth are about evenly matched in returns." (For more on the pros and cons of growth and value stocks, see Chapter 3.)

Whether you side with growth, value or a blend of both, we think everyone should have a *blue-chip, large-cap fund* that owns the biggest stocks in the country, such as General Electric, ExxonMobil or Pfizer. (The 500 favorite stocks in the U.S. account for more than 70% of the total value of the U.S. stock

Types of Funds

Funds vary by investment strategy. Here's a quick overview of some of the principal types of mutual funds:

Index funds: When people talk about the long-term performance of stocks, they're usually talking about the Dow Jones Industrial Average or the Standard & Poor's 500-stock index. An index fund can be based on one of several different benchmarks used to track stocks and bonds. Four of the most popular indexes:

- **Standard & Poor's 500 Stock Index:** covers large U.S. companies
- **Russell 2000 Stock Index:** covers small U.S. companies
- **Wilshire 5000 Stock Index:** covers large, medium and small U.S. companies
- **Lehman Brothers Aggregate Bond Index:** covers the total U.S. taxable bond market. (For more on indexing, see "The Joy of Index Funds" on page 106.)

Growth funds: These invest in the stocks of companies whose profits are growing at a rapid pace. Such stocks typically rise more quickly than the overall market—and fall faster if they don't live up to investors' expectations.

Value funds: Value managers buy companies that appear to be cheap based on their earnings, cash flow or assets. In many cases, these are mature companies that send some of their earnings back to their shareholders in the form of dividends.

Other funds: Since there is a lot of overlap in the stocks held in each of these fund types, you'll need to branch out to get any kind of meaningful diversification. That's where the more aggressive funds, like *aggressive growth funds*, *capital appreciation funds*, *small-cap funds* and *midcap funds*, among others, fit in. Typically, these funds, which tend to be more volatile than large-cap funds, pursue one or more of the following strategies:

- Invest in smaller companies, whose earnings aren't as reliable as bigger firms', but which have the potential for larger gains (and losses).
- Invest in pricey, high-growth stocks.
- Invest in stocks that are in "hot" industries, such as technology or health-care.
- Invest in just a handful of companies.

market.) You should also own a fund, such as a *domestic small-cap* or *midcap stock fund*, that complements your large-cap holding by moving up or down at different rates and times.

International or foreign funds: These come in three basic flavors. The first, *international funds*, typically buy stocks in larger companies from relatively stable regions like Europe and the Pacific Rim. *Global funds* do likewise, but they can also invest heavily in the U.S. And *emerging market funds* invest in less developed, and therefore riskier, countries, most of which are in Latin America, Eastern Europe, Asia and Africa.

Bond funds: Finally, these tend to be segmented across the risk spectrum, with those that specialize in *U.S. Treasury securities* being the safest (and the lowest-yielding) and those that specialize in *junk bonds* being the riskiest, but offering the highest yield. They also divide according to whether the bonds they hold are taxable or tax-free. One thing to remember: When the stock market is headed down, funds that invest in U.S. Treasuries tend to rise in value as investors flock to the safest investments around. When the stock market is going up, junk bonds funds tend to do the best, as improved business conditions make it more likely that even the riskiest bond bets will pay off. (For more on bonds, see Chapter 5.)

Balanced funds and life-cycle funds: These all-in-one funds can provide simplicity and convenience. They are for investors who want their money to grow, but view being actively involved in the investing process as a worrisome hassle. *Balanced funds* include stocks (usually dividend-paying shares) and bonds. The mix is usually 50-50 or 60% (stocks)-40% (bonds). *Life-cycle funds* hold stocks, bonds and cash in proportions that are considered appropriate for investors at specific ages. Even the most conservative life-cycle funds tend to outperform CDs or money-market accounts. The main benefit of these funds is that they help investors make prudent asset allocation adjustments as time progresses. The main drawback is that they don't change their mix to take advantage of changing market conditions.

Money-market funds: Stash your cash (ideally six months to one year's worth of living expenses) in a *money-market fund* that sticks to U.S. Treasury debt, the safest stuff around (This is your emergency fund and it may take you some time to build up.) If you live in a state with high taxes, such as California, Massachusetts or New York, or if you're in the highest federal tax bracket, consider a *municipal (or "tax-free") money-market fund*. But if you live in a tax haven like Nevada, Texas or Washington—or you're in a low federal tax bracket—you may be better off with a taxable money-market fund.

You might also add a *concentrated* or *focused* fund, which holds only a small number of stocks that the fund manager studies closely, or (if you really like a heavy dose of risk) a *sector* or

The Joy of Index Funds

We've long believed that most individuals should use indexing in building a well-diversified portfolio. Index funds, after all, have many virtues. Their performance has been excellent, their expenses are low and you don't have to make hard decisions about which stock or fund to buy.

Indexing is easy, but it's not a no-brainer. Here's what you should keep in mind:

• **There's a lot more to indexing than the S&P 500.** You can, in fact, easily index most of the worldwide stock market and a major portion of the U.S. bond market. You can build a fully diversified portfolio using nothing but index funds.

But if you own only an S&P 500 index fund, you're not getting the full benefit of indexing. By definition, the S&P 500 ignores all small-cap and many midcap stocks. If large-caps underperform their smaller brethren, your returns will suffer if you're too heavily weighted in the S&P 500. That, in fact, is exactly what happened in the first five months of 2001.

The solution? Consider using a total stock market fund—not an S&P 500 fund—as your core index holding. Such funds typically track the Wilshire 5000, which means, in effect, that you are indexing 99% of the U.S. equity market and you will capture the performance of small stocks.

• **Understand the benchmark that you're following.** Make sure that the index fund you're buying holds securities that truly represent the asset class whose returns you're trying to capture. If you aim, for example, to track the performance of the entire non-U.S. stock market, then you want the Vanguard Total International Stock Market fund, which tracks the Morgan Stanley EAFE (Europe, Australasia and the Far East) and emerging market indexes, rather than the Schwab International Index, which sticks to the 350 largest companies in 15 developed countries.

• **Don't assume all index funds are low cost.** You probably equate indexing with bargain-basement expenses. Yes, the average index fund carries an expense ratio of just 0.5%, vs. 1.46% for actively managed funds. But dozens of index funds are saddled with high expenses, 12b-1 fees, even sales loads.

• **Make the most of indexing's tax efficiency.** Because index funds buy and sell stocks less frequently than the typical actively managed fund, they tend to distribute less in capital gains. So it usually makes sense to use these funds in the taxable portion of your portfolio and put actively managed funds in your non-taxable accounts. (For more on smart tax strategies, see Chapter 10.)

Investing with Style

To help investors assess U.S. domestic funds, researchers at Morningstar Inc. developed a style box, a tic-tac-toe grid that displays both a fund's investment approach and the size of the companies in which it invests. According to Morningstar, combining these two variables offers a broad view of a fund's holdings and the amount of risk it takes.

The rows denote the average size of a fund's stocks: large, medium and small. The columns sort a fund's holdings by average price: cheap value stocks, more expensive growth stocks, or a blend of the two. So every domestic stock fund falls into one of nine pigeon holes: small-cap value, blend or growth; midcap value, blend or growth; and large-cap value, blend or growth. Large-cap value would be considered the safest investment; small-cap growth would be the riskiest.

MEDIAN MARKET CAPITALIZATION	INVESTMENT STYLE		
	VALUE	BLEND	GROWTH
Large	Large-cap value	Large-cap blend	Large-cap growth
Medium	Medium-cap value	Medium-cap blend	**Medium-cap growth**
Small	Small-cap value	**Small-cap blend**	**Small-cap growth**

■ LOW RISK   ■ MODERATE RISK   ■ HIGH RISK

specialty fund that buys stocks in one industry, such as technology or health care.

Finally, everyone should own an *international-* or *foreign-stock fund* that invests in companies based outside the U.S. (not a *global fund* that holds some stocks here, overlapping with the U.S. funds you already own). After all, two-thirds of the world's stocks are traded in markets outside our borders. We recommend that you buy one fund that covers the earth, owning hundreds of stocks in several dozen countries in all the major regions of the world (except the U.S.). That way, if something goes wrong in Rome, you'll still have Paris—not to mention Buenos Aires, Helsinki, Singapore, Sydney, Toronto or Johannesburg.

You'll also need at least one bond fund to help reduce the volatility of your portfolio. (See Chapter 5 for your options, and to learn if a municipal bond fund is right for you.) But regardless of whether you buy a taxable or tax-free fund, you're probably best off in one with an *intermediate* or *medium-term* maturity, meaning that its bonds generally come due in seven years or less, and are thus subject to less volatility than long-term bonds. And most smart investors belong in a fund that mainly buys bonds issued by the U.S. government, or corporations with AAA ratings, not by Acme Shoe Stores or the Republic of Kazakhstan.

The MONEY 100 at www.money.com can help guide you to top choices in each of these categories.

BE CAREFUL WHEN CHASING PERFORMANCE

Just as stock investors want to find "the next Microsoft," fund investors are all in search of the "next Peter Lynch"—the great portfolio manager who led Fidelity Magellan from 1977 to 1990, turning a $1,000 investment into a mind-blowing $28,000.

The good news: Fund performance has been analyzed exhaustively by finance professors and statisticians, including several Nobel Prize winners, for clues about exactly what works. The bad news: They've concluded that not very much actually works. But this rigorous research can help you make better, more confident decisions with a higher probability of success.

The first thing you need to understand about fund performance is that the single biggest factor in determining a fund's return is what kind of investments it owns. For example, a fund that owns small-cap value stocks is almost certain to perform poorly when most investors have decided that large-cap growth stocks are in fashion. Thus, a small-cap value fund manager is likely to perform poorly not because he's inept, but simply because he's in the wrong place at the wrong time. And, conversely, even the most bumbling large-cap growth fund manager can look good when big stocks are hot. Only when a fund manager earns extremely high returns over long periods—as Bill Miller, Marty Whitman, Sig Segalas, Peter Lynch and John Neff have—can you be reasonably sure it's because of skill, not luck.

Research has also shown that performance has a tendency to fade and even to reverse. The best funds in one measurement period—say, the past three years—tend not to be the best over the next three years. American Heritage fund, for example, returned an annual average of 48.9% from 1991 through 1993; then, from 1994 through 1996, it lost an annual average of 24.8%. In 1997, it gained 41.6% but slumped the next two years. And when Princeton finance professor Burton Malkiel studied hundreds of stock funds to see how many had sustained

What Kind of Fund Investor Are You?

How your funds behave is important—but how you behave toward your funds is at least as important. We'd like to believe that the key to investment success is buying the best investments. It's not. The key to investment success is self-control.

- **Put yourself on autopilot.** Nearly every fund company will allow you to set up an *automatic investment plan* enabling you to buy a small amount—often as little as $50—of fund shares once a year, once a quarter or once a month. Also called *dollar-cost averaging*, it's perfectly safe and very simple: The fund company automatically transfers money from your bank account to the fund of your choice. It's a great way of forcing you to save painlessly—and to stick with your fund through thick and thin.

- **Take an oath.** Make a promise—out loud to a friend or family member, or in writing to yourself—that goes like this: "If the market crashes, I will not sell, I will buy more."

above-average returns for two years in a row, he found that the percentage of repeat winners ranged from a high of 62% to a low of just 36%. Over the 11 years he studied, an average of 51.7% of funds were winners for two years running—statistically no better than random chance. While yesterday's best funds do not tend to turn into tomorrow's worst, they do end up finishing all over the map. Short-term performance has very little predictive value.

Interestingly, there is a way to predict when actively managed funds as a group will beat the market. If you study mutual fund returns all the way back to their beginnings 75 years ago, you'll find that one thing, and one thing only, explains when the average fund outperforms the market. When small stocks do better than big ones, funds will beat the market. When big ones do better, the market will outperform the funds. Of course, it's hard to know which market segment will outperform in the near future.

So what's the point of trying to pick a good fund when the odds are so lousy and the information is so unreliable? We promised you good news, and there's plenty.

- **Costs.** The statistical research does show that there's one great way to identify funds that will perform well in the future: Buy

Some of Our Favorite Funds

All of these funds have outstanding long-term track records and savvy managers who have been at the helm a long time.

FUND FUND MANAGER	% TOTAL RETURN[1]			STYLE	% ANNUAL EXPENSES	TELEPHONE (800)
	THREE YEARS	FIVE YEARS	TEN YEARS			
Brandywine Foster Friess/William D'Alonzo	15.0	13.0	17.4	Midcap growth	1.0	656-3017
Gabelli Asset Mario Gabelli	11.0	17.1	15.8	Midcap blend	1.4	422-3554
Harbor Capital Appreciation Sig Segalas	10.2	17.0	18.3	Large growth	0.6	422-1050
Scudder-Dreman High-Return Equity A[2] David Dreman	10.9	17.1	17.7	Large value	1.2	621-1048
Legg Mason Value Prime Bill Miller	15.2	25.7	21.8	Large value	1.7	577-8589
Mairs & Power Growth George A. Mairs III	11.6	16.9	17.8	Midcap blend	0.8	304-7404
Strong Opportunity Dick Weiss	15.2	18.1	18.2	Midcap value	1.2	368-1030
Third Avenue Value Marty Whitman	12.4	15.8	16.2	Small value	1.1	443-1021
Torray Robert Torray/Douglas Eby	6.6	17.0	17.1	Large value	1.1	443-3036
Tweedy, Browne Global Value Christopher Browne/John Spears	11.0	15.7	-	Foreign stock	1.4	432-4789
White Oak Growth Stock James Oelschlager/Donna Barton	12.3	19.4	-	Large growth	1.0	462-5386[3]

[1] Through May 24, 2001. [2] 5.75% front-end load. [3] Area code 888.
Source: Morningstar

those that charge low annual expenses. Generally speaking, shop for U.S. stock funds that charge no more than 1.19% a year in total operating expenses; for a small-cap fund, which can have higher research costs, you might go as high as 1.37%. But if you're paying over 1.5% a year for a U.S. stock fund, you're overpaying. The typical stock fund charges 1.46%, and that's way too much—especially when you consider that the vast majority of all funds underperform the market.

Another key finding is that funds that trade their stocks a lot—buying and selling in a big hurry—will tend to perform worse than those that hold their stocks for several years. That's because it costs money—commissions, bid/ask spreads and market impact (the way a fund's own trading makes a stock move in the wrong direction) to buy and sell. At the average stock fund—which holds its typical stock for about 14 months—trading costs probably eat away about 1.6% in total return each year. The faster a fund trades, the higher that cost.

When you add up 1.46% in total operating expenses and 1.6% in trading costs, you'd logically expect the average fund to underperform the market by about three percentage points a year. And over the decade ending December 31, 1999, the average U.S. stock fund returned an annual average of 14.89%, while the S&P 500 returned 18.05%—a difference of almost three and a quarter percentage points, or about what we'd expect. That's why there's one inescapable conclusion: The best way for you to improve your results is to focus on funds with below average expenses and trading costs.

• **Taxes.** After expenses, the next big factor that you can control is taxes. Whenever a fund sells stocks at a profit—without having realized losses to offset that profit—it must "distribute" the gain to you. Even though you don't sell anything, you owe capital gains tax on the amount of the distribution.

And that's why tax efficiency is so vital. As a general (but not universal) rule, the more a fund manager trades—the higher her portfolio turnover rate—the higher your tax bill is likely to be. A fund manager with a *portfolio turnover rate* of 50% or lower, meaning that the typical stock stays in the fund for two years, will often produce lower tax bills than managers with itchier trigger fingers.

What's a good low turnover rate? Well, 0% would be good. Two studies—one by Morningstar, one by three finance professors published as a research paper by the Brookings Institute—found separately that if you froze a fund's portfolio, essentially stopping the manager from trading anything, the fund would do better than if you let the manager do his usual hot-potatoes routine. (Hmm, in this regard, the pros are just like individual investors.). So, in general, lower turnover is always better. But certain fund categories—like small-cap growth—will tend to have higher turnover, since their stocks move very quickly into other categories and the manager has to move quickly too. In short, for a blue-chip U.S. portfolio, 20% (translating to an average holding period of five years) is pretty reasonable.

Finally, there's another controllable aspect of taxes: you. Every time you sell one fund in a taxable account to buy another, you have to fork over roughly 20% of your profits on the first one. And that means your new fund will have to perform even better just for you to break even. Thus, one of the most powerful tools to lower your tax bill is simply not to trade; instead, buy and hold. (For more on lowering your tax bill, see "Taming Fund Taxes" on page 167.)

- **Size.** Another element you can control is how big a fund gets. When funds take in a lot of money from investors in a hurry, their performance tends to suffer. To begin with, there may not be enough cheap stocks to fill a much bigger portfolio; it costs more to trade stocks in big blocks; and, Federal law limits how much of any given stock a fund can own. So, especially for funds that invest in little stocks, bigger is not always better. One way to prevent this problem is to look for fund companies that have closed their funds, or temporarily declined to accept accounts from new customers. Among them: Longleaf Partners, Numeric Investors, T. Rowe Price. Wait and see if they reopen to new accounts and try to join. It will be worthwhile; these companies have shown in the past that they are willing to limit their own growth before it hurts the best interests of their investors.

- **When the manager leaves.** Let's say you bought a certain fund because you really like the experience and investment approach of its manager. Then one day you find out the manager has left the firm—and suddenly your money is being run by a guy so young he thinks the Crash of 1987 was a failed test run for Y2K compliance. These surprise changes in fund management happen all the time: Brian Posner left Fidelity for Warburg Pincus; John Wallace left Oppenheimer for Robertson Stephens; Charles Albers left Guardian for Oppenheimer. The investors who bought those managers' funds ended up with somebody else.

There are several ways to combat this problem. First, you can buy an index fund, which is essentially run on autopilot by a bunch of computers. Second, you can simply avoid fund companies whose funds have a history of rapid management changes. You can get a good handle on this by asking a telephone rep how long the current manager has run the fund you're interested in—and who ran it for how long before that. If each answer isn't at least two years, you don't want to climb onto this carousel. Finally, focus on funds whose managers are big owners. A couple of examples: the Davis funds, the FPA funds and Longleaf Partners. The managers there have put millions of dollars of their money where their mouths are.

Star power?   What about shopping for funds based on Morningstar's enormously popular star ratings available at www.morningstar.com? Ranging from one star to five stars, they provide a simple snapshot of how well a fund has performed and how often it has lost money. If you think this is a good idea, just ask yourself why Don Phillips, Morningstar's president, and John Rekenthaler, its director of research, have said over and over again that buying funds based solely on their star ratings is a bad idea. The reason: Star ratings are based on past performance, and we've already discussed how inadequate a predictor that is. For details about the pitfalls of the Morningstar ranking system, see "Stars in Your Eyes" on page 114.

THE LOAD/NO-LOAD DEBATE

Should you buy direct or use a broker? Most funds are sold with a sales load, or commission for a broker's advice. But many, like those offered by Vanguard or T. Rowe Price, carry no sales charge. Which is better? Neither! If you feel you need a broker's handholding to help you make decisions, you shouldn't try investing on your own. Certainly an honest, intelligent broker who gives clear and sensible advice is worth every nickel you pay him. (Unfortunately, some brokers don't meet that description.) But if you're the kind of person who enjoys doing investment research, then no-load funds are your cup of tea.

If you're willing to do the work, we certainly prefer no-loads because they can enrich you by eliminating unnecessary fees. That seems like a simple idea but, increasingly, many investors are heading in the opposite direction.

In 2000, Scudder—no-load since its founding in 1924—announced that it was switching to a load-only format, following a similar decision by Denver-based Founders in 1999. Rumors now abound that several other traditional no-load firms will soon follow. The reason: Sales are gaunt. While the no-load companies

Stars in Your Eyes

Eat at a restaurant with a top rating from the famed Michelin Guide, and you're virtually assured a fine dining experience. Buy a fund with a top five-star ranking from Morningstar and, well, you could end up with a case of financial heartburn.

To understand why, you've got to know how Morningstar's star system works. The company begins by divvying up its database of nearly 5,600 funds into four large categories: U.S. and international stocks, and taxable and municipal bonds. Next, Morningstar grades each fund based on its risk-adjusted total return after expenses for the past three and, if available, five and 10 years. The funds are then ranked by their scores within their categories. The highest scoring 10% in each category are awarded five stars, the next 22.5% merit four, the following 35% receive three, the next 22.5% get two stars and the 10% with the lowest scores receive one lone star. The ratings are updated every month.

As mathematically precise and soothingly symmetrical as this process is, it's not particularly good at identifying future superior performers. One big problem: The four categories are so broad that the rankings tell you more about which investing style is hot than which managers are doing a great job.

In October 1996, for example, 19% of domestic-stock funds with five-star ratings were growth funds. By September 2000, however, growth funds had taken over 66% of the five-star slots. Had growth fund managers become far better investors than their value-oriented counterparts? Of course not. The surge in five-star growth funds had nothing to do with the relative prowess of growth and value managers. It simply reflected the fact that growth stocks like Intel and Cisco Systems had been all the rage the past few years. (Until 2000, of course.)

Recent research takes a dim view of stargazing. When researchers at the TIAA-CREF Institute tracked the performance of funds with four or five stars as of January 1998, they found that less than a third of those funds maintained a four- or five-star rating continuously over the following two years. Finance professors Christopher Blake and Matthew Morey also found that a high Morningstar rating is not a good predictor of future superior performance, although their research does suggest that funds with low rankings—one or two stars—tend to keep them. "If you want to predict the turkeys, the star ratings are good," says Blake. "But if you want to predict the winners, don't look to the stars."

So where should you look? We'd be more apt to use Morningstar's category ratings, which are also available at Morningstar's website (www.morningstar.com). The category ratings aren't perfect, but at least the funds are stacked up against their true peers—large growth vs. large growth, small value vs. small value and so forth. So you get a sense of how a manager has performed vs. managers of similar funds.

still rake in a respectable 45% of new retail-fund sales, much of these greenbacks come in via 401(k) plans—Fidelity and Vanguard being the two largest 401(k) providers—or the rapidly expanding army of fee-based financial advisers. Investor-to-fund (or investor-to-fund supermarket) purchases have dwindled to the point where they account for only about one-fifth of net sales.

No-load sales have not stalled because of their performance—although load-fund sponsors would like you to think that is the case. Balderdash. Aside from annual expenses (which tend to be higher with load funds because more of them tack on 12b-1 marketing fees), research shows that the performance of load funds and no-load funds is statistically indistinguishable. This was entirely to be expected. The two types of funds hire their portfolio managers from the same schools, equip them with the same research and pay them equally well. Naturally, their results are similar.

Our conclusion: Buy load funds only when you're sure you're getting your money's worth from a professional adviser. However, if you buy a load fund, be sure to consider what share class you're getting. That's because mutual-fund share classes have varying fee structures.

A shares charge a fee when you purchase the fund, called a front-end load. This fee, which is a percentage of your initial investment, compensates the broker who sold you the fund.

B shares charge redemption fees, or back-end loads, which you don't pay until you pull out your money. The amount of the back-end load usually declines the longer you keep your money in the fund. You pay less upfront, but you end up paying more each year in expenses.

C shares (or *level-load funds*) usually, but not always, charge front- and back-end loads, though they charge less than you'd pay on A shares or B shares. Again, you pay higher expenses along the way.

Whether one share class is better for you than another depends on your circumstances: how much money you are investing, how big the fund is, the annual expenses and your time horizon. But, in general, if you have to buy a load fund, you're better off with A shares.

CAN TWO FUNDS BE WORSE THAN ONE?

Morningstar's stars may be overrated, but the firm does offer the most effective tool to help you avoid one of the banes of the mutual fund investor: overlapping holdings, which can undermine an otherwise sound mutual fund strategy. When buying a new fund, don't make the classic mistake of looking only at its performance. Instead, check to see what it owns and whether those holdings duplicate what you already have. You can get a rough idea of how much your funds overlap by eyeballing their annual and semiannual reports. Look at the tables of their 10 largest holdings, then note how much they have in each industry sector (see the "schedule of portfolio investments"). If they share three or more top holdings or their biggest industry weightings are within a couple percentage points of each other, you've got an overlap problem. For an instant analysis of the overlap among funds, use Morningstar's Portfolio X-Rays feature, at www.morningstar.com.

THE BEST ETHICAL FUNDS

Fund proliferation has hit the socially responsible sector as well, and it is no longer easy to choose the right socially responsible fund for your portfolio. There are now more than 60 of them, each with a slightly different ethical focus. So the first step is to decide what matters to you. The Green Century Balanced fund, for example, inspects companies' environmental records but doesn't shun firms that profit from liquor or gambling. The American Trust Allegiance fund will have nothing to do with alcohol and gaming but skips the "green" screen that would weed out polluters. To get a sense of a fund's ethical focus, visit the Social Investment Forum's website (www.socialinvest.org), which lists the issues that each fund emphasizes.

We've selected funds with two criteria in mind. First, they all focus on a broad range of social concerns, screening out firms that profit from tobacco, firearms, military weapons, alcohol and gambling. They also scrutinize corporate records on the environment, human rights and product safety. Second, they pass muster financially, based on a combination of low expenses and quality of management.

The granddaddy of these funds is Domini Social Equity, which has returned an average of 16% a year since its 1991 launch. It holds about 400 mostly large companies with solid growth rates. In 2000, Vanguard launched a rival index fund, Vanguard Calvert Social Index, which invests in about 620 stocks. Like Domini, the Vanguard fund has a bias toward growth stocks. Says manager

Top Socially Conscious Picks

These socially conscious funds stand out from their peers.

FUND (TICKER)	TELEPHONE (800)	WEB ADDRESS	THREE-YEAR RETURN[1]	EXPENSE RATIO
Citizens Emerging Growth (WAEGX)	223-7010	www.citizensfunds.com	19.3%	1.69%
Domini Social Equity (DSEFX)	762-6814	www.domini.com	3.0	0.96
TIAA-CREF Social Choice Equity (TCSCX)	223-1200	www.tiaa-cref.org	N.A.	0.27
Vanguard Calvert Social Index (VCSIX)	662-7447	www.vanguard.com	N.A.	0.25

Notes: Data as of June 18, 2001. N.A.: Not applicable. [1]Annualized. **Source:** Morningstar.

George Sauter: "In a market that favors value, it's probably going to underperform." Vanguard's fund does have one key advantage—it charges annual expenses of just 0.25% vs. 0.96% for Domini.

With an expense ratio of 0.27%, TIAA-CREF Social Choice Equity is also cheap. It now has 26% of its assets in tech—fairly cautious for a socially conscious fund. More aggressive investors should consider Citizens Emerging Growth. It has beaten 96% of its peers over five years by betting on fast-growing midcap stocks. One caveat: It has hefty expenses of 1.82% a year.

SIZING-UP EXCHANGE TRADED FUNDS

Exchange-traded funds (ETFs), which date back to 1993, are similar to regular index funds, but they trade on a stock exchange just like stocks. Instead of buying directly from (or selling directly back to) a fund company, you buy or sell ETFs through a broker. The best-known ETFs are SPDRs (based on the S&P 500 index), Diamonds (based on the Dow Jones Industrial average), QQQs (or "Qubes," based on the Nasdaq 100 index) and iShares from Barclays Global Investors, which follow dozens of different stock indexes.

ETFs have some big pluses. First, they're cheap. Once you pay the broker's commission, an ETF may cost as little as 0.1% a year to own; a traditional fund can easily cost 15 times as much. Second, unlike many traditional mutual funds, ETFs won't whack you with capital-gains tax bills. If you're a buy and hold investor, you could keep one of these babies for decades and seldom—or never—pay a dime in capital-gains tax. (See page 172 for more information about ETFs and taxes.)

What are the minuses? First, not all ETFs are cheap. The iShares Dow Jones Healthcare Sector Index fund charges 0.6% in annual fees—nearly twice the cost of a traditional fund like Vanguard Health Care. If you pay a $14.95 commission to invest $1,000 in an ETF through an online broker, you've forked over 1.5% of your money; at a no-load mutual fund, buying and selling cost nothing. And dollar-cost averaging—investing a fixed amount every month—makes no sense with an ETF, since you pay a commission on each purchase.

The bottom line is that ETFs are a good option if you're in a high tax bracket and you're making a one-time lump sum investment of at least $3,000—the level at which most online brokerage commissions drop below 1%. But if you want to invest additional money on a regular basis, then ETFs are not for you. Even the low commissions at an online broker will eat you alive.

One of the benefits of ETFs is that you can buy or sell them at any time during the trading day.

Holders. State Street Global Advisers offer ETFs that track nine S&P 500 sectors, ranging from consumer services to technology, but Merrill Lynch offers ETF sector investing with an attractive twist.

Merrill Lynch HOLDRs (commonly called Holders) are fixed baskets of stocks in nine specific sectors (including biotech, oil services and semiconductors). One of the advantages of Holders, as opposed to mutual funds or other ETFs, is that you own the underlying shares themselves. For a modest fee of $10, you can swap a 100-share round lot for the individual stocks, and then tinker with them. Because of that nifty conversion feature, Holders must be bought 100 shares at a time.

Chapter 7
HOW A PROFESSIONAL ADVISER CAN HELP YOU

Spend less, cut debt, save more, invest smart. That, in a nutshell, is all the financial planning you'll ever need. Unfortunately, it's not as easy to figure out how much less you should spend or owe, and how much more you should save and invest. Of course, you could ask your best friends to spell out how close they are to being on track, but you'd sooner get a woman to tell you her weight or a man to admit he wears a rug.

Following the turmoil of the end of that great bull market, an increasing number of successful investors are turning to professional financial advisers for guidance. These days, even diehard do-it-yourselfers are admitting that that building wealth requires more than finding the next high-tech wonder. What's the secret? You gotta have a plan. How much advice you require, though, may vary. For instance, if juggling the demands of saving for college, securing your nest egg and figuring out how much insurance you need to protect your assets has left you in a quandary, you may opt for a full-scale financial plan. These sometimes hefty documents can run you anywhere from $400 to several thousand dollars, depending on the level of detail. However, if you're simply concerned that your portfolio isn't growing fast enough to meet your goals or the volatility of your investments keeps you awake at night, you might benefit from a once-a-year checkup for $500 to $750. In this case, an adviser will examine your holdings and make recommendations for investments that are better suited to your needs. In addition to plans and check-ups, advisers can inspire financial discipline and keep your portfolio on track no matter what the market may bear.

Studies show that mapping out your long-term financial goals in a well-thought-out written plan can make a dramatic difference in your overall net worth. In fact, a survey conducted by the Consumer Federation of America and NationsBank found that people with an annual income of $20,000 to $100,000 who had a financial plan (developed by themselves or a pro) had double the savings of others in that income bracket who didn't; people with income over $100,000 and a financial plan had 60% higher savings than their planless peers.

Still, people avoid getting professional investment advice for all sorts of reasons. Some fret about the expense, while others worry about trusting another individual with their money. More than a few people, of course, say they'll talk to an adviser soon— and then never get around to doing it.

Today, brokers, bankers and accountants are all vying with traditional financial planners to put your financial house in order. But not every adviser can provide the guidance or the game plan that will help you reach your goals. Here's what you should know about the shifting world of financial planning and how to get the most out of the advisor you finally choose.

THE FINANCIAL ADVISER SMORGASBORD

Deciding to seek professional advice is a crucial step, but it's only half the battle. You next have to decide what type of adviser to select. Among your choices are:

• **Traditional planners.** They focus on all aspects of your financial life, not merely investments. Planners stand behind an alphabet soup of certification credentials that require a glossary to

The ABCs of Financial Planners

Here's a brief rundown on the most common certifications you're likely to encounter in your search for an adviser. Most planners with these designations have a bachelor's degree and at least three years of experience providing business or financial advice. Since a planner should be comfortable addressing a range of financial objectives, these certifications generally require extensive course work in insurance, investment management, retirement planning, risk management, benefits and estate planning.

A **certified financial planner** (C.F.P.) must graduate from a C.F.P. Board-approved college, pass a rigorous exam, have no criminal or major regulatory record and complete continuing education requirements.

To find out more about C.F.P.s or to begin your search, check with the industry's two main trade groups: the Financial Planning Association (www.fpanet.org), which has about 4,000 members, and the National Association of Personal Financial Advisors (www.napfa.org), a smaller outfit that represents more than 700 fee-only planners. Both organizations can provide a list of planners in your area.

A **chartered financial consultant** (Ch.F.C.) must master a 10-course financial planning curriculum developed by the American College, a non-profit accredited self-study school in Bryn Mawr, Pa. Candidates have to pass a comprehensive course and complete continuing education requirements. To find out more about this designation, go to www.amercoll.edu, and click on certifications.

A **chartered financial analyst** (C.F.A.) is an experienced investment professional who has completed a 10-course self-study program and has passed multiple intensive examinations covering economics, portfolio management, securities analysis and ethics. This certification is sponsored by the Association for Investment Management and Research (www.aimr.org).

---

decode. The three you're most likely to encounter are certified financial planner (C.F.P.), chartered financial consultant (Ch.F.C.) and chartered financial analyst (C.F.A.). A candidate for any of these certifications must undergo a rigorous training program and pass an exhaustive exam that covers all the elements of a full-scale plan. (See the box above for more information about these credentials.)

• **Brokerages, mutual fund companies, insurance firms.** If what you're really looking for is investing advice, a broker or mutual fund rep may be just fine. However, their expertise on broader planning issues depends largely on their training. In fact, a growing number of financial service firms, brokerages and insurance companies are offering financial advice. And more brokers and insurance agents are getting certified as planners. Some consumer advocates question whether the primary objective of many pros-turned-planners is to construct an overall plan for clients or to recommend investments that generate healthy commissions or fees. "Some of these so-called advisers are simply changing the way they portray themselves without changing the way they do business," complains Barbara Roper, director of investor protection for the Consumer Federation of America.

- **Accountants.** Certified accountants are also migrating to financial planning as the prevalence and popularity of tax software packages such as Turbotax continue to erode their income. A C.P.A./planner with expertise in investing and insurance can be especially helpful for business owners or individuals with complicated taxes or uneven cash flow. With the proper training, "the transition can be a natural fit," contends Peggy Ruhlin, a C.P.A. in Columbus, Ohio who has been a planner for nearly 20 years. "But many C.P.A.s mistakenly assume that buying the right software is all the training they require."

- **Wealth managers.** More traditional planners and financial services firms are now positioning themselves as "wealth managers" who go beyond recommending investments. They either run clients' money directly or match them with private money managers, in exchange for a percentage of clients' assets or net worth. That's perfect for folks who don't have the time, patience or expertise to manage their own portfolios.

  "Managing investments is very profitable," says Roy Diliberto, president of the International Association of Financial Planners. "However, developing plans and helping clients walk through the financial minefields of life is the most important part of the process, even though it's labor-intensive and not a big moneymaker."

- **Specialized planners.** Increasingly, advisers are developing planning specialties. Some focus on helping corporate executives manage stock options and retirement plan assets, for instance, while others concentrate on divorced or widowed women. One hot target: people who come into "sudden wealth" because they sold a business, received an inheritance or cashed in stock options.

THE TRUTH ABOUT FEES

If you think finding the best pro to suit your needs is tough, try figuring out the best way to pay them for the service. The bottom line: The amount you pay is more important than the method used to calculate it.

Traditionally, planners have been paid set fees—per hour ($75 to $350), per project or as a percentage of your assets (typically .8% to 1.5%)—or in the form of commissions on financial products they sell you. A commission-based planner usually won't charge you for drawing up the plan, but you may pay as much or more than you would a fee-only planner once you factor in the sales charges and investing costs for the investments the adviser recommends. That's why it's essential to clarify the services you'll get and the dollar amount of all the costs you'll pay before signing on with anyone. The ranks of fee-only planners arc growing, and a relatively new category of "fee based" advisers is emerging who will reduce their fees if you buy commission-generating investments from them.

Consumer advocates contend that fee-only advisers are superior because their recommendations are not influenced by potential income from products. Others in the planning industry argue that conflicts of interest exist for fee-only planners too. "Say a client asks a fee-only planner whether he should take a million-dollar lump-sum distribution vs. a monthly pension payout," says fee-only planner Diliberto. "There's clear potential for conflict of interest if that planner's fee is based on a percentage of assets under management. It boils down to the integrity of the adviser, regardless of how he or she is compensated."

But remember, no matter how proficient you are with spreadsheets, your plan is only as good as the assumptions you plug into it. Projecting a 25% annual return, for instance, will get you to your retirement savings target faster, but only on paper.

Before you start scouting for recommendations and negotiating fees, think about how you want to use an adviser. To clarify your needs, check out the following four scenarios.

A comprehensive plan. The guidance of a skilled planner can help you build wealth faster than you could on your own. That's been the experience of Pleasanton, Texas dentist Billy Morgan. After losing $30,000 in bad real estate and oil-well investments during the '80s, Morgan had virtually no investable assets—and college expenses were looming for his three teenaged children. On the recommendation of a colleague, he hired certified financial planner Joe Kopczynski to overhaul his sinking portfolio and help him face the financial challenges that lay ahead. "You reach a point where you realize you need help to get to the next level," says Morgan. He got that help from Kopczynski. Today, Morgan has a net worth of around $1 million.

In addition, the Albuquerque planner helped Morgan fund his kids' education by investing in a portfolio of mutual funds. Kopczynski also suggested that Morgan prepay college expenses through the state-sponsored Texas Tomorrow Fund, which guarantees that all expenses except room and board will be covered for his three children at state schools, regardless of what the tuition is at the time they enroll. If one chooses an out-of-state school, the prepaid tuition for that child is refundable.

Kopczynski also helped Morgan obtain construction financing for a 4,000-square-foot professional medical building; the loan will be paid off in 2004. "Then we'll use the income from the leases to fund a retirement nest egg for me and my wife Jeanette," Morgan explains. (If you're considering the benefits of a full-scale financial plan, check out "Is a Wealth-Building Financial Plan for You?" on the opposite page.)

A portfolio that's losing money.   When you're faced with a deteriorating financial situation that requires an immediate solution, an experienced planner can get you back on track. Consider the plight of Lisa Horton of Columbia, Md. After discovering that a stockbroker had placed her ailing parents' retirement savings in high-risk stocks that had reduced the value of their account by 25%, Horton sought the aid of certified financial planner Kevin Hutt. For an initial fee of $750, Hutt, who is also a C.P.A., developed a plan for Horton to manage her parents' finances. By reallocating their assets into a portfolio of blue-chip stock funds and bond funds, he increased the amount of their estate by 40% over six years.

Horton was so impressed, she hired Hutt to review her own finances. Following his plan helped the pediatrician double her net worth in four years, even during a two-year period when her earnings were the lowest in her career. She now invests regularly in mutual funds and accumulates stocks through dividend-reinvestment plans.

Is a Wealth-Building Financial Plan for You?

The classic model in the planning process is the comprehensive financial plan. This blueprint can run you from $400 to $15,000, depending on how much ground you want to cover and how much money you have.

A thorough plan provides an accurate snapshot of your current financial status, maps out strategies to help you achieve long-term goals and sets up a safety net of insurance to protect your financial stability. In the traditional scenario, an adviser will meet with you for a couple of sessions to discuss how you spend and invest your money. He or she will want to see your pay stubs, a description of your benefit plans, your investment statements and tax returns. These will provide the numbers to crunch. A good planner will ask you about your wants as well as your needs: Do you crave a vacation home? Are you planning to move to a golf community when you retire? Can you stomach losing money in the stock market, or would you prefer safer alternatives?

The report may be only a few pages or a booklet-size document that includes a full estate plan. A hefty printout full of tables and pie charts is not necessarily a symbol of quality, however. "A document that boils everything down to the four really important things you need to do is what's most valuable," argues Robin Sherwood of Westbrook Financial Advisers in New Canaan, Conn.

If you're a diehard do-it-yourselfer who is comfortable crunching numbers, you can plot out your own plan using low-cost software programs or free websites. In fact, many pros use similar programs, which are essentially financial calculators.

Some software packages and websites have almost all the tools you could ever need, including goal planning, budgeting, investment advice and portfolio management. (Some programs also offer Web links for online banking and updating your portfolio.) To be effective, these programs should help you forecast personal obligations (for your parents and children), identify risks, minimize taxes and write a will. Some even have estate-planning tools.

Good software packages include Quicken and Microsoft Money. See Chapter 11, "Online Resources: The Path to Profits," for the best financial sites on the Web.

"Kevin has given me a good financial education," says Horton, who pays Hutt about $750 a year for quarterly meetings and periodic phone calls for investment and tax advice. One smart move Hutt convinced Horton to make was to rent out her townhouse instead of selling it for a $10,000 loss. Not only did the doctor cover her mortgage, she also reaped tax benefits.

Just a checkup. It's natural to wonder if your investment strategy is still on course or if you're adrift—especially in this market. For a modest fee, many advisers and some financial service companies will perform a one-time checkup focusing in specific areas such as your investment plan, retirement planning analysis or estate planning. In the end, you should receive a written plan of action that reflects your financial profile (based on a questionnaire that you fill out) and addresses your major concerns.

A pro to manage your money. If you're too busy or not experienced enough to manage a sizable portfolio, your best bet may be to find a highly qualified, highly recommended wealth manager to do the job. Most brokerages, fund companies and financial service firms provide asset management services, typically requiring minimum investments of at least $100,000 or more.

When Jim Zimmerman of Libertyville, Ill. sold his engineering services company four years ago, he turned over $300,000 (from the proceeds and IRA account balances) to certified financial planner David Kliff to manage. The entrepreneur says he was too busy starting a software company to give his portfolio the attention it needed to grow. At the time, Zimmerman was invested in a stock-index fund, T-bills and other short-term income investments.

Kliff reorganized the portfolio to provide retirement savings for Jim and his wife Loraine, and a college education fund for Zimmerman's two children. Kliff also convinced Zimmerman to invest monthly. Now the portfolio includes 15 funds and eight individual stocks, which Kliff manages for a percentage of the assets. "Under this arrangement, David has an incentive to have more assets under management, so the better I do, the better he does," says Zimmerman.

CHOOSING THE RIGHT FINANCIAL COACH

It's crucial to find an adviser with whom you feel comfortable. You want to be sure your adviser listens to your concerns and helps you develop a strategy based on your life goals. Does that person understand your biggest financial issues, your strategies and your tolerance for various levels of risk? And if you're looking for a comprehensive plan, your adviser should be able to help steer you through all things financial, including retirement and asset allocation, tax strategies, insurance and estate planning.

Begin your search by asking the right people for recommendations. If you were searching for a pediatrician, you'd solicit names from other parents, preferably those whose kids have the same health issues as yours. Why? They share your needs. That's why colleagues with similar earning power and benefit plans are the best source of planner recommendations. Other good sources: accountants and estate-planning attorneys who are familiar with your finances. Even when a planner comes with glowing recommendations from a friend, the fit has got to be right for you. Before signing on with an adviser, review these five pointers:

1. Consider only advisers who are properly licensed or accredited.

The box on page 121 explains certifications you may find on an adviser's business card. While no form of accreditation guarantees competence or honesty, certified financial planners are monitored by the C.F.P. Licensing Board of Standards, which disciplines members who violate ethics codes. Although brokers may not be certified as planners, they must have a Series 7 license to sell securities.

2. Make sure the adviser has at least five years of experience addressing your major challenges.

Not every planner is qualified to draft estate plans, for example.

3. Confirm the adviser's regulatory record and financial disclosure forms.

Anyone compensated for dispensing financial advice must be registered with the Securities and Exchange Commission if he or she oversees assets of $25 million or more and with state securities regulators if assets are less than $25 million. Being a registered adviser doesn't guarantee competency; it means the adviser filled out an ADV (short for advisers) form and paid a fee. Advisers are legally required to give you a copy of ADV Part II, which discloses the terms of their compensation, including all commissions and payments received from sponsors of financial products that the adviser recommends. Review this carefully for any potential conflicts of interest.

Also ask for Part I, which details any run-ins with regulators or other disciplinary history. If a planner refuses to give you this information, find someone else, suggests Nancy Smith, director of the SEC's Office of Investor Education and Assistance. You can also get a copy of an adviser's ADV Part I from the SEC (www.sec.gov) or from your state securities regulators (call the North American Securities Administrators Association at 888-846-2722—www.nasaa.org—for a local contact).

You can also call: The National Association of Securities Dealers Regulation (800-289-9999; www.nasdr.com) keeps records of securities brokers' regulatory violations that you can review.

4. Meet with at least three planners before making a decision.

Most planners will agree to a free half-hour session to learn what you need and to present their qualifications. The Certified Financial Planner Board of Standards (303-830-7500; www.cfp-board.org) provides questions to ask a planner. Here are a few of the most important ones:

• **What is your typical client like, and what are your areas of expertise?** The planner may not be the best fit if you're in your thirties and the planner targets retirees.

• **How do you prepare a plan?** Planning requires more than knowing the financial details of your life; understanding your family, career goals, lifestyle and the challenges you may face when implementing the plan are critical.

• **What's your investment philosophy?** Although there's no right or wrong answer, you should feel comfortable with the response. If you want a mix of individual stocks and bonds and the planner is a mutual fund devotee, you're not a good match. Chat about current market conditions to see how up to date the adviser is. And pose questions about some challenge you face to see how different planners would approach these problems. Be concerned if the planner offers answers without asking follow-up questions—or quickly changes answers if you express reluctance.

• **How often will we meet once the plan is implemented?** Meeting once a year to review your progress may not be enough, especially if you have short-term goals. Find out how you will be charged for these sessions.

Don't be shy about peppering your potential planner with questions or even requesting a sample plan for a past client. It's not the least bit rude to want to know more about the adviser you're intending to trust with your financial future.

5. Follow up on client references.

"You'd have to be Jack the Ripper not to be able to provide three positive references, so ask for a list of clients who have worked with the adviser for at least five years," says Louis Harvey, president of Dalbar, a financial services research firm in Boston. Call three clients, and ask specific questions such as: Did recommended investments perform as expected? Did you have any problems with the plan, fees or arranging meetings?

Finally, once you choose an adviser, ask for a written agreement that outlines the services you will receive and how much they will cost.

GETTING THE MOST OUT OF YOUR FINANCIAL ADVISER

Forging a productive relationship with a pro can be difficult if you are not accustomed to discussing the details of your financial life. To help you get the most out of the planning experience, we turned to New York City certified financial planner Michael Terry of Financial Asset Management Corp. for advice. Here are his eight strategies to make sure that your time (and money) are well spent:

• **Write down your financial goals and objectives before your first meeting with a planner.** Be as specific as possible: Do you need advice on how to take your pension distribution? Do you want to reorganize your estate to reduce taxes? Or, are you concerned about managing your money during retirement? No matter what your challenges may be, go to the meeting prepared to discuss them. Throwing spaghetti up against the wall to see what sticks is not a good recipe for wealth management.

• **Be willing to open up.** A good financial planner is a professional listener. Don't be afraid to share your dreams, your anxieties, your wants and your needs. And don't be put off by probing personal questions. Planners aren't judging you, they need lots of details about your needs and lifestyle to provide the most appropriate advice.

• **Bring all of your financial documents to the meeting.** Try to have at least three years of tax forms, current brokerage or mutual fund statements, retirement plan documents, life insurance policies, annuity contracts, bank statements and current Social Security statements. If you're looking for estate-planning advice, bring copies of your current will and any trusts that you may have already set up. Don't hold anything back. There's nothing worse than working out a plan and then remembering another $50,000 or so that you had squirreled away in a CD somewhere.

• **Know the basis for all your taxable investments.** A good decision on repositioning your assets can't be made without assessing the tax consequences. If you're not sure about a tax issue, ask your planner to talk to your tax preparer.

• **Be honest about your risk tolerance.** If you say that you're a very aggressive long-term investor who is looking for growth, the chances are good that your recommended portfolio will be heavy on equities. But if you can't sleep at night when the Dow goes down, then such a portfolio will not be a good fit. Better to explain all your worries and let the planner show you the trade-offs between risk and return.

• **Don't have an investment return figure locked into your mind.** Even if the market is forging ahead, you should not automatically expect high double-digit annual returns. If a planner guarantees a specific rate of return, take your money and run.

• **Once the plan is delivered, ask lots of questions.** Here are a few to start with: Why is a particular asset allocation model used? Why was a particular stock, bond, or fund chosen? How risky is the portfolio? What are the fees? What are the expense ratios of the suggested funds? Are there any early-withdrawal penalties or back-end loads? Are the recommended funds tax efficient? If your planner refuses to answer your queries, find someone else who will provide better service. True, that may mean starting over, but what's the point of having a plan that you don't understand?

• **Establish a monitoring plan to watch over your investments.** Don't let your plan sit on the shelf gathering dust instead of wealth. First outline steps to implement the plan and then develop a systematic review system for you and your adviser.

Chapter 8
THE PSYCHOLOGY BEHIND INVESTOR MISTAKES

Among the reasons that financial advisers can be so helpful is that they help protect us from ourselves. Clearly, one of the greatest obstacles to achieving investment success is human nature, which encourages us to make many moves that are financially counterproductive. Often, we try to be too clever for our own good. As Pogo said, "We have met the enemy, and he is us."

The best way to fight this enemy is to understand what makes him tick. People often say that investor behavior is guided exclusively by two emotions—greed and fear—but that seems overly simplistic to us. Investors who bought Internet stocks for the first time right before the market peak in March 2000 surely weren't motivated by greed alone. Many could no longer tolerate being left out of the great Internet bash that Wall Street was throwing, and more than a few could not abide the idea of attending yet another cocktail party at which neighbors or colleagues discussed the obscene profits they had made in Yahoo, Infospace and MicroStrategy. So, in a vain attempt to keep up with the Joneses and eliminate their regret for not having bought these gargantuan winners sooner, they snagged these stocks at the top and watched them plummet by 95%, 99.3% and 99.5%, respectively.

We believe that investors can improve their returns by understanding the mental processes that underlie the most common investment mistakes. The better you understand how your mind works, the more you'll achieve as an investor.

So, while we can't prevent you from buying a clunker stock in the future—in fact, we guarantee that if you buy enough individual stocks this will happen—we think you'll be more likely to dump the loser sooner rather than later if you realize why that voice in your head is urging you so vehemently *not* to sell it. It is bad enough to buy Yahoo at its all-time high of $250.06, but it is even worse to ride it all the way down to $11.38 before finally saying good-bye and good riddance.

THE TROUBLE WITH HUMANS

Humans have a remarkable ability to detect patterns. That's helped our species survive, enabling us to plant crops at the right time of year and evade wild animals. But when it comes to investing, this incessant search for patterns causes more heartache than anything else.

We see that value funds have stunk for years, so we dump them outright and pile into fashionable growth stocks like Intel and Cisco—right before they hit the skids. We buy a stock because some guy at a neighborhood barbecue recommended it, and everything he talks about seems to go up—but this one plunges. We put every dime in stocks after hearing that they've trounced bonds forever—only to see bonds zoom past stocks in 2000 and in the first months of 2001.

Our incorrigible search for patterns leads us to assume that order exists where it often doesn't. Many of us believe, for example, that it's possible to foresee where the market is heading or whether a particular stock will continue to rise. In reality, these things are far more random and unpredictable than we like to admit. (Warning: Our memory is selective when it comes to market predictions. We tend to remember our successful predictions and forget most of the rest.)

Remarkably, scientists are now finding that this tendency to look for patterns is hardwired into the human brain. Psychologists have long known that if rats or pigeons knew what the Nasdaq is, they might be better investors than most humans are. That's because, in some ways, animals are better than people at predicting random events. If, for instance, you set up two lights in a laboratory and flash them in a random sequence, humans will persistently try to predict which of the two lights will flash next. Stranger still, they'll keep trying even when you tell them that the flashing of the lights is purely random. Let's say you flash a green light 80% of the time and a red one 20% of the time but keep the exact sequences random. (A run of 20 flashes could look something like this: GGGGRGGGGGGGR-RGGGGGR.) In guessing which light will flash next, the best strategy is simply to predict green every time, since you stand an 80% chance of being right. That's what rats or pigeons generally do in a similar experiment that rewards them with a crumb of food whenever they correctly guess the next outcome.

But humans are apparently convinced that they're smart enough to predict each upcoming result even in a process they've been told is random. On average, this misguided confidence leads people to get the right answer in this experiment on only 68% of their tries. In other words, it's precisely our higher intelligence that leads us to score lower on this kind of task than rats and pigeons do. (Interestingly, experts in behavioral finance say that such "overconfidence" often diminishes the returns of individual investors.)

The man with two brains.   A team of researchers at Dartmouth College, led by psychology professor George Wolford, has been studying why it is that we think we can predict the unpredictable. Wolford's team ran light-flashing experiments on "split-brain patients"—people in whom the nerve connections between the hemispheres of the brain have been surgically severed as a treatment for epilepsy. Here's the group's key discovery, which was recently published in the *Journal of Neuroscience*: When the epileptics viewed a series of flashes that they could process only with the right side of their brains, they gradually learned to guess the most frequent option all the time, just as rats and pigeons do. But when the signals were flashed to the left side of their brains, the epileptics kept trying to forecast the exact sequence of flashes—sharply lowering the overall accuracy of their predictions. (See "How the Other Half Thinks" on page 137.)

Wolford's conclusion: "There appears to be a module in the left hemisphere of the brain that drives humans to search for patterns and to see causal relationships, even when none exist." His research partner, Michael Gazzaniga, has christened this part of the brain "the interpreter." Wolford explains: "The interpreter drives us to believe that 'I can figure this out.' That may well be a good thing when there is a pattern to the data and the pattern isn't overly complicated." However, he adds, "a constant search for explanations and patterns in random or complex data is not a good thing."

The dance of happenstance.   Trouble is, the financial markets are almost—though not quite—as random as those flashing lights. On CNBC and countless websites, investment strategists and other so-called experts scan the momentary twitches of the market and predict what will happen next. Far more often than they're right, they're wrong—and the Dartmouth discovery about the interpreter in our brains helps explain why. These pundits are examining a chaotic storm of data and refusing to concede that they can't understand it. Instead, their interpreters drive them to believe they've identified patterns upon which they can base predictions about the future. (The forecasts of professional economists concerning interest rates and economic growth are notoriously inaccurate—and it's their business to make predictions! No wonder mutual fund legend Peter Lynch said he never wasted time trying to make economic predictions.)

Meanwhile, the interpreters in our own brains impel us to take these seers more seriously than their track records deserve. As Berkeley economist, and John Bates Clark medal winner, Matthew Rabin has pointed out, just a couple of accurate predictions on CNBC can make an analyst seem like an ace, because viewers have no way to sample the analyst's entire (and probably mediocre) forecasting record. In the absence of a full sample, our interpreters take over and lead us to see the analyst's latest calls as part of a pattern of success.

The interpreter also helps explain what's called the gambler's fallacy—the belief that if, say, a coin has come up heads several times, then it's "due" to come up tails. (In fact, the odds that a coin will turn up tails are always 50%, no matter how many times in a row it's come up heads.) The gambler's fallacy is as common on Wall Street as hairballs under a couch: Some pundits will say emerging markets are sure to rebound because they've been doing badly for years, while others say tech stocks will crash because they've risen so much. In reality, the market makes mincemeat out of most of our predictions; apparent trends often foretell little about the future.

In its constant search for patterns, the interpreter also tricks investors into believing that hot performance streaks are sure to persist. Based on a few months of scorching returns, investors piled into Internet stocks late in 1999—and are now sitting on returns as cold as liquid nitrogen. What's happening here is simple: As soon as a pattern seems to emerge in the market, the interpreter in our brains sees it as part of a predictable trend—rather than a random happenstance that may never be repeated.

Finally, we think the Dartmouth research helps solve another puzzle. Even when we have only a small sample of our own performance at risky tasks—a few yanks on a one-armed bandit or a handful of big scores on tech stocks—we tend to decide either that we know what we're doing or that we're on a lucky streak. We almost never conclude that our success is the result of chance alone. Dutch psychologists Willem Wagenaar and Gideon Keren have found that professional gamblers, when accounting for their wins and losses, greatly overestimate the role of skill, attributing just 18% of the outcome of each bet to chance.

Similarly, when a day-trader makes a fat profit off a stock after doing no research and owning it for only seconds, he's likely to conclude that he's an analytical genius or has an uncanny feel for the market. In truth, that profit is probably an accident—but his mind won't allow him to see things that way.

Mind over matter.   So how can you keep your brain from giving you a garbled view of the investment world? You could disable your interpreter once and for all by having a neurosurgeon separate your brain's two hemispheres, and then by scrutinizing investment information in the leftmost part of your field of vision. That way, only the right half of your brain would be able to process investment data, and the interpreter would be shut down. However, it won't be easy talking a surgeon into carving your cranium open for this, and watching CNBC out of the far corner of your eye might be an uncomfortable experience. So here are some less drastic options.

Don't obsess.   In one of his most startling findings, George Wolford of Dartmouth says people in his experiments earned higher scores when they were distracted with a "secondary task" like trying to recall a series of numbers they'd recently seen. In other words, interruptions improved their performance by preventing the interpreter in their brains from seeking spurious patterns in the data. Likewise, continually monitoring your results will probably make them worse—as you fool yourself into seeing trends that aren't there and trade too much as a result. If you're spending more than a few hours a month on investing, you're not only taking valuable time away from the rest of your life, but you're almost certainly hurting your returns.

Remember what's at stake.   John Staddon, a professor of psychology at Duke, says rats or pigeons will generally bet on the option that has had the highest probability of success over time. But, notes Staddon, "humans will consistently do that only when the stakes are large and the consequences really matter." So you'll make better financial decisions if you convince yourself that there's no such thing as a small or casual investment. Just think of the thousands of dollars you could squander—and the blissful retirement you could jeopardize—with a few careless stock picks.

Track your forecasts.   Whenever you've got a strong opinion about where a stock, or the market, is headed, jot it down and note the date. This will keep you from conveniently forgetting your failed forecasts and may provide you with a humbling reminder of your limitations as a soothsayer. And whenever some analyst seems to know what he's talking about, remember that pigs will fly before he'll ever release a full list of his past forecasts, including the bloopers.

Defy the chaos.   Not everything about investing is chaotic, however; a few things really are predictable. On average, over time, investors who keep costs low (either through index funds or buy-and-hold stock portfolios) are mathematically certain to outperform investors who trade too frequently or buy funds with high expenses. So before you focus on your returns—which are entirely unpredictable—make sure that your investments are not overpriced.

Diversification is another principle that defies chaos. Consider the danger of investing almost exclusively in tech stocks. Many investors who bet heavily on the sector in 1982—the last time it was as hot as it was in early 2000—loaded up on market darlings such as Alpha Microsystems, Commodore, Tandy, Vector Graphic and Wang Laboratories, which later tanked. If you diversify—by owning a wide range of U.S. and foreign stocks and

How the Other Half Thinks

Normally, what you see in each eye is analyzed by both sides of the brain (see arrows, panel 1). But if the brain's two hemispheres are split by a surgeon (for example, to treat epilepsy), this interchange breaks down. When the right side of the brain does the work (panel 2), people make better forecasts than when they use the left side (panel 3)—suggesting that a function on the brain's left side tricks us into finding patterns even when they don't exist.

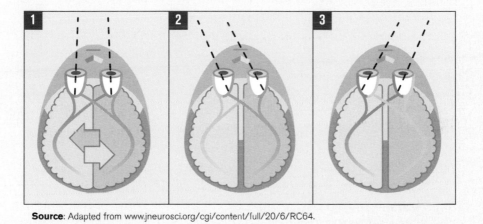

Source: Adapted from www.jneurosci.org/cgi/content/full/20/6/RC64.

bonds—you virtually eliminate the chance that a few duds like these will ruin your financial future. Broad diversification is still the best insurance against the risk of making an investment mistake. And there's nothing random about that.

DON'T GIVE IN TO "GET-EVEN-ITIS"

Investors' buy and sell decisions are often the product of psychological habit rather than rational design. Consider: If you owned two stocks—one that was up, say, 25%, and another that was down by the same amount—which do you think you'd be more likely to sell? If you're like most investors, you'd unload the winner. Indeed, when University of California-Davis finance professor Terry Odean studied trading patterns between 1987 and 1993 in 10,000 retail discount brokerage accounts, he found that investors were about 50% more likely to sell investments in which they had a gain and hang on to those in which they had a loss.

Does this make sense? From a tax standpoint, the answer is almost certainly no. When you sell a stock in which you have a gain, a piece of your profit goes to the IRS, leaving you less to plow into your next investment. Now, if you were sure the winner was about to head south and the loser was on the verge of a comeback, dumping winners and clinging to losers would be the right thing to do. But when Odean examined the performance of the winners that investors sold and the losers they kept, he found that the winners outperformed the losers by an average of almost four percentage points over the subsequent two years. (If that doesn't alarm you, it should.)

Why are we so hesitant to dump losing stocks and so eager to jettison the winners? Odean says that the answer lies in something called "prospect theory," a tenet of behavioral finance that says we tend to avoid loss and regret whenever possible. Selling a stock in which we have a loss forces us to admit that we've blown it. We don't have to face that uncomfortable admission if we just hold on to the stock and don't realize the loss.

We also hold on to losers because we suffer from a malady called get-even-itis. Simply put, once we're underwater in a stock, we'd do anything—undergo root canal without anesthesia, attend an Adam Sandler film festival—rather than sell that baby until it gets back to even. This makes no sense, of course, because the Amazon.com stock you paid $70 a share for at the beginning of 2000 and that recently traded at around $13 has no idea how desperate you are to see it claw its way back to 70 bucks.

As for our penchant for cutting loose our winners, that may be a case of the "take the money and run" syndrome. Once we've got a decent gain in a stock, that paper profit starts burning a hole in our pockets; we can't wait to cash in at a profit and then crow about what terrific investors we are.

Clearly, the decision to sell a stock should be based on your estimate of its future prospects, not whether you're ahead or behind in it. If you own tech stocks that are down 50% from their highs but that your analysis leads you to believe still have excellent long- term growth potential, then by all means hold on to them. (If you have a loss in these shares, you might consider selling and buying them back 31 days later to book a loss for tax purposes.) On the other hand, if you're sitting on a 90% loss in shares of a dotcom whose entire business plan was spending all its cash on a 30-second Super Bowl commercial in hopes of generating some buzz...well, the game's probably over, and it's time to sell and move on.

AN ICON OF BEHAVIORAL FINANCE

When some people are asked to name the investment thinker they have learned the most from, they do not say Warren Buffett, Peter Lynch or John Bogle. Instead they reply: Daniel Kahneman.

Kahneman is not a great stock picker like Buffett, a masterful fund manager like Lynch or a crusader for investors' rights like Bogle. Instead, Kahneman is a psychologist at Princeton University who studies how people estimate odds and calculate risks—the very essence of investing. Kahneman may have done more than anyone else alive to shed light on how to improve our investing judgment and manage risk intelligently.

Citing research on everything from American entrepreneurs to Swedish drivers, Kahneman explains how prone humans are to "overconfidence," or the belief that we know more than we really do. He bolsters his case with tales from his own life, confessing that he'd once underestimated by seven years how long it would take to help write a textbook. He asks "Do you know how little you know?" and challenges people to re-examine everything they assume to be true.

Kahneman and his late research partner, Amos Tversky, have helped answer some of the great questions of finance. Why do people buy high and sell low, when they know they should do the opposite? Why do investors listen to analysts who are clearly clueless?

In essence, Kahneman and Tversky discovered that people are not the rational, sensible investors they assume they are. Their investigations of how people actually make financial decisions led them to conclude that the majority of investors make foolish decisions more often than not. But, paradoxically, the single smartest thing any investor could do is to recognize the limitations of his ability and the extent of his irrationality.

In this age of instantaneous information, any of us can find out almost everything there is to know about any stock. Why, then, have so many of us recently earned the worst returns of our lives? Because information is useless if we misinterpret it or let emotions warp our judgment. Kahneman's research throws us a lifeline that can save us from our own self-defeating behavior.

Pigeons, pilots and IPOs. Kahneman captured his first great insight by observing his own students. In the late 1960s, he was teaching a class on the psychology of training to flight instructors in the Israeli air force. Concerned at how the instructors screamed obscenities and pummeled trainees' helmets until they cried, Kahneman told his class that research on pigeons showed reward to be a better motivator than punishment. One flight instructor burst out, "With all due respect, sir, what you're saying is for the birds." He heatedly told Kahneman that trainees almost always did worse on their next flight if they'd been praised—and tended to fly better just after getting yelled at.

Kahneman was dumbstruck. He realized he was staring into the face of a profound misperception: The flight instructor believed that his own praise or criticism caused the trainee's performance to reverse. In reality, Kahneman knew, chance alone dictates that an unusually good or bad event is typically followed by a much more ordinary one—what statisticians call "regression to the mean."

Regression also explains why hot funds go cold and why the Nasdaq, after more than tripling from 1998 to 2000, subsequently imploded. But, like the Israeli flight instructor, most investors fail to see how powerful a force regression is. We know in theory that "what goes up must come down"—but, as Kahneman saw that day, we vehemently resist recognizing it in practice.

• **We base long-term decisions on short-term information.** The "law of large numbers" holds that only a vast sample of data (a nationwide poll, say) can give an accurate picture of the population it's drawn from. But Kahneman and Tversky found that the typical person acts on what they christened the "law of small numbers"— basing broad predictions on narrow samples of data. For instance, we buy a fund that's beaten the market three years in a row, convinced it's "on a hot streak"—even though a mountain of research shows that three-quarters of all funds underperform in the long run. And many investors concluded in 1999 that growth stocks would clobber value stocks indefinitely, since they'd done so for five—yes, five!—years running. Sure enough, value stocks trounced growth by almost 39 percentage points from January 1, 2000 to April 12, 2001. The people piling into hot growth stocks at the peak clearly should have been buying value instead.

• **If something is easy to recall, we think it happens more often than it does.** Kahneman and Tversky had people listen to a list of male and female names, both famous and obscure, and then recall whether it contained more men or women. When more of the famous names were female, 81% of people concluded that women made up more than half the list—when, in fact, there were more men on the list.

Likewise, it's easy to recall initial public offerings that have been famously lucrative, like Cisco and Microsoft. Yet IPOs that flop—like, say, 3DO Co. or Quarterdeck Software—vastly outnumber those that soar. Historically, IPOs have actually underperformed the rest of the stock market by three to five percentage points a year, but many gung-ho investors fail to recognize that the majority of new stocks are stinkers.

• **When estimating future values, we "anchor" our projections on any number that happens to be handy.** In one experiment, Kahneman and Tversky asked people to estimate various statistics, such as the percentage of African countries in the United Nations. Before each person guessed, the researchers spun a "wheel of fortune" to generate a number between 0 and 100. When the wheel landed on a low number, people tended to guess that African nations made up a small percentage of UN members; when it landed on a high number, they guessed that Africa accounted for much more of the UN's membership.

Experiments like this prove that the mere suggestion of an outside number is enough to distort people's views. That's just what happens when an analyst publicizes a price target for a stock. Such targets often are utter garbage—but investors still "anchor" on them. On Dec. 29, 1999, PaineWebber analyst Walter Piecyk slapped a 12-month target of $250 (split-adjusted) on Qualcomm. That day, the stock soared 31% to $165, as investors headed toward Piecyk's anchor. But 12 months later, Qualcomm had belly flopped to $82, 67% below his target; it now wallows around $60.

Risk.   In the late '70s and early '80s, Kahneman and Tversky focused on how people perceive risks. Economists had long argued that a rational person will wager an equal amount for the chance to win $100 or avoid a $100 loss. After all, either gamble leaves you $100 better off. But Kahneman and Tversky showed that most people don't think that way. Try one of their experiments yourself: Imagine a coin toss in which you'd lose $100 if tails came up. How much would you have to win on heads to be willing to take the bet? Most people insist on at least $200. The lesson: Losing $100 feels roughly twice as painful as gaining $100 feels pleasant.

In fact, Kahneman and Tversky concluded that we hate losses so much that we make inconsistent gambles in the hope of avoiding them. Their findings help explain, for example, why people tend to sell their winning stocks too early, while holding on to losers for too long: We want to lock in a sure gain before something jeopardizes it, but we'll hang on to a losing stock in a bet that it will eventually break into the black. (Remember the ol' "get-even-itis" that we discussed earlier in this chapter?)

Kahneman and Tversky's proofs of the pain of loss also show why more investors don't stake all their money on stocks. History suggests that stocks should outperform bonds over any period of 30 years—but few of us bet every cent on stocks. That's because the short-term pain of owning them in a disastrous year like 2000 overwhelms our perception of the long-term gain they should eventually produce.

Other insights we can apply to our portfolios:

- **Distrust data.** Rather than leaping to conclusions based on scant data, look at as many numbers as possible. Don't rely just on recent performance; look at several time periods. "It doesn't take many observations to think you've spotted a trend," warns Kahneman, "and it's probably not a trend at all." Merrill Lynch, for instance, recently told investors to slash their exposure to overseas stocks since foreign returns have lately resembled those of U.S. stocks. But what if that proves to be an aberration?

- **Chill out.** The hotter an investment's recent returns are, the more skeptical you should be about its future. Remember to ask what eventually became of other similarly faddish investments. Until lately, years of easy profits had made investors much too confident. As Kahneman wryly notes: "In a rising market, enough of your bad ideas will pay off so that you'll never learn that you should have fewer ideas."

- **Anchors aweigh.** When pundits like Goldman Sachs' Abby Joseph Cohen predict where the Dow is heading, or when analysts like Morgan Stanley's Mary Meeker forecast Amazon.com's stock price, the market often moves magnetically in their direction. But don't anchor your expectations to the tea leaves of the so-called experts. At best, they're making educated guesses; at worst, they're manipulating you to make money for their own companies.

- **Use mad money.** If you can't resist the temptation to make some high-risk bets on individual stocks, do so with only a small portion of your portfolio. Use a little of your money (10% tops) to "play the market." This way, you keep your hunches on the fringe, where they belong. "It's like going to the casino with only $200," says Kahneman. "It helps protect you from regret."

- **Step back.** In scary times like these, force yourself to look at your whole portfolio. Instead of selling a good stock because it's down a lot, use "global framing" and look at the sum total of everything you own.

- **Stop counting.** "If owning stocks is a long-term project for you," says Kahneman, "following their changes constantly is a very, very bad idea. It's the worst possible thing you can do, because people are so sensitive to short-term losses. If you count your money every day, you'll be miserable."

  Studies repeatedly show that the more investors trade, the worse they do. The combination of transaction costs, wrong guesses and emotional upheaval takes a dreadful toll on one's portfolio.

- **Fly on autopilot.** Many of the people who loved the Nasdaq when it was at 5000 in 2000 won't touch it now that it's at less than half that level. Such irrational mood swings lead people to trade too much as they veer erratically between glee and dismay. "All of us," says Kahneman, "would be better investors if we just made fewer decisions."

  Luckily, there's a solution called dollar-cost averaging. That means mechanically shoveling cash into your investments each month, regardless of what's happening in the market. Putting your portfolio on "permanent autopilot" prevents you from trying to guess what will happen next—a game many researchers say can't be won.

- **Look within.** Most financial advice, especially on TV and the Internet, suggests that investing is an endless race to beat the market. Every day brings a breathless stream of bulletins about who's ahead or behind. If anyone else wins, it seems, you lose.

But Kahneman's insights teach us something very different and vastly more profound: Investing isn't about beating others at their game. It's about controlling yourself at your own game. You're not a penny poorer if someone in Dubuque beats the S&P 500 and you don't. But you can ruin your family's financial future if you lose self-control and let greed or fear trick you into buying high or selling low.

For each of us, risk doesn't reside only in the market. It lurks inside ourselves—in the way we misinterpret information, fool ourselves into thinking we know more than we do or overreact to the market's swings. Never forget the paradox that the most powerful thing we can learn is how little we can ever possibly know. It may save you a fortune someday.

Chapter 9
SMART WAYS TO INVEST FOR RETIREMENT

Retirement. It's a daydream that for many of us involves visions of 10 a.m. tee times, 3 p.m. naps and 6 p.m. mojitos by the pool. Or maybe of teaching a course at the local college, learning to fly or moving to the mountains of Oaxaca, Mexico. Thanks to the strong economy and remarkable bull market of the 1990s, that dream has in recent years seemed within reach for many Americans. According to a survey taken in 2000 by the Employee Benefit Research Institute, 26% of the respondents said they were confident that they'd have enough money to live comfortably in retirement, up from just 19% in 1993.

In mid-2001, with the major stock indexes down and the economy slowing, some thought the ideal retirement looked harder to achieve. That need not be the case.

In fact, the new tax law President Bush signed in June 2001 will make it easier for retirement savers to achieve their goals. Beginning in 2002, you'll be able to contribute more to tax-deferred accounts. The maximum IRA contribution will rise from $2,000 to $3,000 in 2002, and will reach $6,000 in 2008. The limit on 401(k), 403(b) and 457 contributions will increase from $10,500 in 2001 to $16,500 by 2010.

This chapter will help you better manage your retirement investment strategy so you can realize your dreams. As new miracle medicines are introduced and longevity increases, the amount of time you spend in retirement is likely to be longer than you had imagined. That is potentially wonderful news—if you are financially prepared. If not, however, the consequences can be dire.

The best way to assure that your retirement is joyous rather than nerve-racking is to start saving early, take full advantage of all your tax-deferred investment opportunities and follow some of the specific advice in this chapter. If you haven't figured out how much you'll need to put away each year to meet your retirement goals, let our online calculators crunch the numbers for you at www.money.com/retirement or plug in your numbers in the worksheet on the opposite page.

AN ANNUAL CHECK-UP FOR YOUR RETIREMENT ACCOUNTS

For the nation's 39 million 401(k) investors and 42.5 million American households with IRAs, the 2000-2001 bear market was a shocking reversal of fortune. After nearly a decade of fat double-digit returns, investors were lulled into thinking that this retire-a-millionaire thing was just a matter of signing up for your plan. Well, by the beginning of 2001, investors were facing major losses in their portfolios, often for the first time in their investing careers. So, how do you protect your retirement fund and still improve performance? The answer is simple: Develop a clear retirement investing strategy. To do this, you must max out on any tax-deferred account that you are eligible to make contributions. (For a rundown of accounts, see the "Tax-Deferred Plans" table on page 148.) You must also be absolutely clear that IRAs should fit into your retirement strategies even if you have a 401(k) plan. (Check out "FAQs on IRAs" on page 153 and the IRA rollover section later in this chapter.) Finally, you also must be willing to put into action the risk management, diversification and asset allocation investment tactics we discussed in Chapter 2. To help you with this last point, we've included some specific suggestions pertaining to retirement investing.

Although no one enjoys watching their investments take a dive, a market crash highlights the dirty little secret of 401(k)s

What's Your Number?

When you consider what can change before you retire, estimating how much you'll need seems hopeless. Yet as a reality check, it's useful. This worksheet solves for two stakes. The first assumes you'll leave money behind; the second that you'll spend it all. Both assume 3% inflation, an 8% return and a life expectancy of 90. But beware: If a bear market hits early in retirement, these projections may prove too optimistic.

1. Enter your desired annual **retirement income**. (We recommend using 100% of pre-retirement income, less what you are saving.) $_____

2. Multiply line 1 by Factor A below, based on a target retirement age. This is the **income you'll want** in the first year of retirement. $_____

3. Subtract expected pension and Social Security income (available at www.ssa.gov). This is the **income your assets must generate**. . $_____

4. Multiply line 3 by Factor B, based on your age at retirement. The result is your **ideal retirement stake**, which should generate enough income without tapping your principal. $_____

5. Multiply line 3 by Factor C, based on your age at retirement. This is your **minimum retirement stake**, which should generate enough income only until age 90. $_____

YEARS UNTIL RETIREMENT	INFLATION FACTOR A	RETIREMENT AGE	FACTOR B	FACTOR C
0	1.00	50	24.2	20.7
1-5	1.09	55	21.8	18.6
6-10	1.27	60	19.9	16.2
11-15	1.47	62	19.0	15.5
16-20	1.70	65	18.1	14.1
21-25	1.97			

Source: Tarbox Equity Inc., Newport Beach, Calif.

and IRAs: You, the employee, bear full responsibility for ensuring that you have enough money to retire on. If your portfolio comes up short when it's time to call it quits, these savings vehicles are not like a corporate pension fund; the company won't make up the difference. But if you develop a sound strategy and follow

Tax-Deferred Plans

To get the most from your retirement savings, you should take full advantage of tax-deferred plans. But which ones? Here's an overview of the eight major plans. In all, your earnings grow tax deferred. With a Roth IRA, you also get tax-free withdrawals. But keep in mind that in exchange for the tax perks, you have to leave the money untouched until age $59\frac{1}{2}$ (with certain exceptions). Otherwise, you could owe a 10% early-withdrawal penalty, income taxes or both.

Note: The maximum annual contributions listed below are for 2001. Contribution limits rise starting in 2002, as discussed on page 145.

PLAN	WHO'S ELIGIBLE FOR FULL BENEFIT	MAXIMUM ANNUAL CONTRIBUTION	PRETAX CONTRIBUTION
401(k)	Employees of companies with plans, typically after one year of service	$10,500 or the plan limit[3]	Yes
403(b)	Employees of nonprofits	20% of gross income or $10,500[3]	Yes
KEOGH	Self-employed or small business employees	15% of net income or $30,000[3,4]	Yes
SEP-IRA	Self-employed or small business employees[1]	15% of net income or $25,500[3]	Yes
SIMPLE IRA	Self-employed or small business employees	$6,000 plus match of 3% of income	Yes
DEDUCTIBLE IRA	People not covered by pension or those who earn below certain income caps[2]	$2,000	Yes
ROTH IRA	Singles with adjusted gross income of $95,000 or less; couples with $150,000 or less	$2,000	No
NONDEDUCTIBLE IRA	Anyone with earned income	$2,000	No

Notes: [1]If compensation is $170,000 or less. [2]Eligible for full deduction if adjusted gross income (AGI) is less than $32,000 for singles, $52,000 for married couples filing jointly; if married and spouse is covered by an employer plan, you can take full deduction if total AGI is under $150,000. [3]Whichever is less. [4]25% if money-purchase plan.

through with regular portfolio maintenance, you can reach your retirement goals. Here's a plan you can follow:

1. Figure out where you stand.

If you haven't opened your retirement account statement lately, grit your teeth and do it. And if the "personal rate of return" cited on your account statement is a negative number, don't waste time daydreaming about how rich you used to be or kicking yourself over everything you might have done. "It's irrelevant where your portfolio stood before," says Robert Bingham, principal at San Francisco investment advisory firm Bingham Osborn & Scarborough. "That money is gone. You need to start over from where you are now."

What you do need to look at is your current asset allocation: how much you have stashed in each fund and what type of investments each fund holds. If you have other retirement portfolios—a spouse's 401(k), a rollover IRA and so on—be sure to include them. Make a list and add up how much you have in each fund; software such as Quicken or Microsoft Money can help.

Next, determine what kinds of stocks your account or equity funds contain—large-cap growth or midcap value, for example. To get an accurate picture, look beyond the fund's name and find out what stocks the manager actually buys. Legg Mason Value fund, for example, has been peppered with growth companies like Amazon and Dell, while Fidelity's Equity-Income II fund is loaded with stocks that don't pay dividends. You can see a fund's holdings data by looking at its annual report online; you can also check a fund's investing style and get a portfolio analysis on sites such as www.morningstar.com.

Don't be surprised if you find that you were more heavily weighted in risky stocks than you realized. Many formerly stodgy stock funds loaded up on tech during the glory days. In addition, as growth funds like Janus Twenty and Putnam Voyager rocketed higher year after year, many investors couldn't resist leaping on board. "You can't get higher returns without taking risk, but investors turned that notion around," says Scott Lummer, chief investment officer at mPower, an online investment advice firm. "They thought if they took higher risks, they automatically got higher returns."

Take Greg and Gayle Hayhurst. In 1999, Greg rolled over a 401(k) from an old job into a brokerage account and invested almost the entire amount in tech stocks. As of early April 2001, that account had dropped 87% from its $63,000 peak in March 2000. Luckily, the rest of the Hayhursts' retirement money was less tech-heavy; all told, their combined retirement portfolios, now totaling $249,000, were down by 29% by the beginning of 2001.

Numerous online calculators, including those at the websites Financialengines.com or Morningstar's ClearFuture, can help you get an estimate of what you really need to save with about 15 minutes' work. The key to making a realistic plan is assuming a reasonable—not turbocharged—rate of return. Count on a conservative annual growth rate of 8% for a diversified portfolio.

Once you work through the numbers, you may be shocked to learn how much you need to sock away to finance your retirement. Vanguard, for instance, calculates that the average investor earning $100,000 will need to stash about 20% of his or her salary, on average, over 30 years in order to retire by age 67 with a $75,000 annual income (including full Social Security benefits but no pension). Remember, however, IRS rules often restrict the amount you can contribute to your retirement accounts. Therefore, not only should you contribute the most your plan allows, you should also pump up your after-tax savings. So for instance, if you're saving 10% of a $75,000 salary in a 401(k) or SEP-IRA (for the self-employed), try increasing that to 15%. Over 20 years, assuming a 7% return, the extra savings will add $160,000 to your retirement stash.

2. Design a realistic asset allocation.

The recent market massacre serves as a reminder, in case you needed one, that diversification is still essential protection against market wipeouts. Unfortunately, a study by benefits firm Hewitt Associates found that 36% of 401(k) participants invest in only one fund and another 19% in just two funds, which suggests that workers are badly underdiversified. Some 80% have never rebalanced their asset allocations.

Start your asset allocation check-up by reviewing your overall split between stocks and bonds—this proportion will have the biggest impact on your returns and your level of risk. Although many investors put all their retirement assets in stocks during the bull market, very few investors are comfortable over the long term with a 100% stock allocation. In fact, anyone over 30 should consider adding a healthy dose of bonds to his or her 401(k) or IRA for ballast. (See page 30 for suggested allocations.)

Of course, these allocation suggestions are starting points. Customize your mix based on your own financial needs, risk tolerance and time horizon with the Asset Allocation Wizard at www.money.com. In choosing allocations, again, be sure to take your other retirement portfolios into account, as well as any other long-term savings.

Over time, you may want to adjust your asset mix to reflect your changing life circumstances. It's particularly important to revisit your asset allocation once you are within five years of retirement; most advisers recommend scaling back on stocks at that point. In fact, many workers in their fifties and sixties who were too aggressively invested in equities are suffering now, notes Martha Priddy Patterson, director of employee benefits policy analysis at Deloitte & Touche.

Troy Perry wants to make sure he won't have a fiftysome-thing portfolio crisis. Perry, the 38-year-old co-owner of an Omaha construction firm, currently has his 401(k) 100% in stocks, but he intends to move a portion to bonds well before retirement. "What is scary is seeing the guys in their early to mid-fifties who got tired of hearing about people making money in tech stocks and moved into that market," he says. "Now they're in trouble. That's exactly what I want to avoid."

Experts recommend that you rebalance your portfolio annual-ly. To explore the best ways to rebalance your portfolio, review the rebalancing section that begins on page 40 of Chapter 2.

3. Watch out for company-stock time bombs in 401(k) plans.

About 20% of 401(k) plans offer company stock. If yours is one of them, consider this cautionary tale from Michael Scarborough, president of Scarborough Group, an Annapolis, Md. 401(k) advice firm. Scarborough recently got a call from a 58-year-old Lucent employee. Early in 2000, the man had $400,000 in his 401(k), 90% of it in Lucent stock, and he planned to retire in two years. Then Lucent's stock tumbled; his account is now worth just $80,000. "It's tragic," says Scarborough. "There's really nothing you can do in that situation but keep working."

We've said it before, but we can't say it enough: Don't put more than 10% of your 401(k) into company stock. "You are tak-ing a tremendous amount of risk for average returns," says UCLA accounting professor Shlomo Benartzi. Market history is littered with examples of major companies that ran into financial trou-ble, costing workers both their jobs and their nest eggs. Remember IBM in the early '90s? Gillette in '99? How about Procter & Gamble and Dell in 2000?

Even so, company stock seems to be an offer that employees cannot refuse. In some cases, that's literally the case: Of plans that offer company stock, 25% use it to fund matching contribu-tions. More often, though, employees simply perceive the stock as safer than a diversified equity fund (though the opposite is true) or as a superior investment (though that's rare). A 2000 sur-vey by the Investment Company Institute and the Employee Benefits Research Institute found that in plans with a company-stock option, workers in their forties and fifties allocate 30% of their portfolios to that risky asset, on average. Among 401(k) plans that also match contributions solely with company stock, the average stake is 50%.

4. Get help if you need it.

As your retirement account grows and your finances become more complicated, you may find it difficult to handle your investments on your own. Workers nearing retirement, in particular, may be daunted by the many decisions they need to make. If that's the case, by all means consult an expert. Many 401(k), IRA and KEOGH administrators offer advice, whether online or one-on-one. If your plan doesn't meet your needs, search for financial planners by taking the advice in Chapter 7.

For Malvin and Donna Green of Gonzales, Texas, hiring an adviser proved to be timely. The 51-year-old bank president aims to retire at age 65 and wanted advice on managing his $182,000 portfolio from a former job, which was invested primarily in large-cap growth funds. He turned to a financial adviser in December 2000, and she rolled over his money into blue-chip stocks just before the market meltdown. "I had been very aggressive," says Green, whose rollover was down 25% in March 2001 but regained some ground in April. Meanwhile, he continues to contribute to his current 401(k). "The market will rebound," says Green. "I have no doubt that things will work out fine for our retirement." And after renovating your 401(k), you too will be on your way to a more secure retirement.

THE ROLLOVER: THE BIGGEST RETIREMENT DECISION YOU'LL MAKE

While almost 50 million boomers will begin rolling over their retirement plans during the next 20 years, few are prepared for what may be the most important financial decision they'll ever make, with probably the biggest pile of money they'll ever handle. Ideally, any lump-sum distribution from your 401(k) plan—whether you're changing jobs or retiring—should be funneled into either an IRA or another employer's plan, where you can invest it to last a lifetime. But it doesn't often happen that way. "Most employees are ill equipped to handle rollover distributions, and they don't even know it," says Dee Lee, a financial planner in Harvard, Mass. "But a mistake could easily cost you more than half your nest egg in unnecessary taxes, penalties and poor investments."

Don't count on much rollover guidance from your company. Although many employers are starting to offer advice on investing for retirement, few have focused on workers who are actually

FAQs on IRAs

If you think managing your IRA just means pumping money into your account and sitting back to watch your money grow, think again. Since the first IRA was established 27 years ago, the number of plans, as well as the number of rules governing these tax-advantaged savings accounts, has mushroomed, creating colossal Excedrin headaches for investors.

Since each IRA comes with its own set of features, choosing the one or ones that best meet your needs can be difficult if you don't have all the facts. You probably know that a traditional IRA lets your earnings grow tax deferred—but did you know that you'll never pay taxes on earnings in a Roth if you follow the rules? Or that, if you're self-employed, you can sock away up to $25,500 in a SEP-IRA? (To find the most appropriate plan or plans— or to assess your current one—see "Tax-Deferred Plans" on page 148.)

But choosing the right IRA is only part of the challenge. MONEY magazine is flooded with queries from readers asking for advice about how to properly manage their IRAs. Following are eight frequently asked questions about IRAs.

Note: The contribution numbers used in this section are for 2001. The limits rise in 2002, as discussed on page 145.

Q. Can I contribute to a Roth IRA if I'm not working?

A. That depends on how you define working. To contribute to a Roth, you must earn at least the amount of your contribution in taxable compensation, which includes wages, tips, professional fees, bonuses, commissions and alimony, but not pensions. Dividends, interest and capital gains also don't count, no matter how hard you worked on your portfolio.

Q. Can I still set up an IRA for my spouse who does not work outside of the home?

A. With both a traditional and a Roth IRA, contributions can be made in the name of a spouse who earns less than $2,000, if the couple files a joint tax return. The maximum annual contribution for a spouse is $2,000, assuming the working spouse earns at least that amount. (If the working spouse—in this case, your husband—also wants to contribute $2,000 to his own IRA, his total compensation must be at least $4,000.)

Q. What's the income threshold to convert an IRA to a Roth?

A. If you want to make a conversion, your adjusted gross income for the year must not exceed $100,000, whether you're single or married. Married individuals who file separately cannot make Roth conversions, period. Plus, regardless of your marital status, a 401(k) must first be rolled over into a traditional IRA before a Roth conversion can take place.

Q. Can you commingle the funds in a traditional IRA that was converted to a Roth with another Roth account? Can you deposit into both?

A. You can combine the rollover and the new Roth into one account. But while one Roth means less paperwork, it could also mean headaches if you take any money out in the next few years. New Roth contributions can be withdrawn anytime, with no penalty; rollover contributions, however, cannot be tapped penalty-free in the first five years unless you're over $59\frac{1}{2}$ or using the money for such things as major medical or college expenses or for a first-time home purchase. (Earnings are subject to different rules.) So keep careful records.

And, yes, you can contribute to two Roths, as long as your total IRA contributions don't exceed the maximum contribution (up to $2,000) for your income.

Q. What happens when you make a contribution to your Roth IRA, but by the end of year you realize that you'll make more than the $160,000 adjusted gross income limit for contributing to a Roth? Do you recharacterize your contribution as a traditional IRA, should you withdraw $2,000 in cash (plus earnings) or should you withdraw the number of shares that you purchased (plus earnings)?

A. Do not withdraw the money at all. Just ask your financial institution to redesignate the money (which will be the current value of your 2001 contributions plus any reinvested dividends and earnings or losses) to a traditional IRA. (If you want to move the money to another institution, ask for a trustee-to-trustee transfer.) You must do this before October 15, 2002.

Even if you file your federal tax returns on April 15, you can file an amendment for a recharacterization.

Q. What makes more sense to trade on a regular basis—the stocks in IRAs or the ones in taxable accounts?

A. Frequent trading in any account can be dangerous. Although you may be lucky some of the time, constantly trying to time the market has been shown, over time, to fail. That said, if you still can't help yourself, it's best to do most of your stock trading in your IRA. You won't pay capital-gains taxes that would otherwise be triggered by trades. One drawback: If your investments in a tax-deferred account tank, you are not allowed to write off the losses as you could in a taxable account.

Q. Can IRA funds be invested in undeveloped land?

A. Only cash—not land—can be contributed to an IRA. Although you could choose to invest IRA funds in land, why would you want to? First of all, the land would have to be purchased entirely with IRA funds and held in the name of an IRA trust. (A bank, credit union or savings and loan that is insured by the federal government would qualify, but not all such companies would agree to the job.) Also, land is not a liquid asset, which could complicate making the required minimum withdrawals on schedule.

Q. In case of a divorce, what's the best tax strategy for dividing an IRA in the husband's or wife's name?

A. Just as the song says, breaking up is hard to do. But even if tempers flare, staying focused on all things financial will keep Uncle Sam from benefiting from your misfortune.

To avoid triggering unnecessary taxes, consider these two alternatives for splitting your nest egg: A direct transfer lets you simply move your share of the holdings from your spouse's IRA into an IRA account in your name. Or if your spouse has more than one IRA, he or she can sign over one of his accounts to you. Your spouse must agree to give you 100% of what's in that account, though. Whichever method you happen to choose, have the exact terms of distribution clearly outlined in the divorce or separation agreement.

retiring. Too bad, because the rollover decision is much more complicated than it may seem. (Internal Revenue Service rules governing IRA rollovers alone run to more than 70 pages.) Plus, your moves should fit into a comprehensive retirement planning and tax strategy.

When making any rollover, you'll want to mind these points:

• **Be sure to do a direct, or trustee-to-trustee, transfer to the financial institution that will hold your IRA or manage your new 401(k).** If your old employer ends up writing a check in your name, 20% of the money will be withheld for taxes; therefore, in order to roll over the full amount, you will have to come up with the extra 20% yourself. If you do receive a check directly, you will have just 60 days to make the transfer. If you miss the deadline, the IRS will deem the amount a withdrawal and will impose an additional 10% penalty.

• **If you're rolling over into an IRA, the money must go into a regular IRA.** You can convert later to a Roth, if you wish to take advantage of its post-retirement tax benefits. And if you want to retain the option of transferring your money from the IRA into a new employer's 401(k), keep the IRA separate from your other savings accounts and avoid mixing contributions. More on that particular rollover tactic in a bit.

You may find it easier to work with a financial adviser, especially if you have a big bundle or are hoping to retire soon. Even if you hire a pro, however, you still need to understand the basics. We've broken them into three life stages for managing your rollover.

Stage 1: Changing Jobs

Rule No. 1: Don't cash out your lump sum and spend it. Seems pretty obvious, right? Yet too many workers opt for instant gratification. A survey by benefits firm Hewitt Associates found that 57% of 401(k) plan participants who are changing jobs choose a cash payment rather than a rollover. Of those with balances under $5,000—mostly younger employees—nearly 80% take the moolah and run. "People look at the money as a big windfall, so they spend it," says Hewitt consultant Mike McCarthy. But cashing out carries a price. You'll owe income taxes plus a 10% penalty if you're under age $59^1/_2$, and you'll lose the opportunity for future tax-deferred growth.

So let's assume you don't cash out. When deciding what to do with your 401(k), you basically have three choices: You can keep it in your company plan (assuming your balance is more than $5,000), move it to your new 401(k) plan (if its rules allow) or roll it over into an IRA. The right strategy for you will depend on your specific plans and retirement goals, but you'll almost always want to consider these issues:

Keeping the money where it is. If you like the investments in your previous plan or don't want to go through the trouble of choosing new ones, there's little downside to staying put. It also may make sense to stick with the plan if you've made a significant amount of after-tax contributions. Why? You can't roll over dollars that have already been taxed (although you can roll over the earnings on those contributions).

Moving the money to your new 401(k). This makes sense if your new plan has more or better options, or lower fees, than your previous one. Old plan or new, a 401(k) can be helpful if you'll ever need to borrow against the assets during an emergency. You can't do that with an IRA. Also consider a 401(k) if your job involves a high risk of lawsuits or if you fear bankruptcy: Company plans are federally regulated, so they're exempt from creditors; IRA assets, by contrast, are subject to state law, which may not protect them from creditors.

Choosing an IRA.   With all the benefits of 401(k)s, why would you opt for an IRA rollover? There are several reasons. First, an IRA lets you select virtually any investment option. It also provides more flexibility in choosing your beneficiary and (if you are retiring early) taking distributions. "Company plans tend to be far more restrictive than IRS rules," says Ed Slott, a C.P.A. in Rockville Centre, N.Y. who publishes the newsletter *Ed Slott's IRA Advisor.* "Most employers don't want to keep track of their ex-employees and all their descendants—it's a paperwork nightmare." Finally, today's good 401(k) plan might morph into tomorrow's bad one, especially if your old company merges or goes through a bout of cost cutting. In fact, most financial advisers prefer IRA rollovers to 401(k)s for their clients.

Stage 2: Approaching Retirement

The clock is ticking: It's time to decide what to do with your retirement plan money—keep it where it is or make the final rollover that will serve you throughout your retirement. You first need to determine when you will start making withdrawals. The payout procedures can differ significantly between 401(k)s and IRAs, but if there's one universal rule, it is this: You should draw first from your taxable accounts, so that your IRAs and 401(k)s can compound tax deferred as long as possible. After all, your retirement could last 30 years or more, so you need to maximize growth.

Before making any rollover choice, check the rules of your company plan—details can vary widely from company to company. And consider these key rollover options for pre-retirees:

An early withdrawal from your 401(k).   If you have a sizable 401(k) but little money in your taxable accounts, you may want to stick with your company plan. That's because at many companies you can retire between 55 and $59^1/_2$ and make regular withdrawals from your 401(k) without paying a penalty. (Your distribution schedule can continue if you later return to the work world—or even rejoin the same employer.) Of course, once you turn $59^1/_2$ at any company, you're free to take out your 401(k) money at will without penalty if you're retired. But how you take advantage of the 401(k)'s early-withdrawal opening depends on your particular plan's policies. In most cases, you can choose only among the regular retirement withdrawal schedules set by the plan or take a lump-sum distribution. Simply pulling out your money may, in fact, end up being the best choice, since it offers the greatest flexibility. You could set aside what you need to spend in the next few years—taking the income tax hit—and roll over the rest tax deferred into an IRA.

Turning your IRA into a 401(k).   This could be an intriguing option if you have little in a 401(k) but a lot in an IRA rollover. Moving that IRA money into a 401(k)—if the plan rules allow such a switch—will let you tap into your nest egg while avoiding the more restrictive early-withdrawal schedule of IRAs, which we note below. But the move may not be worth the hassle if you intend to roll out of your 401(k) in a few years.

401(k) limitations. If you're older than $59^1/_2$ and retiring, there's little reason to stick with your 401(k). Many company savings plans simply aren't that accommodating to retirees, and some plans force workers to take out all their money by the official retirement age, typically 65. If you don't make prior arrangements, such as a direct rollover into an IRA, you could be automatically mailed a check for the distribution—minus the 20% withholding tax.

IRA limitations. If you really need to make withdrawals from your nest egg before age $59^1/_2$, think twice about an IRA rollover. Generally, the only way to avoid paying an early-withdrawal penalty on an IRA is by taking periodic payments based on your life expectancy. (This rule for determining payment schedules applies to all IRA owners regardless of age.) The younger you are, the smaller your income stream will be. Plus, once you start taking withdrawals, you must continue for at least five years or until you turn $59^1/_2$, whichever is later.

A chance to unload company stock.   If you own a big helping of company shares in your retirement plan and you can't touch your company stock while you're still working, use an IRA rollover as an opportunity to diversify. Retiring workers with a bigger chunk may want to consider taking an in-kind distribution, which can substantially lower your tax bill. Here's how it works: If you keep your company stock in your 401(k), you'll pay regular income taxes on it as you withdraw money. But before you roll over the money into an IRA (or take a lump sum), you can choose to withdraw some or all of your company stock separately. At that point, you'll pay tax not on the full value of the stock but only on the cost basis, which is what the shares were worth when they went into your account. When you sell the stock, you'll owe taxes only at capital-gains rates on your long-term profits. This strategy is a no-brainer if your stock has zoomed in value, notes accountant Twila Slesnick. But if gains have been modest, you may do better paying ordinary income taxes. Check with an accountant. Of course, if you can diversify out of company stock while you're still working, so much the better.

Stage 3: In Retirement

Okay, you're no longer working. Time to chill out. Your chief task these days is managing your rollover and other retirement accounts. If you haven't already rolled out of your former company's 401(k) plan, consider doing so now, since IRAs generally offer the widest investment options for keeping your portfolio on track, as well as the best alternatives for distributions and estate planning. Here's what you need to consider:

Staying with stocks or stock funds. If you have a hefty nest egg, you will need to be well diversified among stocks, bonds, funds and other assets. Clearly, an IRA rollover to a good brokerage firm or other money-management outfit offers more choice than the typical 401(k) plan. But even though you may be changing your account, don't assume you all of a sudden need to make major changes in your asset allocation and run for the safety of fixed-income investments. "There are several stages of retirement," notes Ronald Yolles, a financial adviser in Southfield, Mich. "And in the early stages, you usually need as much growth as you did when you were working."

Updating your beneficiaries. If you wish to pass money on to your heirs, IRAs are the more flexible choice. For example, nearly all 401(k) plans require that your spouse be listed as the primary beneficiary of your account, unless he or she signs a waiver. That makes it more difficult to pass money to your children or other heirs. By contrast, major brokerage and mutual fund companies generally offer plenty of beneficiary options on IRAs. (If yours doesn't, attach a customized form that spells out your wishes—or move your money to a firm that offers more flexibility.)

Retirement Plan Payouts Made Easier

In a move that should make retirement accounts more manageable in one respect, the IRS has simplified the rules for calculating the minimum distribution from an IRA, 401(k), 403(b), Keogh and SEP that most seniors must start taking at age $70^1/_2$. Instead of deciding between complicated withdrawal methods—single-life expectancy, joint life, term certain, recalculation— you'll now rely on one uniform life expectancy table, and the age of your beneficiary no longer figures into the calculation (unless, in the one remaining exception, your spouse is your beneficiary and is more than 10 years younger). Plus, naming and changing your beneficiary has become easier.

Even if you're already taking your required minimum distributions, you can switch to this new payout method. Why do that? For most, this new system will produce smaller minimum distributions (because your life expectancy often grows as you age), thereby letting your money grow tax-free for longer. One caveat: Company plan administrators have the option of sticking with the old system in 2001, and they may choose to do so if the new rules necessitate amending the plan. To see the new life expectancy tables, go to www.irahelp.com, the site run by tax expert Ed Slott.

Always double-check your beneficiary forms, and update them if necessary. To pass your IRAs to desired heirs, the people must be specifically named on the forms—stating your wishes in your will does not override the account documents.

Watching your withdrawals.   When it comes to mandatory withdrawals, IRAs rule, since they offer more options than company plans do for setting withdrawal schedules. Bear in mind, though, that by April 1 of the year following the year you turn $70^1/_2$—we told you these rules can get thick!—you must begin withdrawing the required minimum distributions from your tax-deferred accounts, be they IRAs or 401(k)s. As we indicated earlier, the federal penalty for not taking out at least the minimum is stiff: a full 50% of the amount you should have withdrawn. And you are the one who is responsible for figuring out the number. As you've no doubt guessed, calculating the precise amount of that minimum distribution is no easy task, since the rates are based on your life expectancy and, in one specific instance, those of a beneficiary. (See "Retirement Plan Payouts Made Easier" above for a full discussion.)

After all these details, there's just one other thing about rollovers to note: If you've got a sizable pile, consider getting expert advice.

Rollover Resources

- **Taking Your Money Out: IRAs, 401(k)s and Other Retirement Plans**
  by Twila Slesnick and John C. Suttle (Nolo, $24.95); not exactly light reading but an excellent starting point

- **www.irajunction.com**
  A site offered by mPower, which also runs another top investor website called 401kafe.com

- **www.irahelp.com**
  Sponsored by C.P.A. and IRA newsletter publisher Ed Slott, the chief attraction is a forum where he'll help answer your IRA questions.

- **www.quicken.com/retirement**
  A comprehensive though cluttered website that offers the lowdown on various IRAs and rollovers, along with links to expert advice and planning tools

- **www.onmoney.com**
  This sleek site is backed by online broker Ameritrade, but it seeks to offer independent financial planning advice.

Few things grab the attention of a money manager more than a big, fat IRA rollover walking through the door. You're certainly more likely to get better advice on investing and estate planning than if you keep the money in your company plan. Of course, you needn't rush to an expensive adviser. Depending on your financial needs, you can select from a growing variety of lower-cost resources, ranging from books to online advice to one-shot financial planning services (see "Rollover Resources" above for some suggestions). Most major brokerages, investment firms and fund companies such as T. Rowe Price, Fidelity and Vanguard also offer retirement income management advice. Shop around. That way, you can really ensure that your money keeps working, even if you don't.

CHOOSING FUNDS FOR YOUR RETIREMENT ACCOUNTS

To create a mutual fund portfolio that will meet your retirement needs, you need a step-by-step plan. Go grocery shopping without a list, and you're liable to go home with two flavors of Godiva ice cream, a jar of raspberry mustard and no milk or cereal. So don't browse among all those fascinating funds without a clear idea of what you need. If you focus solely on the flashiest returns, you may end up with a very unbalanced, and highly risky, portfolio. Here's how to make the right choices:

Step 1: Hunt for bargains.   You know the boilerplate: "Past performance does not guarantee future results." But there is a way to determine which funds are likeliest to outperform: Look at expense ratios.

Your plan packet might not include expense ratios, but you can find them at fund websites or at Morningstar.com. Go through the list of funds and eliminate those with above-average annual expenses, using these benchmarks:

- Bond funds: 0.85%
- Domestic stock funds: 1.19%
- Small-cap stock funds: 1.37%
- International stock funds: 1.56%

If these expense figures are lower than other averages you may have seen, it's because they exclude the highest-cost types of shares (such as B and C classes). A good 401(k) plan these days is a Price Club of fund investing—your company buys in bulk and gets a discount. Since any decent 401(k) offers funds with cheaper shares, why pay expenses higher than these?

Step 2: Consider index funds.   This is a corollary to the bargain-hunting rule above: Index funds tend to outperform actively managed funds in the long run, partly because their fees are almost always much lower. The other reason to favor index funds is that most of us, pros included, can't consistently pick winners. Some money managers make a convincing case that indexing isn't the best strategy in less efficient markets, such as small-cap or international stocks. But it's hard to argue against indexing the large-cap market in the long run.

Step 3: Check your master lists.   Compare your list of funds (offered by your 401(k) plan or IRA or Keogh administrator) to those recommended by reliable sources, such as the MONEY 100 list of top mutual funds (available at www.money.com) or Morningstar.com.

Step 4: Trust the old standbys. When in doubt about choosing a fund, says John Rekenthaler, Morningstar's director of research, consider giving the nod to an offering from heavyweights like Fidelity, Vanguard and American. These families boast three times as many funds with above-average category ratings as below-average funds.

"They attract top-quality people and have below-average expenses, which leads to better funds overall," he explains. "Besides having a higher percentage of winners, they have almost no real dogs. When they have a problem fund, they can throw resources at it, as both Fidelity and Vanguard have done in recent years. They have a will to win and higher standards than most."

Step 5: Checks and balances. Instead of considering only whether funds buy large-cap stocks or smaller names, it can also pay to offset aggressive, risky growth styles with more conservative value-priced plays.

You could make a guess on style by the fund names, but that method has a high margin of error. Any good mutual fund website, however, should categorize each fund in a helpful way. (Of course, a broad U.S. equity index fund would cover both growth and value.)

You might, for example, choose MAS Mid Cap Growth, a great aggressive play, and pair it with Fidelity Low-Priced Stock, which holds cheaper and smaller names. Similarly, you could pair the fairly aggressive Harbor Capital Appreciation, a large-cap growth fund, with a stake in the Fasciano fund, which specializes in smaller-cap growth stocks, with less of an emphasis on technology. (For a list of MONEY magazine editors' all-time favorite funds for retirement accounts, go to page 110.)

STOCKS TO RETIRE ON

You also can create a fine retirement portfolio by using individual stocks as opposed to funds, or you can use individual stocks to supplement the funds already in your portfolio. If you think the costs of doing so are too high, think again.

With a small IRA, this may not be practical, which explains why some financial advisers used to caution against holding stocks in retirement accounts. If you have a small account and want to buy the number of securities needed to achieve diversity, the math is deadly. The amount invested in each stock would be so minute that commissions will kill any chance of a decent return.

But for most Americans it is a reasonable idea. Retirement balances have swelled as commissions have dwindled. The 42.5 million American households with IRAs hold an average of $72,000 in their accounts at a time when the average online-brokerage commission is hovering around $15. At the same time, the percentage of large companies offering 401(k)s with a so-called brokerage window, through which investors can purchase any securities they please, has jumped to 10% from nearly zero in just seven years. All of this means that folks with sizable IRA or brokerage-enabled 401(k) balances can invest, even actively, and actually keep their expenses competitive with mutual funds.

Scott Lummer of mPower believes that an investor ought to hold 20 to 30 stocks to achieve a well-diversified portfolio. He notes that an investor who sets up a retirement account equally divided among 20 stocks pays about $300 in transaction fees through an online broker. Assume you make some additional trades during the year—perhaps five sells and five new buys—which add another $150. If you hold a $100,000 IRA, that $450 in commissions is only 0.45% of your portfolio. Sure, that's more than the lowest end of the mutual fund cost spectrum—Vanguard offers index funds with expense ratios as low as 0.06%—but it's far lower than the average expense ratio of actively managed domestic equity funds, which, at 1.46%, is the equivalent of a $1,460 charge every year on a $100,000 portfolio.

You get a tax break, so use it. By sheltering capital gains in retirement accounts, the government is actually encouraging investors to trade stocks in them. Consequently, they are a purer trader's environment than taxable accounts, allowing you to make buy-and-sell decisions based exclusively on investment analysis. A stock that's rocketed after eight months need not linger in your portfolio for another four just to escape the short-term capital-gains tax.

And make no mistake: Managing a retirement stock portfolio takes diligence. Despite the fact that a third of the $2.5 trillion in IRAs is already invested in individual securities, people tend to pay less attention to their retirement accounts than their taxable ones. That's not good. It may be tempting to assume that you can simply select several good stocks from several different sectors and literally ignore them for decades. Unfortunately, there's no such thing as a "widows and orphans stock" anymore. Says Dave Foster of Foster & Motley, a money-management firm in Cincinnati: "There are no more one-decision stocks like AT&T once was. I mean, Procter & Gamble took a 30% haircut in one day."

In general, you should buy a retirement stock for the same reason you would any stock—you believe in its fundamentals. Beyond that, however, there are a few factors that may make some stocks more appropriate for a retirement portfolio than others. With that in mind, we've outlined five general categories below that can help lead you to the kind of solid, consistent performers that you don't have to monitor every minute of the day yet are likely to be long-term winners.

Consider these stocks as candidates for your portfolio, but don't forget to use other strategies discussed in Chapter 3 and to seek out bargains in the Sivy 100.

- **Oversold favorites in established industries.** There are plenty of Amazons and Yahoos—companies that have fallen 90% or more and have made the trip from overvalued to, arguably, undervalued. But we're not ready to haul out the word bargain for those former rockets just yet. Even though we suspect the Internet's leaders will shine again, the negative sentiment surrounding them might take years to overcome. For your retirement accounts, consider some value-priced old-world firms such as Bear Stearns that might not soar this month or this year but will eventually justify your faith. (See page 53 for a more details on the company.)

- **Consistently focused firms.** These are companies that know how to do one thing very well, to dominate their market, and not to indulge their wanderlust—or their egos. They're perfect for retirement accounts, since investors who look the other way are less likely to discover that the company they own is no longer in the sector they thought it was. Two long-time favorites: Wal-Mart and FedEx.

- **Companies with manageable debt loads.** A very large debt burden means you're no longer investing only in the outcome of your stock's core business. You're also betting on the financial winds. That extra layer of volatility is the last thing you need in a retirement portfolio. For this category, consider high-cash-flow businesses that distribute most of their cash to shareholders and operations, not mean old banks waving IOUs. Good examples: Pfizer and Coca-Cola.

• **Companies with the right kind of risk.** There's good risk and there's bad risk—the trick is to distinguish between the two. Paying a premium for companies experiencing fast, sustainable growth is usually a risk worth taking. But that strategy can backfire (as investors in Cisco know too well) when growth rather than the underlying business becomes the reason investors come to the stock. For a retirement account in particular, your reasons for taking a risk have to be aligned with an underlying belief in the long-term strength of the company, rather than a simple guess that its shares are headed higher.

The risk we prefer for retirement stocks can be found in companies like BellSouth and Philip Morris whose near-term outlook may have sufficient uncertainty to ensure a low stock price, but whose long-term prospects are healthy, especially relative to competitors.

• **Clear leaders in emerging industries.** Retirement investing rewards the spotter of long-term trends more richly than short-term pickers. Recently, "long term" in investing had come to mean a year at best. As much as one might love the products of Krispy Kreme or the WWF, these stocks are clearly of the moment. The trick is to find companies such as E-Trade and JDS Uniphase that have established themselves in industries that will be around long after the Rock's heart specialist has told him to lay off the doughnuts.

Chapter 10
TAX STRATEGIES INVESTORS NEED TO KNOW

We've focused a lot on how investors can make money. In this chapter, we'll show you how to keep it. Millions of investors earn less than they should because they don't pay sufficient attention to tax consequences. However, even though the 2001 tax reforms haven't given us any capital gains relief, there are strategies for reducing your tax bite. The key is to pay close attention to the tax cost of every investment move you make.

Be aware, though, that radical moves to avoid taxes often lead to lousy investment decisions, as many investors who got burned in fee-heavy limited partnerships discovered in the 1980s. So don't do anything crazy, and never focus on taxes to the exclusion of other investment criteria. Remember, though, that becoming a tax-smart investor is one of the most powerful steps you can take on the road to increased investment success.

TAMING FUND TAXES

Many mutual fund investors get eaten alive by taxes without even knowing it. Millions of fund investors think their performance is better than it actually is. "The return you get after taxes is often nowhere near the return you see reported," says Vanguard fund taxation specialist Joel Dickson. One of the best ways to wring the maximum possible gain out of your investments is to keep your fund tax bill low.

How much difference can fund taxes make? Here's a tale of two funds with seemingly similar returns. Over the five years through February 2001, Fidelity Asset Manager: Growth averaged a 12.3% annual gain, while Legg Mason Focus averaged 12.1%. But after taxes it was a different story: The Fidelity fund returned 8.8% for an investor in the 39.6% federal tax bracket; Legg Mason shareholders got an 11.7% after-tax return.

What explains the gap? The culprit was portfolio turnover. By law, mutual funds must distribute essentially all the year's income and realized capital gains to shareholders, who are then responsible for paying taxes on that money. Managers who trade frequently tend to create more capital gains than those who hang on to their winners. Sure enough, over the past five years, the team running Asset Manager: Growth bought and sold actively, while Focus manager Robert Hagstrom made far fewer moves.

Some managers factor taxes into their trading strategies while others make them a secondary consideration—or ignore them altogether. Over the past five years the average U.S. stock fund was 78% tax-efficient, according to research firm Morningstar. That means an investor in the 39.6% tax bracket was left with 78% of the fund's return after paying taxes on the income and capital gains it distributed. Looking at all domestic-stock funds, tax-efficiency varies dramatically—from a low of 10% (Alliance Quasar B and C shares) to a high of nearly 100% (IPS Millennium and White Oak Growth Stock).

Trouble is, identifying funds that will be tax-smart in the future is more art than science, and an abstract art at that. You can find a fund's tax-efficiency figure in MONEY's annual fund rankings, and tax-adjusted returns are available at www.morningstar.com. But like all performance figures, these numbers don't guarantee future results. Strategy shifts, manager changes and asset outflows can all affect a fund's tax characteristics. And the portfolio turnover rate is not always a reliable guide either. Some fast-trading managers are able to offset gains by taking losses, while even low-turnover managers must sometimes cash in big winners, which can lead to sizable taxable distributions.

Consider Legg Mason Value. Manager William Miller has not only outperformed the S&P 500 for an almost unheard-of 10 years straight. He has also kept turnover low and taxable distributions to a minimum—until the year 2000, that is. That is when Miller decided it was finally time to take profits on longtime holdings like America Online (now AOL Time Warner) and Dell. As a result, the fund distributed more than $14 a share in taxable gains in 2000—even though its return for the year was a 7.1% loss. Investors who bought into Legg Mason Value in 2000, before its June and December distributions, got hit with a huge tax bill for gains they weren't around to enjoy.

The lesson: while a low-turnover fund can grow almost tax-free for years, when it finally does sell a highly profitable holding, the resulting distribution can be a doozy. So some advisers favor new funds with no built-up tax liability. Under that theory, young Longleaf Partners International would have seemed a tax-savvy purchase early in 2000, given the Longleaf team's brilliant record and low-turnover strategy. The fund has indeed been a smashing success—from a pretax perspective. The managers' value picks soared right past their targets in 2000, prompting them to sell shares, which generated a whopping distribution.

In the end, it's so hard to predict the distributions of actively managed funds that you may be better off holding them in a 401(k) or IRA account, where you needn't worry about annual tax bills. In any case, before you invest in an actively managed fund, be sure to call the fund and ask for the "ex-dividend" date, and then hold off investing until that date has passed.

Consider index funds.   As for your taxable accounts, index funds are hard to beat before taxes because of their low expenses—and they're even harder to beat after taxes because they don't shuffle their portfolios. They aren't totally tax-proof: They may have dividend income to distribute and also need to buy and sell stocks when their benchmark index makes adjustments. But Vanguard 500 Index has been 95% tax-efficient over the past five years. Small-cap index funds often make greater capital-gains distributions because they must sell successful stocks as the names outgrow the index. For instance, Vanguard Small-Cap Index's after-tax five-year return is only 74% of the pretax return.

Capitalize on losses.   If index funds are still too taxing for your taste, you could select another breed of funds—tax-managed

After-Tax Winners

These funds, representing a variety of styles, are all solid performers that follow strategies designed to keep distributions to a minimum and shareholders' tax bills low.

FUND	THREE-YEAR RETURN[1]	THREE-YEAR TAX-EFFICIENCY
Eaton Vance Tax Man. Growth 1.1A	9.6%	100.0%
Fidelity Tax-Managed Stock	5.6[2]	99.6[2]
J.P. Morgan Tax-Aware U.S. Equity	8.3	97.4
Schwab 1000 Investor Shares	7.0	95.8
Third Avenue Value	10.3	83.5
T. Rowe Price Tax-Efficient Bal.	8.2	90.3
Vanguard Tax-Managed Capital App.	9.1	98.0
Vanguard Tax-Managed Small-cap	18.6[3]	98.7[3]

Notes: Data as of Feb. 28, 2001. [1]Annualized. [2]Since Nov. 2, 1998. [3]Since March 25, 1999. [4]5.75% sales charge.

funds—that purposely try to minimize, if not eliminate, taxable distributions. Tax-managed funds execute a careful balancing act, offsetting gains with losses whenever possible to minimize distributions to shareholders. Many also charge a redemption fee if you sell within a few years; that's to dissuade shareholders from active trading, which can force a manager to realize taxable gains. Tax-managed funds typically follow low-turnover, benchmarked strategies much like index funds. There are also a few active managers, including Martin Whitman of Third Avenue Value, who focus on achieving strong after-tax returns. We've listed eight outstanding tax-savvy funds in the table above.

If you like the idea of indexing but also want the benefits of a tax-managed fund, you can find both those qualities rolled into one in what you could call tax-managed index funds. The Schwab 1000 fund (800-435-4000), for example, tracks a Schwab index of the 1,000 largest U.S. companies. To avoid taxable distributions, manager Geri Hom employs proprietary software to harvest losses in certain stocks that can cancel realized gains in others.

Gus Sauter employs similar strategies at Vanguard's stable of tax-managed funds. Vanguard's Tax-Managed Growth & Income, for example, follows the S&P 500 index, much as the Vanguard 500 Index fund does, although the tax-managed version occasion-

ANNUAL EXPENSES	MIN. INITIAL INVEST.	TELEPHONE (800)	COMMENT
0.68%[4]	$1,000	225-6265	Fund is closing, but an identical offering, 1.2, is open.
0.97	10,000	343-3548	Predictable S&P 500-like performance
0.85	2,500	521-5411	Risk-conscious investing, tax-sensitive trading
0.46	2,500	435-4000	Tracks a custom large-cap index
1.10	1,000	443-1021	Occasional big distributions, long-term tax-efficiency
1.00	2,500	541-4975	Conservative combo of blue-chip stocks and munis
0.19	10,000	871-3879	Tracks the Russell 1000
0.20	10,000	871-3879	Tracks the S&P SmallCap 600

Sources: Morningstar, fund companies.

ally deviates from the index to take losses in some stocks. So far, tax-managed funds have pretty much lived up to their promise of limiting taxable distributions.

Look for funds with hidden tax breaks.   Under IRS rules, mutual funds must distribute capital gains to shareholders each year, but they don't distribute capital losses. Instead, the funds are allowed to use them to offset future gains for up to eight years. So a fund that recently realized $50 million in losses will not have to distribute its next $50 million in capital gains, giving shareholders a free ride. (In looking for these built-in tax breaks, it's important to understand that only funds that booked their losses by selling stock are entitled to the benefit; funds that held on to losing stocks will get no relief.)

How can you tell if a fund you're interested in has large tax losses? You'll have to do some digging. If you become interested in a fund that had a negative return, check its annual report. You can get one from the fund company, or at websites such as www.FreeEDGAR.com, which makes SEC filings available to the public. In the footnotes to the fund's financial statement, you will usually find an item describing the fund's tax loss carry-forwards (also called "capital loss" carry-forwards), if it has any.

Of course, you don't want to latch on to a fund simply because it has a potential tax break; tax strategy should never drive investment decisions.

TAX-FAVORED INVESTMENT VEHICLES

The problem with any mutual fund—even a tax-managed one—is that shareholders can't control the timing of gains distributions. Stock investors, on the other hand, can avoid all capital gains by simply choosing not to sell. But what if you have no interest in doing the work—crunching numbers, scouring annual reports, monitoring company news—involved in picking stocks? Consider the following investment vehicles that give you the convenience of funds plus some of the tax advantages of stock ownership.

Exchange-traded funds (ETFs) are essentially mutual funds that trade like stocks, but their taxable distributions are low because they do almost no trading. ETF shareholders don't get off tax-free, however. There's still dividend income to be distributed, and ETFs must follow the same diversification regulations that apply to mutual funds. That means an ETF may be forced to sell some shares of a particular stock when it grows to occupy too large a position in the portfolio. When it comes to the mainstream indexes, though, ETFs are proving tax-efficient so far. From their 1993 inception to the spring of 2001, SPDRs (the State Street ETF that tracks the S&P 500 index) made a capital-gains distribution only once.

Another alternative: Merrill Lynch's Holding Company Depositary Receipts (Holders), which may be more tax-efficient still. These portfolios of stocks are fixed—there's no buying and selling to track an index, and they aren't subject to diversification requirements. And when you own a Holder, you can, for a small fee, exchange it for the underlying stocks and sell them when you wish (you can offset winners with losers to lessen your tax bite).

Because of their structure, buy-and-hold philosophy and the fact that they don't track an index that changes over time, Holders will not sock you with hidden, mutual fund-style capital gains charges. You'll only owe tax on any profit you realize when you sell your shares.

FOLIOfn takes up where Holders leave off. This online service, at www.foliofn.com, offers preselected stock packages. For a flat fee of $295 a year, you can choose three folios and hold as long as you like. To keep the cost below 1.5% of assets (competitive with actively managed mutual funds), you'd need to invest at least $20,000—but you can, at no extra charge, customize your folios by buying and selling individual stocks, and the site's tools will help you minimize taxes when you sell.

BUILD YOUR OWN STOCK TAX SHELTER

A simple yet effective strategy can help you shelter money from the government when you invest in taxable accounts. All you do is buy stocks that have superior long-term prospects and pay little or no dividends—then hang on to them unless their prospects sour or you need the money.

Following this strategy accomplishes two things. First, you get tax-deferred compounding of gains. "You're earning a rate of return on money you otherwise would have sent to Uncle Sam," says Neil Wolfson, national partner in charge of investment consulting at KPMG LLP. Second, by holding a stock longer than a year before selling, any gain is taxed at the maximum long-term capital-gains rate of 20% rather than at ordinary income rates of up to 39.6% (not including state taxes). This combination of deferral and lower rates does not eliminate taxes, but it dramatically reduces the IRS' take. If you pick your stocks wisely, this strategy can beat the after-tax returns of most mutual funds and even index funds.

FOUR TAX-CUTTING STRATEGIES TO KEEP IN MIND

Selling stocks, on the other hand, can sometimes give you tax nightmares if you're not careful. Uncle Sam could abscond with up to 40% of your annual gains—unless you intervene. Luckily, it's not all that hard to shield your profits from tax. But there's no one-size-fits-all tax-avoidance strategy. Our advice: Don't put off investment tax-planning until the end of the year. Always keep taxes in mind. It may be much smarter to take a tax loss in May rather than in early December, when thousands of others are scrambling to unload the same stock as well.

Did you sell appreciated stock or mutual funds shares this year? Did you sell stocks or funds at a loss? Are you holding on to bonds that have dropped in price? Below are four typical investing scenarios, followed by the appropriate tax-saving strategy.

Scenario No. 1:
You recently sold stock, and your gains exceed your losses.

Say, for example, that you sold shares earlier this year for a $5,000 capital gain, but that you haven't sold any investments at a loss. Before year-end, you should identify securities in your portfolio on which you're $5,000 in the hole—and sell them. By pairing a $5,000 gain with a $5,000 loss, you shield the gain from tax, for a savings on your return of $500 to $1,980, depending on your top income tax rate and how long you owned the profitable stock before you sold it.

The problem with this strategy is that you may not want to sell your loser(s). If so, here's your out: Sell the loser and then buy new shares of the same stock after 31 days, counting the date of sale—but no sooner. Under the tax law's so-called *wash-sale rule*, you can't write off the loss if you purchase substantially identical securities within 30 days before or after the sale. Obviously, the stock could go up during the time you don't own it. That's the risk you take. If you're uncomfortable with that, you can reinvest as soon as you wish in a security that would not be considered substantially identical to the one you sold.

If you invest in funds, however, your situation is more flexible, and that could help many investors who own large-cap growth and tech funds that slumped badly in the 14 months between March 2000 and May 2001. You're allowed to sell a losing fund and immediately buy one that's remarkably similar in style—and still claim your tax loss. This is one area in which fund investors have a dramatic advantage over stock investors.

For example, you could sell one family's index offering and get identical exposure by buying the same index from a different company. The IRS has never challenged this tactic. You can also swap actively managed funds, as long as you understand that the portfolios won't be identical. The key is to find funds that play in the same part of the market. See the "Stop and Swap" table on page 176 for a list of fund substitution ideas. With mutual funds, when you've got a lemon, it's easy to make lemonade.

Scenario No. 2:
You sold stock this year, and your losses exceed your gains. You
can deduct your capital losses dollar for dollar against your capital

gains; if your losses exceed your gains, you can deduct up to $3,000 of the excess against your other income. Say, for example, that you haven't realized any capital gains this year and your losses come to $3,000 or less. You don't need to monkey with your portfolio at all. Simply write off the loss against your ordinary income when you file your return. The savings on a $3,000 write-off in 2001: $450 to $1,188, depending on your top tax rate.

If your capital losses total more than your capital gains plus $3,000, you have two choices. One option is to sell stock on which you have enough of a gain to absorb the excess loss. If you don't want to part with your appreciated stock permanently, sell it and then buy new shares of the same stock. Doing this works to your advantage in two ways: You'll generate a capital gain to absorb your loss, and you'll have a higher cost basis on the new shares than you had on the ones you sold. Assuming the stock continues to appreciate, you'll have a lower gain—and hence lower taxes—the next time you sell. What makes this strategy even more attractive is that you don't have to wait any length of time to buy those new shares, since the wash sale's wait period applies only to stock that you've sold at a loss.

Your second option for dealing with excess losses is to do nothing—for now. The tax law lets you carry forward unused losses to later years.

Scenario No. 3:
You're holding on to appreciated stock—and you have some big cash outlays coming up.

If you intend to give to charity this year, your best tax move may be to give the stock instead of cash. Or, if you were planning to sell stock soon to pay a big expense for a child, such as college tuition, you may be better off taxwise giving the stock to the child. Consider:

If you've owned the stock for more than a year and you give it to charity by year-end, you can claim its full fair market value as an itemized deduction and you avoid tax on the gain. Say you paid $1,000 years ago for stock now worth $5,000. If you sell the stock and give the proceeds to charity, you could deduct the $5,000 donation. But you would also owe as much as $800 in tax on the long-term gain. If, instead, you donate the stock, you get the $5,000 deduction and pay no tax.

Alternatively, you could give the stock to a child who is age 14 or older. Your child can then sell it and pay tax at his or her

Stop and Swap

See if the tax-savings steps below—and the various fund shifts we recommend—are right for you.

1. Assess. Is your $10,000 investment now worth, say, $8,000? There may well be a bright side if you consider the tax advantages.

2. Maximize losses. Identify your highest-cost shares. If you dollar-cost average, you may have bought shares at less than today's price.

3. Lock in tax savings. Sell the shares with the greatest losses—and stockpile the tax write-offs to offset future investment gains and income.

4. Maintain your exposure. Buy a similar investment the day you sell, so you don't miss any moves up. The goal is to cut taxes, not time the market.

Take losses here...		...and make a similar investment here, or vice versa.
■ Vanguard Total Stock Market Index (–14.2%)	⟷	Fidelity Spartan Total Market Index (–14.6%)
■ S&P Depositary Receipts (Spiders) (–14.9)	⟷	Vanguard 500 Index (–14.4)
▲ T. Rowe Price Blue Chip Growth (–14.9)	⟷	TIAA-CREF Growth & Income (–14.1)
▲ Fidelity Magellan[1] (–14.3)	⟷	Vanguard Primecap[3] (–13.9)
▶ American Century Ultra Inv. (–26.3)	⟷	American Century Growth Inv. (–27.2)
▶ Fidelity Blue Chip Growth (–19.1)	⟷	Vanguard Tax-Managed Capital Apprec. (–18.4)
▶ Vanguard U.S. Growth (–38.1)	⟷	Harbor Capital Appreciation (–26.8)
● Janus Mercury (–31.3)	⟷	White Oak Growth Stock (–31.1)
● Janus Olympus[1] (–34.3)	⟷	Janus Mercury (–31.3)
◆ AIM Constellation A[2] (–22.5)	⟷	Invesco Dynamics Inv. (–22.8)
◆ Putnam Vista A[2] (–29.0)	⟷	Janus Enterprise (–41.3)
✖ Pin Oak Aggressive Stock (–42.3)	⟷	Red Oak Technology Select (–46.3)
✖ T. Rowe Price Science & Technology (–43.0)	⟷	Dresdner RCM Global Technology N (–41.2)
✖ Qualcomm (or any fallen tech stock) (–40.3)	⟷	Nasdaq-100 Trust shares (QQQs) (–47.6)

■ Market index   ▲ Large-cap blend   ▶ Large-cap growth   ● Agg. large-cap   ◆ Midcap growth   ✖ Tech

800 numbers: AIM, 959-4246; American Century, 345-2021; Dresdner, 726-7240; Fidelity, 343-3548; Harbor, 422-1050; Invesco, 525-8085; Janus, 525-8983; Putnam, 225-1581; TIAA, 223-1200; T. Rowe Price, 541-4975; Vanguard, 871-3879; Oak, 888-462-5386. **Notes:** Losses are for 12 months ended April 24, 2001. [1]Closed. [2]Has front- or back-end load. [3]$25,000 minimum. **Sources:** Morningstar, Baseline.

rate, generally 10% on a long-term gain vs. a 20% hit for you. A few caveats: The tax savings don't add up as nicely if the child is 13 or younger, because his or her unearned income above $1,400 will be taxed at your rate. Moreover, think twice before you give stock to a college student who qualifies for financial aid, since your gift could reduce the amount of aid.

That said, be aware that giving stock to family members is also a simple way to lighten the potential tax on your estate, since you can give away assets worth up to $10,000 per person per year free of gift tax, $20,000 per person each year if you and your spouse make the gift together. (When the recipient sells the stock, he or she will owe tax based on the price of the stock when you bought it.) Note: To ensure that such a gift is "made" this year, you must complete all of the paperwork transferring your securities and the recipient must assume full ownership of the assets before year-end.

Scenario No. 4:
Your bonds have slumped.
Now could be a good time to sell them and reinvest in a different bond. Done right, such a swap can save taxes and preserve your investment position, says Hugh R. Lamle, president of Chase & M.D. Sass Partners, an investment management firm in New York City, who prepared the following example:

Assume you paid $106,500 in January 1999 for Treasury notes with a par value of $100,000, a coupon rate of 5.5% and a maturity date of Feb. 15, 2008. As interest rates rose during 1999, those Treasuries would have declined in value to $96,125. If you had sold at the end of 1999, you would have had a short-term capital loss of $10,375. If you used that loss to offset gains on your 1999 return, you would have saved from $1,038 to $4,109, depending on your top income tax rate and whether the gains you're offsetting are long term or short term.

Now assume that you turned around and paid $96,687 for Treasury notes with $100,000 face value, a coupon of 5.625% and a maturity date of May 15, 2008. True, the new notes cost $563 more than the price you got for the old ones, but your tax savings from claiming the $10,375 loss outweigh that extra cost. More important, your income over the life of the notes increases by $1,077. Indeed, when you factor in the tax savings and your extra income, the swap leaves you ahead by $1,552 to $4,623.

A warning: You can't claim the tax loss if you buy a new bond that is substantially the same as the old one during a 30-

Think Ahead—and Save

Good accounting can be rewarding to an investor who wants to minimize his or her tax bill. Before selling shares of a mutual fund or stock, always determine what your cost basis is, especially if you've sold shares you bought over time. [Cost basis is usually the price of your shares plus the commission you paid to buy them.] And if you've bought mutual funds and reinvested dividends, that affects the cost basis of your mutual fund shares.

The tax law contains four different accounting methods for computing your capital gain (or capital loss) when you sell mutual fund shares. Surprisingly, these methods—known as *specific identification, single-category averaging, double-category averaging* and *first-in, first-out* (FIFO)—can yield vastly different results. So before you redeem shares in a fund, you (or your tax pro) should project your tax using each of the methods, and then structure the sale to use the one that is best for your taxes.

In many cases, specific identification gives you the best tax result. With specific ID, you specify in writing the particular shares you want to redeem at the time you sell. By selling your costliest shares, for example, you generate the smallest possible taxable gain, or the largest possible tax-deductible loss. To identify the shares you're selling, note their purchase date and the price you paid. Also ask the fund for a confirmation that you traded shares bought on those dates and keep a copy of your letter and the confirmation.

If you don't use specific ID, you can wait until the time you file your return to choose one of the other three methods to calculate your tax. It's possible that one of those methods will yield a better tax result than specific ID. But you can't know that unless you examine the tax consequences of the sale before you sell.

Note: Specific ID and FIFO are off limits if you sold shares from your fund in the past and used averaging back then to figure the tax. In that case, you must continue to use averaging for every subsequent sale.

You are allowed to use the specific identification strategy for stocks as well. But call your brokerage firm first to find out exactly how it wishes to be notified.

day period before or after the sale. If you don't want to wait, you can buy a new bond that differs from the old one in at least one—and preferably two—of the following ways: the issuer, credit rating, maturity and yield.

Chapter 11
ONLINE RESOURCES: THE PATH TO PROFITS

T here's no doubt about it. The Internet continues to be an empowering revolutionary force for individual investors. Today, you have virtual access to unfathomable amounts of corporate data and investment research that were once solely the province of professionals. Plus, with just a few clicks you can access sophisticated analytical tools—from stock screeners to portfolio trackers—and execute trades using online brokers for as little as $8.00.

This could be a good thing. Then again, for some investors, it is anything but. The Internet has turned some people into frenetic traders, and studies show that such gunslingers underperform investors who adopt more of a buy-and-hold approach. In many ways, the Web can make investors overconfident—and too much confidence has led some to financial recklessness. Another downside: The Net can be a time bandit—we constantly hear stories about investors who spend so many hours researching their investments that they hardly recognize their families.

That is definitely not a good thing.

Nonetheless, we are big fans of the Internet and believe it is one of the great allies of the self-directed investor. Supersites like

MSN MoneyCentral, Yahoo! Finance and Quicken.com provide investors with almost all the tools anyone could need. One of our favorite websites, www.money.com, has many terrific features as well, while dozens of specialized websites provide more esoteric information.

In this chapter, we want to guide you to some of the Web's better tools, with insights and advice on how to make your Net time more productive and effective. Specifically, we review the best sites on the Web, rank the best online brokers and look at tools to analyze your investments and track your portfolio.

THE TOP FINANCIAL WEBSITES

The Web is aptly named—it's so easy to get tangled up. And the Web moves fast, growing by nearly 2 million pages every day. That's why MONEY's writers, reporters and editors spent months clicking and comparing our way through nearly 1,500 sites (disqualifying those that charge a regular subscription fee) to find the most useful investing and money-management sites around. We found some terrific sites—and eliminated hundreds that will waste your time.

The Supersites

Everyone needs a page to call home. And MSN MoneyCentral, Quicken.com and Yahoo! Finance remain the best places to make your default stop whenever you first hit the Web. These information supermarkets are more than just an investor's paradise of one-click access to quotes, news and data. They're also stocked with advice and resources on virtually every personal-finance topic there is, from mortgages and credit cards to insurance, taxes and home buying.

But no one site can be all things to all people. Each of the three portals sports a distinct personality, and each one's unique strengths may appeal to some users more than others.

• **MSN MoneyCentral** (www.moneycentral.com)
MoneyCentral is the single best all-around financial destination on the Net. Its step-by-step planning guides and high-powered portfolio tracking and screening tools continue to be the site's hallmarks, easily outpacing those of its nearest competitors. But MoneyCentral has unveiled a number of significant improve-

ments, with an emphasis on personalization. At My MoneyCentral, you can now aggregate information from multiple credit-card, brokerage and bank accounts, allowing you to check all of your balances on one Web page. The site will also e-mail you reminders about upcoming bills and create a customized clip file of news stories from sources like the *Wall Street Journal* and MSNBC. Both real-time and extended-hours quotes on U.S. stocks are available for free, as are full financial data on companies located in France, Germany, Japan and the U.K.

MSN MoneyCentral is also a good data source, especially for beginners. Its Research Wizard explains the fundamentals of any stock you select so you can learn the language of Wall Street. With more than 100 criteria, ranging from the obvious (price) to the obscure (receivables turnover), the site's Stock Finder (www.moneycentral.com/investor) is tough to beat for serious stock screening. For the more advanced investor, MoneyCentral also alerts you to key events, including earnings announcements and analyst upgrades or downgrades, for companies you select. The high-powered portfolio tracker on the site automatically updates prices every five minutes, categorizes your stocks by six criteria, including risk and market capitalization, and provides advice on how to better diversify your holdings. (For details and advice on using MoneyCentral's tracker, see "Tune-Up Tools for Your Portfolio" on page 192.)

Virtually any finance site can draw you a chart, but the best tools, like the ones found on MoneyCentral, let you customize the graphic with technical indicators such as intraday pricing, moving averages and trading volume, compare stocks with one another or with indexes and manipulate a wide range of dates.

There is one dent in MoneyCentral's armor (although, admittedly, it affects only 4% of all computer users). Most of its interactive tools do not work on Macintosh computers.

- **Quicken.com** (www.quicken.com)

Quicken.com excels at offering basic, solid information on a broad range of topics. It is also exceptionally user-friendly. QuickAnswers—flash overviews of popular subjects—are available on each topic to save you the hassle of digging through the layers of info.

Quicken's editorial content isn't your typical regurgitation of yesterday's news. The IdeaCenter in the Investing section, for example, digests and analyzes recent stock picks from journalists and professional money managers. And while Quicken's gadgets may not pack the punch of MoneyCentral's, they're well worth a look. Many of the tools use real-life data. The College Planner, for instance, incorporates actual college tuition figures to create a savings guide based on hard numbers rather than estimates. Quicken has caught the personalization bug as well, and it's easy to create your own personal-finance center at MyFinances.

Quicken.com also has an outstanding (and Mac-compatible) tracker that uses icons to note if one of your stocks made headlines, was upgraded by a Wall Street pro or hit a 52-week high or low. The site's Stock Screener (www.quicken.com/investments) uses only 33 criteria, making it a good choice for quick, simple searches.

- **Yahoo! Finance** (finance.yahoo.com)

Need information fast? Yahoo! Finance is the best bet. It lacks the bells and whistles of both MoneyCentral and Quicken, but that's often a blessing for the self-directed surfer. Its clean, spare design is free of intrusive advertising, making it easy to navigate the 10 primary sections, which range from Today's Markets and Mutual Funds to Loans and Insurance.

For a global perspective, visit Yahoo's International Finance Center. At this new addition, you can get economic profiles, news and exchange rates for countries all around the world. The upgraded Tax Center has a complete library of links to federal and state tax forms. Yahoo is quickly establishing a notable presence in the banking world as well, leading the pack in online account-aggregation and bill payment services.

Investing Sites

Directories: If you're looking for a Web directory a tad more expansive than our list, head to **Superstar Investor** (www.superstarinvestor.com), an obsessively detailed guide to virtually every significant investing site on the Web. This formidable collection of over 20,000 well-organized links is enough to satisfy any investor's needs.

Financial News: Many destinations offer a daily dose of market chatter and business stories, but none do so as expertly as **CBS MarketWatch** (www.cbsmarketwatch.com) and **CNNfn** (www.cnnfn.com). CNNfn (owned by MONEY's parent company, AOL Time Warner) spices up the standard news fare with relevant audio and video clips.

A Site We Call Home

Conflict of interest be damned. We can't help mentioning just one more financial website. At the site that bears our name, you'll find some of your favorite writers from the pages of MONEY, educational resources for newcomers, financial planning aids and a guide to the best of the Net.

As a MONEY reader, you may already be familiar with our Web sibling, www.money.com. If not, here's what you'll find. Along with the stock and fund quotes, business news headlines (from CNNfn) and the portfolio tools you'd expect, the site offers a regular lineup of columnists drawn from the magazine's ranks. Three times a week, stock expert Michael Sivy shares his insights on blue chips in Sivy on Stocks. In his twice-weekly Tech Investor column, David Futrelle examines the businesses of the New Economy. Bethany McLean lends her irreverent outlook to the day's financial news in MarketRap. And personal-finance expert Jean Chatzky answers readers' questions every day. You can sign up for free e-mail delivery of all these columns.

The Money 101 section teaches newcomers the basics of everything from finding a home to managing your debt. Our calculators can help you buy a car, home or insurance policy.

Stock Quotes and Data: Market Guide (www.marketguide.com) is the best place to look up stock prices and other fundamental data. That shouldn't be surprising once you consider that Market Guide feeds financial data to more than 135 major websites, including Yahoo! Finance and Charles Schwab. Search by ticker or company name for free real-time quotes or a handy Snapshot that includes tons of information, ranging from P/E ratios and revenue figures to insider sales and institutional ownership.

Company Research: You can now get a complete background check on a company via the Web. Among the handful of websites specializing in retrieving quarterly and annual reports from the Securities and Exchange Commission's EDGAR database, **10K Wizard** (www.10kwizard.com) is the easiest to use, allowing you to search for documents by company name, ticker symbol or keyword. Register for free at the site, and it will send you an e-mail any time one of the companies you specify files a report.

BestCalls.com (www.bestcalls.com) maintains a calendar of upcoming conference calls, searchable by name or symbol. Investors can then sit in on the meetings via telephone or streaming audio links at the site. Recent calls are archived for up to 90 days.

You can investigate up to 10 companies at a time with **Company Sleuth** (www.company.sleuth.com), which snoops the Web and e-mails you daily updates on recent press releases, patents, trademarks, federal litigation, domain name registrations and other juicy tidbits.

Stock Analysis: To get the full picture of a company, you'll also want to exploit third-party resources for a different take on the numbers and news. **Multex Investor** (www.multexinvestor.com) is the leading source for those much hyped buy-sell-hold stock reports put out by brokerage houses and research groups. Multex Investor warehouses over 300,000 reports from hundreds of firms, including blue-chip names like J.P. Morgan and Bear Stearns. The catch: Most files cost between $4 and $150 to download. Even so, the site is worth a look. Each week, Multex Investor posts a handful of free reports and hosts Q&A sessions with prominent analysts.

Stock Screeners: Mac users, try **Wall Street City's ProSearch** (www.wallstreetcity.com) for advanced screens. Wall Street City flaunts an impressive set of more than 70 variables. Or run one of the 39 preset screens, including one that hunts for undervalued growth stocks and another that tracks possible turnaround plays.

Charts: **BigCharts.com** (www.bigcharts.com) boasts a range of offerings that's almost as varied as MoneyCentral's—and plays nice with Macs. BigCharts lets you alter a graph's look with nine different designs from mountain and bar chart to candlestick and logarithmic.

Bulletin Boards: **The Motley Fool** (www.fool.com) has cultivated a sophisticated group of followers, many of whom espouse a long-term buy-and-hold philosophy. Noise is kept to a minimum by a self-policing membership and vigilant employees who stroll the most active boards looking for yahoos.

It's harder to dig through the trash at **Raging Bull** (www.ragingbull.com), but the sophisticated level of the discussion makes the effort worthwhile. "Membermarks," a Siskel and Ebert-style peer review, honors the most respected posters.

Silicon Investor (www.siliconinvestor.com) has among the most highly trafficked tech boards, and for good reason—the site tends to foster relatively intellectual stock discussions. Though posting messages will cost you $60 for six months, reading is free.

Direct Investing: Want an even cheaper way to invest directly in your favorite company? **Netstock Direct** (www.netstockdirect.com) is the premier place to participate in company-sponsored dividend-reinvestment plans and direct investment programs. The site provides access to over 1,600 plans, which sometimes require no more than $25 to start. Transaction costs are generally lower than with a broker.

Mutual Funds: Fund coverage on the Web has exploded in the past year; there are now hundreds of sites covering the $5 trillion industry. But **Morningstar.com** (www.morningstar.com) is still the king. A quick search unearths a report on any of the 5,548 funds the site covers. Dig through the front-page clutter for fund manager chats, daily industry news and tools like Fund Selector and Portfolio X-Rays to help analyze your options.

FundAlarm (www.fundalarm.com) posts an informative listing of funds that have underperformed their benchmarks over the past one, three and five years. But FundAlarm's biggest draw is founder Roy Weitz's quirky, charming monthly column, a gossipy, insightful look into mutual fund industry mayhem whose audience includes scores of fund company executives and insiders.

International: Worldlyinvestor.com (www.worldlyinvestor.com) is the international investor's forum. Daily columns and e-mail newsletters dissect trends in stocks, bonds and mutual funds around the globe. The ADR Screener filters foreign stocks traded on U.S. exchanges by sector, country or return. **FT MarketWatch** (www.ftmarketwatch.com) is the place for up-to-the-minute news on offshore companies and foreign markets. A joint venture of the Financial Times and MarketWatch.com, the site combines insightful in-house commentary with a roundup of world news.

IPOs: Investors need to be pickier about snapping up IPO shares these days, so it pays to do your homework. Start at **IPO Central** (www.ipocentral.com) for a basic education on IPOs. Then cruise its other sections for company profiles, the latest news and statistics on hot offerings, top underwriters and lagging performers. To help get a feel for which new issues may be long-term winners, check out **Quote.com** (www.quote.com). It ranks recent IPOs' chances for success based on a variety of factors such as first-day gain, market cap and insider trading. It's also crucial to know when insiders can first sell their shares, as that may signal a possible sell-off or indicate when additional shares might become available. **UnlockDates.com** (www.unlockdates.com) keeps a database of IPO lockup periods and will alert you when the date approaches for any stock you choose.

Technology Investing: CNET Investor (investor.cnet.com) is a must for tech hounds. The site stockpiles articles from a variety of sources, including Bloomberg, as well as its own crack coverage. Using one of CNET's 18 proprietary indexes, you can monitor the performance of, say, the wireless industry. The editors at **Next Wave Stocks** (www.nextwavestocks.com) believe that some of the best opportunities in tech are at companies with less than $10 billion in market cap. The Next Wave 100, a listing based on that philosophy, identifies emerging small and midcap players. In addition to the usual news you'll find at any tech site, Next Wave posts original Q&As with gurus like Roger McNamee of Integral Capital Partners and Softbank Venture Capital director Bill Burnham.

THE BEST ONLINE BROKERS

Once you've done your homework online and researched investments that fit within your investment goals, it's time to start trading. Although a major shake-out among the smaller brokerages plying their trade online is a virtual certainty, online investing is no fad—it remains the cheapest, most convenient, smartest way for self-directed investors to put their money to work. Small wonder that about a third of retail trades now go through the Internet.

To determine which online brokers will serve you best, we put 24 sites through a battery of tests. We tallied and weighted the scores in the five categories to determine the best brokers for each of our four investor types. For example, we underweighted costs for mainstream investors (whom we defined as having at least $50,000 to invest and making fewer than 12 trades a year). While the difference between a $9.99 limit order at Datek Online and a $30 one at Fidelity isn't something to ignore, prices are

FAQs about Online Brokers

Q. Is my money safe?

A. While online brokers have hit tough times, they probably won't be the next arrivals at the dotcom graveyard. According to the Securities Investor Protection Corporation, or SIPC (an industry-funded insurance firm that virtually every brokerage is a member of), there has not been any notable rise in online brokerage closings. But some smaller outfits could be takeover candidates in the months ahead.

If your broker is bought, the only change you may see is the logo on your statements—but ruder shocks are possible. When Morgan Stanley Dean Witter took full control of Discover Brokerage, it doubled its basic commission to $30 from $15. If you don't like the changes, you can always move your account. But transfers can tie up your money for weeks or even months, so if you're the customer of a tiny online brokerage, you may want to move a portion of your portfolio to a second, more established brokerage now, just so you'll always have access to some of your funds. If your broker does go under, however, SIPC may be able to help you retrieve your shares. If (note the "if") SIPC can get another broker-dealer to take over your brokerage's accounts, you can expect to receive your property in under three months. As the customer of a brokerage that's being liquidated, you should receive a warning in the mail or see notices in the newspaper with the deadline to file a claim. For more information, visit SIPC's site (www.sipc.org).

Q. How do I move to a new online brokerage? And why do transfers take so long?

A. Ask 10 brokerages how long account transfers take, and you'll get 10 different answers. E-Trade's site says transfers take three to six weeks. Fidelity's says three to five weeks. And at NDB it's seven to 10 business days. That's strange, since the regulatory arm of the National Association of Securities Dealers says the whole process should really take only about six days.

While no one agrees on how long a transfer takes, the process is generally the same everywhere: You download or request a form from your future brokerage, fill it out, send it in—and wait. Any inconsistency in your paperwork will cause a delay. If the firm you've picked chooses not to accept the account, perhaps because it's a large margin account, expect a considerable lag. Delays can also occur if you try to transfer securities from different types of accounts, such as from a taxable account into an IRA.

---

nearly negligible for investors who make only a few trades a year. On the other hand, cost factored heavily in the scoring when we ranked the best brokers for frequent traders, who can quickly rack up massive commission bills.

Scorecard

The table below details how the top 20 brokers of the 24 we surveyed stack up. The ranking reflects category weightings for mainstream investors, with customer service and products and tools counting more than the other three categories. Winners in each category are highlighted in red.

OVERALL RANKING	COMPANY WEBSITE (WWW.)	CUSTOMER SERVICE	PRODUCTS AND TOOLS	EASE OF USE	SYSTEM RESPONSIVENESS	COST	OVERALL SCORE
1	**Fidelity** fidelity.com	★★★★★	★★★★★	★★★★★	★★★★	★	★★★★★
2	**Merrill Lynch Direct** mldirect.com	★★★★	★★★★★	★★★★★	★★★	★	★★★★★
3	**Charles Schwab** schwab.com	★★★★★	★★★★½	★★★★	★★★★★	★	★★★★½
4	**National Discount Brokers** ndb.com	★★★½	★★★	★★★★½	★★★★	★★★	★★★★
5	**CSFBdirect** csfbdirect.com	★★★★	★★½	★★★★	★★★★½	★★★	★★★★
6	**Ameritrade** ameritrade.com	★★★½	★★★★	★★★½	★★★★½	★★★★	★★★★
7	**TD Waterhouse** tdwaterhouse.com	★★★★★	★★★★	★★½	★★★★	★★★★	★★★★
8	**E-Trade** etrade.com	★★★★½	★★★★	★★½	★★★★	★★	★★★½
9	**Datek Online** datek.com	★★★★	★	★★★★	★★★½	★★★★★	★★★½
10	**Muriel Siebert** siebertnet.com	★★★	★★★★½	★★★	★★	★★★★	★★★½
11	**USAA** usaa.com	★★★½	★★★	★★★	★★★½	★½	★★★
12	**Quick & Reilly** quickandreilly.com	★★★½	★★★	★★★½	½	★★½	★★★
13	**Scottrade** scottrade.com	★★	★★½	★★	★★★½	★★★★★	★★½
14	**The Financial Cafe.Com** financialcafe.com	★★	★★	★★★½	★	★★★★★	★★½
15	**JB Oxford** jboxford.com	★★★	★★	★★	★★★½	★★★	★★½
16	**American Express** americanexpress.com/trade	★★★	★★	★★	★★★	★★	★★
17	**Accutrade** accutrade.com	★★	★★½	★★★½	★★★	★	★★
18	**Morgan Stanley Online** msdwonline.com	★	★★★★½	½	★★★★★	★	★★
19	**Web Street** webstreet.com	★★½	★★	★	★	★★★★	★½
20	**A.B. Watley** abwatley.com	★★	★	★	★★	★★★★★	★½

Notes: [1]Based on 100 shares at $50 a share. [2]Based on a $25,000 margin account on April 17, 2001. [3]No-load funds only. [4]Area code 877. [5]Area code 888. N.A.: Not applicable.

INITIAL DEPOSIT	LIMIT ORDER	BROKER-ASSISTED TRADE[1]	MARGIN RATES[2]	NO-FEE FUNDS[3]/ TOTAL FUNDS	MUTUAL FUND FEES[1]	NUMBER OF BRANCHES	TELEPHONE (800)
$2,500	$30.00	$59.00	8.05%	1,151/4,521	$75.00	78	544-7272
2,000	29.95	50.00	10.25	500/2,400	N.A.	600	653-4732[4]
5,000	29.95	55.00	8.25	2,661/3,740	39.00	400	225-8570
0	19.75	27.95	8.25	927/10,892	20.00	2	888-3999
0	20.00	20.00	9.50	1,060/9,933	35.00	2	355-4273[4]
2,000	13.00	23.00	8.75	0/9,828	18.00	0	454-9272
1,000	15.00	48.00	8.00	1,545/11,030	24.00	170	934-4448
1,000	19.95	54.95	9.75	1,250/5,200	24.95	2	387-2331
500	9.99	25.00	8.25	196/3,684	9.99	0	823-2835
0	14.95	37.50	8.75	1,293/9,329	35.00	9	872-0711
0	24.00	37.07	8.25	578/6,288	75.00	0	365-8722
0	19.95	42.50	8.00	600/3,000	35.00	118	837-7220
500	12.00	17.00	7.25	1,400/7,400	N.A.	140	619-7283
0	11.95	25.70	9.50	1,500/10,000	13.75	0	600-6410[4]
2,000	19.50	29.50	8.75	337/6,282	25.00	4	526-9367
0	19.95	75.00	8.73	926/3,426	39.95	227	297-7378
5,000	29.95	30.00	8.25	624/9,828	27.00	0	494-8939
2,000	29.95	39.95	8.00	835/5,629	25.00	530	688-6896
0	14.95	24.95	7.25	1,300/6,000	N.A.	6	932-8723
3,000	9.95	17.95	8.50	2,500/5,000	40.00	0	229-2853[5]

For Mainstream Investors

First place: **Fidelity**   Second place: **Merrill Lynch Direct**   Third place: **Charles Schwab**

The best just keep getting better. Fidelity, which clinched the top spot for the second year in a row, rolled out a ton of new features, such as its account-aggregation area that allows investors to view most of their banking, brokerage, credit-card and retirement accounts (including those not held with Fidelity) on a single page. Thanks in part to a recent facelift, Fidelity remains one of the easiest sites to navigate. The ability to preview a section's content by clicking on menus at the top of the page made it a breeze to find exactly what we were looking for without having to dig deeper into the site or toggle between pages. Fidelity also got points for being one of the few sites to provide cost-basis information online and for allowing investors to download gains and losses directly into most tax-prep software programs. Fidelity's reps answered our calls quickly and proficiently. At $30 for a limit order, Fidelity is among the costliest, but with so many features and an ever-improving product, it's well worth the extra money.

In less than two years, Merrill Lynch Direct has become a formidable presence in the online brokerage world. With a full range of services like cash management accounts, options and mutual funds, plus those highly touted buy-sell-hold reports, ML Direct is hard to beat at $29.95 a trade. Its online bond center is the best around. Customers can get face time with a rep by visiting one of ML's 600 branches, a topnotch perk whether you have $2,000 or $20 million. For quick help, we loved the phone reps and speedy internal e-mail system.

At Charles Schwab, less than stellar customer service—with hold times of up to 30 minutes—prevented it from snagging top ratings in the past. Problem solved. Schwab's reps picked up the phone in seconds and always gave us helpful answers. Schwab shines with an assortment of educational resources on every personal-finance topic imaginable, from estates and trusts to retirement and college planning. Biggest drawback: The site's navigation lags behind the Web's best.

For Wealthy Investors

First place: **ML Direct**   Second place: **Fidelity**   Third place: **Schwab**

When we searched for the best brokers for clients with a minimum of $100,000 to invest, we demanded superlative institutional research and sophisticated tools, such as mutual fund screeners and asset allocators. We required that the sites have the widest range of products and services, from access to IPOs, options and bonds to account aggregators. ML Direct grabbed top honors in this category for the second year running. Quite simply, no other e-broker gives away as much proprietary research as Merrill, and the site makes it a snap to zero in on the firm's latest opinion changes or daily market commentary.

Clients with well above $100,000 may want to consider a related Merrill product, the Unlimited Advantage account. It comes with more personal attention than ML Direct. For a minimum annual fee of $1,500, UA clients get unlimited free trades, a personal broker and a financial assessment report that helps plan for taxes, college and insurance needs. (Reports cost $250 for ML Direct clients.)

Fidelity placed second, thanks to its solid research, and Schwab got third by giving clients with at least $100,000 special investing services and institutional research.

For Frequent Traders

First place: Datek Online   Second place: Fidelity   Third place: Schwab

Datek Online knows the active trader better than anyone else. For three years running, this boutique has snared the top spot by offering a simple, low-cost product that consistently delivers on its promises. Charging just $9.99 for either a market or a limit order, Datek is among the cheapest brokers in the business. While most sites update your positions only once every couple of hours, Datek does so in real time. It also offers free streaming quotes during market hours and after-hours trading. And Datek has finally introduced options.

With powerful stock screeners and in-depth market coverage, Fidelity and Schwab boast attractive complete packages for active traders. Fidelity cuts its limit order tariff to $14.95 if customers make 72 trades in a 12-month period. Schwab slashes its $29.95 commission to $19.95 for those who make more than 30 trades per quarter.

For Beginners

First place: Fidelity   Second place: ML Direct   Third place: National Discount Brokers

Roughly 50,000 households open accounts with e-brokers each month, according to J.D. Power & Associates. With those newcomers in mind, we screened for top all-around brokers that require no more than $2,500 to open an account. Then we looked for sites that are especially easy to navigate and customer service centers with extra-helpful brokers. Fidelity finished first thanks to its reassuring hand-holding and large branch network. Fidelity's customer service folks frequently told us things we didn't realize we'd need to know. It's also one of the few sites that puts Search and Help buttons on the top of every screen.

ML Direct took second, due in great part to its recent neophyte-friendly move of slashing its opening minimum balance from $20,000 to a more manageable $2,000. NDB claimed third place. From an e-mail that confirmed our account was open to the real-time online customer service and a dialog box that warned us once when we overbid a stock, NDB always seemed to be watching over us, making sure that we never made a mistake.

TUNE-UP TOOLS FOR YOUR PORTFOLIO

Anybody can use the Net to make cheap trades, but smart investors explore the Web's wondrous selection of sites and tools (many of which were described earlier in the chapter) that analyze and track your investment portfolio. Our step-by-step plan will help you monitor your holdings, track investments you're eyeing, analyze your assets and consider ways you might want to tinker with your allocations.

Step 1: Set up your portfolio tracker. Your first assignment is to enter all of your stocks and mutual funds in a portfolio tracker—sorry, but finding a reliable bond tracker has been tough. The best ones are on sites that not only update your portfolio throughout the day, they'll also help you track stocks on your watch list. Some will alert you by e-mail when there are big moves or major news on your investments. The most worthwhile portfolio trackers can follow a stable of stocks from the date and price at which they were purchased, adjust for splits and dividends and point out holes in your portfolio.

We recommend MSN MoneyCentral (moneycentral.msn.com), which lets you view your portfolio in terms of prices, valuations and fundamentals. The tracker also lets you customize your view so you can include 52-week highs and lows, news or other details (for more information, see the complete profile earlier in the chapter). If you want something even savvier (though more difficult to master), try **SellSignal** (www.sellsignal.com), a tax-smart tracker that lets you know when to consider shedding a stock for maximum tax advantage.

Step 2: Look at the big picture. Once you get a handle on your holdings, it's time to determine how diversified you really are and how your investments interact to form a sound portfolio. Enter your stocks and funds into the Portfolio X-Rays tool at **Morningstar** (portfolio.morningstar.com) for a snapshot overview of your assets. Say you own a big slug of Intel and, unbeknownst to you, so does one of your funds. X-Rays will tip you off to the fact that you may not be as diversified as you think. X-Rays assesses up to 50 stocks and mutual funds based on eight criteria such as asset allocation, sector, fees and expenses, and geographical diversity. (The site doesn't provide individualized advice unless you cough up $9.95 a month.) An added bonus: Morningstar lets you import your portfolio from the tracker at MSN MoneyCentral, as well as from AOL, Yahoo, Quicken.com and the CD-ROM versions of Quicken and Microsoft Money; Morningstar also allows you to export your data directly onto your PC's hard drive.

Step 3: Assess risk. Now check out just how volatile your holdings are and decide whether you can stomach their potential gyrations. Of all the gizmos purporting to analyze risk, we prefer **Portfolio Science** (www.portfolioscience.com) for its simplicity and flexibility. Just enter the ticker symbol of a stock or a portfolio of holdings and the website expresses risk as the dollar amount or percentage by which that security or portfolio could fluctuate daily, weekly, monthly or annually. A share of Ford, for example, may typically go up or down $1 on a given day or $9.20 over the course of a year, according to the site. **Riskgrades** (www.riskgrades.com) is a similar but more complicated tool; it factors in variables such as market and sector conditions, plus one-time events like earnings surprises. It then assigns individual stocks or entire portfolios a risk score, ranging from zero for cash to beyond 1,000 for the most wildly speculative plays.

Step 4: Check on valuations. Finally, it's time to see if any of your holdings are ripe for thinning based on how they are priced relative to their historical levels. The security evaluation tool at **Quicken** (www.quicken.com/investments/seceval) is an excellent starting point. In February 2001, the tool suggested that Sun Microsystems was overvalued at $23 a share by about $10 and that the company "must grow earnings 19.5% annually for 10 years to justify its current price." Within two months, the stock had fallen slightly more than $10, to $12.85.

For a different view—and often a different opinion on whether a stock is a buy—visit Yale University finance professor Zhiwu Chen's **Valuengine** (www.valuengine.com). Using the professor's mathematical models, this site comes up with what it calls fair market values for individual stocks. In contrast to Quicken.com, Valuengine recently said that Sun was undervalued, 53% below the site's fair market quote of $53. Valuengine also lets you import your portfolio from other websites such as MoneyCentral and Quicken.com. Full access costs $19.95 a month, but a 14-day trial is available for free.

Chapter 12

STOCK OPTIONS: "THE NEXT BEST THING TO FREE MONEY"

Welcome to the world of stock options, at once the most lucrative and highly desired of employee perks (what *Fortune* magazine called "the next best thing to free money") and also arguably the most difficult asset for individuals to manage wisely. Previously a perk solely for the rich and powerful, options have gone mainstream and now are a crucial part of compensation for millions of employees in the U.S.

That's undoubtedly good news. Unfortunately, many employees who receive options don't really understand how to get the most out of them. "Managing stock options is the most complex financial task employees face," says Michael Beriss at American Express Financial Advisors in Bethesda, Md. And many companies that grant options don't give their employees all the information and advice that they need.

That's probably because the complications are many, and hard-and-fast answers aren't easy. When do you exercise options, and when do you wait? How do you value those you haven't exercised, especially when they haven't cost you a dime to acquire? How should you think about potential tax implications? How should they affect your portfolio allocation? The questions seem endless.

The truth is, handling employee stock options is as much art as it is science. There are few immutable rules. Still, it's essential to have a framework in which to make your decisions. We will outline a strategy for managing, exercising and thinking about stock options, offering both specific suggestions and general rules of thumb. (We focus here on nonqualified stock options, the most common type. Incentive stock options, or ISOs, are given primarily to top executives. For definitions of key terms, see our glossary on page 199.) While we can't promise that our approach will make you a multimillionaire—or that you'll never regret a decision—it should provide the tools to help you develop a plan that works for you.

THINK CASH BONUS

Before we start talking strategy, let's be clear about what a stock option really is. An employee stock option is the right given to you by your employer to buy (*exercise*) a certain number of shares of company stock at a pre-set price (the *grant*, *strike* or *exercise price*) over a certain period of time (*the exercise period*).

Now for a few observations—and three critical axioms. First the observations. In recent years, companies have been passing out stock options like candy: Some 10 million people now have them, according to the National Center for Employee Ownership, a tenfold increase since 1992. Yet a recent study by OppenheimerFunds found that 37% of option holders claimed to know more about Einstein's theory of relativity than about the tax implications of options, and 11% admitted that they let in-the-money options expire worthless. "We were shocked," says Marci Rossell, OppenheimerFunds' corporate economist.

Many people think about options as if they were shares of stock. We look at them a little differently. While the value of options fluctuates with the price of stocks, in other ways they are more akin to cash bonuses—in particular because you don't have to put up any cash to generate income. This is what gives options their essential power and appeal, which can be summed up in a single word: leverage.

Usually when you make an investment, you are making a choice about how to deploy your capital: Do you buy a house, a car, a stock, a certificate of deposit? With each choice, you are forgoing other choices. But with employee stock options, the situation is dramatically different. You don't have to tie up any resources, yet your potential gains are limitless—and your potential loss is zero.

That's why stock options are much like a bonus that varies in value depending on the future prospects of your employer. Unlike a regular bonus, however, you don't have to pay taxes when you're granted the option, which gives you the added benefit of tax deferral. The key to managing stock options, then, is taking maximum advantage of these two features—the bonus and the leverage—without getting distracted by other issues. And that leads us to our three primary axioms.

- **Forget taxes.** Don't waste your time worrying about taxes. Remember, your options are like income. You wouldn't turn down a raise just because you'd have to pay taxes; neither should you be focused on taxes when making decisions about your nonqualified options. We realize that's easier said than done. When you exercise options—that is, when you actually buy shares of stock at the price set by your options—the IRS takes a big bite. The gains from your nonqualified options (the difference between your exercise price and the market value on the day you exercise) are taxed as income. The prospect of a hefty tax bill prompts some to exercise their options early to try and limit their tab. It's a faulty strategy. Once you commit capital, you've given up the key advantage of your options: leverage. "Stock options are part of your income stream," says OppenheimerFunds' Rossell.

- **Always flip your options.** For a minor fee, you can ask a broker to do a cashless transaction, in which you simultaneously exercise your options and sell the shares. This way you maximize the inherent leverage of options. You commit no capital, and you reap the windfall. (If you buy the stock, you will have to put up your own money to get the shares at the exercise price.)

- **Think about your net.** Keep track of the value of your options on a net basis. Don't be fooled into measuring unrealized options gains on a pretax basis (and beware of spending option "profits" that could disappear). The true value of your options is your after-tax take. Let's say you've got 2,000 options at $20 and the stock is at $60. That means each option is worth $40, pretax, or $80,000 total. But you'll have to withhold for taxes, including Social Security, Medicare and state tax. If you're in the top federal income tax bracket of 39.6% and live in a high-tax state like New York, your cash-out value is not quite $37,000, according to calculations from www.mystockoptions.com.

OPTIONS STRATEGIES

There is one axiom missing from our list above—one that many academic experts would put at the top of the list: Wait as long as possible before exercising anything. This rule makes perfect sense, in theory, because you maximize the amount of time your options have to work their leveraging magic (and you postpone the tax bill). Since stocks have historically gone up over time, the longer you hold, the more you can get out of them. "Waiting until the end looks like a stupid thing to do, but it is the smartest move," says Kaye Thomas, a tax attorney who runs www.fairmark.com, a tax guide site for investors.

We agree—in theory. But in the real world it's not always that simple. Once options are in the money, it's difficult to ignore them. After all, they could be converted to real dollars easily enough. And as so many tech investors realized to their horror in the past two years, options may be in the money one week and hopelessly underwater only months afterwards. And some of these options might remain underwater forever.

For Jon Greeno, the past year has been a real roller-coaster ride. The up: In August 2000 he exercised 500 options in the stock of his employer, Nortel Networks, and netted himself a quick $18,000. That windfall allowed him to get a head start in paying for college for his three kids. And he still had another 500 options that he would be able to cash in before the following year's tuition bills came due. The down: One week after Greeno exercised, Nortel's stock collapsed—it's off by more than 80%— and he's now sitting on options that are worth far less than they once were. "Unless I was in desperate straits, I wouldn't exercise them at the price they're at today," he says.

Still, we realize that a lot of people will—and should—exercise options well before they expire. The rule we'd apply is sim-

The ABCs of Options

Here are some quick definitions of the most important options terms.

Black-Scholes: The definitive academic formula for valuing stock options. Designed by the Nobel-prizewinning academic Myron Scholes and Fischer Black, it takes into account the cash you could get out now, the time value till expiration and other factors.

Cashless exercise: Exercising your options and selling the resulting shares on the same day. You put no money in and get the cash that remains after paying the exercise price, a small broker's fee and withholding for taxes.

Disqualifying disposition: A tax term that refers to the sale of stock from incentive stock options (ISOs) in the same year you exercised them. It means you give up the tax privileges inherent in ISOs.

Exercise price: The per-share price you pay to turn your options into stock. Also referred to as the strike price.

Grant date: The day the options were awarded to you by your company.

In the money: Describes options when their market price is higher than your exercise price. (If the current price is lower, then they're considered to be underwater.)

Incentive stock options: Also known as ISOs, these options include a tax advantage. A big benefit: The gains from exercising them—unlike those from nonqualified stock options—do not count as income for tax purposes.

Nonqualified stock options: The most common type of stock option, they allow you to take part in your company's price appreciation without putting any money down, but offer no tax advantages.

Stock swap: Using shares you already own to exercise your options. One potential advantage: This could lower your tax bill.

Time value: The component of an option's value that's related to the length of time until expiration.

Vesting: Attaining the right to exercise your options and the ownership of the stock that results. A typical options grant vests in four years at a rate of 25% a year. Some start-up companies now offer monthly vesting.

ple: You should usually have a specific reason to exercise. And, in our view, there are just five worthwhile reasons to do so.

• **You need the money for something very important.** Maybe you want to get some cash to put a down payment on a new home or to pay for your wedding. That's what Anthony Gilmore, a regional vice president at grocer Whole Foods Market, did.

Gilmore, who lives in Austin, used a chunk of his options to foot the big bills for his 1998 nuptials at a winery in California, his honeymoon in Cabo San Lucas and a down payment on a house. By exercising just 1,400 of his 18,000 options, he netted some $40,000. "We were able to pay for our entire wedding in cash," Gilmore says. But before you go for the cash, be sure the expenditure is worth it. Remember, by exercising options you may be giving up future gains.

• **You expect to get more options.** This alone may not be enough, but it can be an important criterion in combination with others. Future options will give you more chances to participate in whatever upside your company's stock has. This is especially true if you get so-called *reload options*, in which you get replacement options when you exercise your existing ones. In that case, you may want to exercise whenever you can.

• **You need to diversify your portfolio.** Many people with stock options find their financial futures overly reliant on their own company's stock. To decrease your risk, you may decide to cash out some of your options, pay the tax and redirect the money. The main issue is how much risk you're willing to take. "It is classic greed vs. fear," says Michael Beriss.

Take the case of Sam Sheng, a chip designer at LSI Logic. When the private chipmaker he worked for, DataPath Systems, was bought by LSI in July 2000, his options made him an instant millionaire on paper. Then, over the next several months, he watched as LSI—his biggest investment—plummeted, from $60 to a recent $15. Now Sheng is struggling to come up with a smart strategy for making the most of a diminished nest egg. "Your entire net worth is vapor," he says.

One way around this dilemma is to exercise and sell some of your options regularly, say once a quarter. It's the options equivalent of dollar-cost averaging. Just as you would invest in your 401(k) in regular increments regardless of where the investments

How to Exercise Your Options

Options can be exercised in three different ways.

- **Cash.** This is the most straightforward route. You give your employer the necessary money and get stock certificates in return. But what if, when it comes time to exercise, you don't have enough cash on hand to buy the option shares and pay any resulting tax?

- **Stock swaps.** Some employers let you trade company stock you already own to acquire option stock. Say your company stock sells for $50 a share and you have an incentive stock option to buy 5,000 additional shares for $25 each. Instead of paying $125,000 in cash to exercise the option, you could exchange 2,500 shares (with a total market value of $125,000) you already own for the 5,000 new shares. This strategy has the additional benefit of limiting your concentration in company stock. Note: You must have held the swapped incentive stock option shares for the required one- and two-year holding periods to avoid having the exchange treated as a sale and, thus, incurring tax.

- **Cashless exercises.** This is the most common method. A broker helps the optionholder to buy the stock at the exercise price and simultaneously sell it at the market price without putting up any money. The optionholder pockets the difference between the market price and the exercise price less taxes and brokerage fees.

Which options go first? It's not uncommon to have multiple grants, at varying exercise prices, with different vesting timetables and expiration dates. Which should you exercise first? Assuming there's no expiration pressure, the answer is simple: the lowest-priced options. This allows you to cash in the fewest options to get the money you need. You'll also have more options to take advantage of future price appreciation.

Let's say you have 1,000 options at an exercise price of $20, another 1,000 at an exercise price of $40, and the stock is currently trading at $60. If you need to raise $20,000 pretax, you'd need to exercise only 500 of the lower-priced options, but all of the higher-priced. With the former scenario, you'd still get $1,500 in incremental gains for every $1 the stock moves up, while the latter scenario would give you only $1,000.

are trading, you could exercise your options (and sell the resulting shares) at regular intervals. This strategy won't get you the biggest gains, but it mitigates potential losses and can help you weather the volatility inherent in options.

- **You think your company's stock is headed for a fall.** If you've lost faith in your company or believe its stock is overvalued, you may want to take the profits you have on in-the-money options rather than worry that your bonus will shrink. That's what Mark Spellman did when he was working at Macromedia, a maker of software for the Internet. In 1996, Spellman worried that Macromedia was losing ground to competitors like Adobe, so he cashed out all of his options for roughly $150,000. He used the proceeds to buy a house in tony Oakland Hills and to repay student loans and credit-card debt. Spellman left the company, and Macromedia's stock cratered, though it has since more than recovered.

- **You stand to lose your options.** If your options are approaching expiration (which typically occurs 10 years after you get them) or you think you might be leaving the company (you'll lose your options if you don't exercise them quickly), you want to be sure you don't leave money on the table. Tim Clancey made that mistake when he left his job at a bank in San Francisco. Clancey had 500 vested options that were $4 in the money. But he didn't realize he'd forfeit them if he didn't exercise within 60 days of leaving the company. He didn't. "I'm embarrassed," Clancey says. "It's not like I was at a dotcom."

OPTIONS AND YOUR PORTFOLIO

Now comes the most difficult part: how to account for stock options in relation to the rest of your portfolio. The key question is: Do you have too much of your wealth tied up in one company? For some option holders, the answer is a resounding yes; but for most people, whose money is spread across a variety of funds, stocks and options, it's a tough call. We suggest you begin by doing two calculations:

- **Value your options.** The easiest way to do this is to figure your options' current market value and what you would get if you cashed them out today. Let's say you've got 2,000 options at $20 and the stock is at $60. That means each option is worth $40—a total of $80,000 pretax. Sure, you'll get far less after tax if you cash out. But since everything else in your portfolio is valued on a pretax basis, we suggest you do the same for your options when trying to figure their position in your portfolio.

This process has one major shortcoming: It ignores the potential future gains of your options. What we're really talking about here is the time value of your options. One way to take that into account is to apply the so-called Black-Scholes valuation to your options, which companies often include in their options offers to employees. The calculation is not simple, but if you want to give it a try, check out the online Black-Scholes calculators at www.stock-options.com or at www.intrepid.com/~robertl/option-pricer1.html. But remember, the Black-Scholes method makes big (and possibly unrealistic) assumptions about the future performance and volatility of your company's stock.

• **Check your portfolio.** The next step is to take the value of your options and compare it to the overall market value of the rest of your holdings, including your 401(k) and other retirement money; your stocks and funds held outside of retirement accounts; your cash; and any other investments. This way you can see what percentage of your portfolio the options represent and get a feeling for just how reliant you are on your company stock.

Let's go back to the cash-out example above. Say you're looking at an $80,000 position on a $500,000 portfolio; that means your options represent 16% of your assets—a bit high, but not unreasonable. Assume instead, however, that your total portfolio size is $250,000. In that scenario, $80,000 adds up to nearly one-third of your assets. If, like many option holders, you also have company stock elsewhere in your portfolio, the actual percentage will be higher.

You may be willing to make a large bet on a single company, but most financial planners suggest limiting stakes in your company to just 10% of your total portfolio. Clearly, this message is not getting through to many Americans. The average participant in a 401(k) has 41% of his or her money invested in company stock.

If you want to minimize your risk by diversifying, think about how you're going to invest your gains before you exercise your options. Let's take the same example again: With 2,000 options of $20, and the stock currently at $60, you have $80,000 in pretax gains. If the stock goes up 10% to $66, you now have $92,000 pretax—an increase not of 10% but of 15%. So if you believe your company's stock will go up 10% this year, you need to ask: What other investment could I make that would return

15% or more? Of course, though, this also works in reverse. If the stock goes down 10%, to $54, you're looking not at $80,000 in pretax gains but at $68,000—a decline of 15%. So you also need to ask: Is the very real possibility of losing 15% too painful to bear?

Steve Legg, 32, has faced these kinds of questions ever since he began receiving options from Starbucks, where he works as a risk manager. But Legg has decided not to cash out of his options. "I don't have huge expenses dangling over my head," Legg says. Instead, the Kirkland, Wash. resident is holding on to his options, betting that Starbucks stock will continue to rise over time.

Whatever course you choose, remember the power of options. Like any bonus, they can make a real difference in your financial life. You may not get rich off options, but you may be able to buy a home or help pay for the kids' schooling—and still have money for something fun. Remember Jon Greeno? He used most of his options money to pay for his kids' college. But the first purchase he made after cashing out was a vintage electric guitar that he had always wanted.

Chapter 13

A GRADUATE-LEVEL COURSE IN INVESTING FOR COLLEGE

One of the hardest things for any parent to do is to set priorities for investing. Which is more important, retirement or paying for college? Okay, they're both important, but if one has to get short shrift, which should it be?

The answer: college. After all, for many families there will be some financial aid available, even if it comes in the form of loans—but no one is going to finance your retirement. (See the "Web Resources" box on page 206 for information on financial aid and different loan programs.) That's why many financial advisers suggest you treat saving for college like saving for a downpayment on a house. You can't expect to pay the whole bill up front, but anything you can put away now reduces the need to borrow later.

And there's some good news for you in this chapter. The spread of 529 college savings plans will be a boon to many parents struggling to save for college. In most cases, the tax breaks they offer make them preferable to other college savings vehicles, including custodial accounts.

In 2001, earnings on 529 plans are taxed at the child's rate, but that will soon change. Beginning in 2002, all 529 earnings will be free of federal tax and will be subject only to minimal state taxes (and even these will not apply in most cases).

CUSTODIAL ACCOUNTS

Putting money in an account in your child's name can be a smart move—but only up to a certain point. Under the Gifts to Minors laws, you can pass along up to $10,000 a year to your child free of taxes (two parents can give $20,000). And that money can be invested however you wish.

The benefit: The first $700 a year in investment income that the account earns is tax-free, and the next $700 is taxed at the child's rate. But that's where the breaks peter out. Any amount above $1,400 a year is whacked at the parent's rate, as high as 39.6%, until the child turns 14. At that point, the entire amount is taxed at the child's rate.

Moreover, putting money in a custodial account can cost more in aid (including loans) than you save on taxes. The formulas for determining aid require a child to contribute as much as 35% of his or her assets per year, while parents are expected to pay up to 5.6% of theirs. That means a sizable custodial account will limit the aid you receive much more than, say, a fund in your name. In addition, there's a risk that by putting the money in your child's name, you give up control. If you need to draw on those funds for some financial emergency, you won't be able to unless it's for your child's direct benefit. And once the child turns 18 (or 21 in some states), there's little to prevent him or her from using the dough to go to Belize instead of Brown.

So here's a reasonable compromise: Put a limited amount into a custodial account, just enough to qualify for the tax break. Then put the rest into a 529 plan. An alternative for those who want to manage their own accounts: If you're certain you won't get aid (and you're confident your child is college-bound), Kal Chany, a New York City financial aid adviser and author of *Paying for College Without Going Broke*, suggests this: Use a custodial account to invest in growth stocks, which appreciate in value but pay small dividends. When the student turns 14, sell the stock and take the capital gain, which is taxed at the child's rate. That's around the time you should start to shift to bonds anyway.

THE 529 SOLUTION

Okay, so custodial accounts leave a lot to be desired. Surely, there must be some other way for parents struggling to save enough money for their children's college bills to take advantage of tax breaks. Anything called the Education IRA must be a godsend, right? Well, so far, all you can put away in an Education IRA is a paltry $500 a year—barely enough for pizza money. (In 2002, however, the contribution limit jumps to $2,000. And now you can use the money to pay for elementary and secondary education, not just college tuition. The phase-out range for married people filing jointly has been raised to $190,000 to $220,000 of AGI.) State-run prepaid tuition plans? They lock you into subpar returns. Little wonder that most parents end up saving in taxable accounts—thereby sacrificing a big piece of their profits to Uncle Sam—or raiding their retirement accounts.

Enter the 529. These state college savings plans are the more attractive younger siblings of prepaid tuition programs. Anyone, regardless of income, can open an account and invest a hefty amount in stock and bond funds (more than $150,000 in many states). The money can be used at any school in the country, and you keep control until the child goes to college. Best of all, after 2001 you don't have to pay federal tax on the money earned in

State by State

In the tables that follow, you'll find the highlights of our survey of the 38 state savings plans that are open or due to open soon. We've identified the five top choices for anyone—and 12 other plans whose tax perks make them great options for state residents. For those who want to shop nationally, we've included the key information you need to compare plans, including resident state tax benefits, typical expenses and investment options. For updated information on any plan, go to the plan's website listed below.

	STATE	MANAGER	PLAN NAME	MAXIMUM CONTRIBUTION[1]
	ALASKA	T. Rowe Price	University of Alaska College Savings Plan	$250,000
	ARIZONA	Securities Mgmt & Research	Arizona Family College Savings Program	168,000
	ARKANSAS	Merrill Lynch	The GIFT College Investing Plan	125,000
	CALIFORNIA	TIAA-CREF	ScholarShare College Savings Trust	165,886[4]
	COLORADO	Salomon Smith Barney	Scholars Choice College Savings Program	150,000
	CONNECTICUT	TIAA-CREF	Connecticut Higher Education Trust	235,000
	DELAWARE	Fidelity	Delaware College Investment Plan	131,480
	IDAHO	TIAA-CREF	Idaho College Savings Program	235,000
	ILLINOIS	Salomon Smith Barney	Bright Start College Savings Program	160,000
	INDIANA	Bank One	Indiana Family College Savings Plan	114,548
	IOWA	Vanguard/state treasurer	College Savings Iowa	140,221
	KANSAS	American Century	Learning Quest	127,000
	KENTUCKY	TIAA-CREF	Kentucky Education Savings Plan Trust[8]	235,000
	LOUISIANA	State treasurer	START Savings Program[8]	281,543[4]
	MAINE	Merrill Lynch	NextGen College Investing Plan	153,000
	MASSACHUSETTS	Fidelity	U. Fund College Investing Plan	171,125
	MICHIGAN	TIAA-CREF	Michigan Education Savings Program	125,000
	MINNESOTA	TIAA-CREF	Minnesota College Savings Plan	100,000

- ▦ **Recommended** for residents and national shoppers
- ★ **Recommended** for state residents only
- ✋ **Caution:** High expenses or sales charges may apply
- ⤳ Plan being **overhauled**
- ⦸ Plan **not open** yet

STATE TAX BREAKS		NUMBER OF NON-AGE-BASED FUND OPTIONS				
MAX. ANNUAL DEDUCTION SINGLE/JOINT	TAX-FREE WITHDRAWALS	EQUITY	FIXED INCOME	EXPENSE RATIO[2]	WEBSITE (WWW.)	TELEPHONE
NO STATE INCOME TAX		2	2	0.95%	troweprice.com/college	800-369-3641
0 S / 0 J	✓	7	3	1.42[3]	smrinvest.com	888-667-3239
U S / U J	✓	2	1	1.80	thegiftplan.com	877-442-6553
0 S / 0 J		2	1	0.80	scholarshare.com	877-728-4338
NO LIMIT	✓	1	2	1.29	scholars-choice.com	888-572-4652
0 S / 0 J	✓	1[5]	1[5]	0.79	aboutchet.com	888-799-2438
0 S / 0 J		2	1	1.10	fidelity.com/delaware	800-544-1655
$4,000 S / $8,000 J		1	1	0.92	idsaves.com	866-433-2533
0 S / 0 J	✓	1	1	0.99	brightstartsavings.com	877-432-7444
0 S / 0 J		2	2	1.06	incollegesave.com	888-814-6800
2,112[6] S / 2,112[6] J	✓	–	–	0.79	collegesavingsiowa.com	888-672-9116
2,000[6] S / 4,000[6] J		–	–	1.22[7]	learningquestsavings.com	800-579-2203
0 S / 0 J	✓	1	–	0.80	kentuckytrust.org	877-598-7878
2,400[6] S / 2,400[6] J	✓	–	1	0.00	osfa.state.la.us	800-259-5626
0 S / 0 J	✓	8	2	1.85[9]	nextgenplan.com	877-463-9843
0 S / 0 J		2	1	1.04	fidelity.com/ufund	800-544-2776
5,000 S / 10,000 J	✓	1	1	0.65	misaves.com	877-861-6377
0 S / 0 J		1	1	0.65	mheso.state.mn.us	800-657-3866

(continued)

	STATE	MANAGER	PLAN NAME	MAXIMUM CONTRIBUTION[1]
★	MISSISSIPPI	TIAA-CREF	Mississippi Affordable College Savings Program	$235,000
▤	MISSOURI	TIAA-CREF	MOST (Missouri Saving for Tuition)	235,000
★	NEBRASKA	Union Bank & Trust	College Savings Plan of Nebraska	$165,000
★	NEW HAMPSHIRE	Fidelity	Unique College Investing Plan	166,600
	NEW JERSEY	State treasurer	NJBEST[13]	150,000
★	NEW MEXICO	State Street	The Education Plan	160,539
▤	NEW YORK	TIAA-CREF	New York's College Savings Program	100,000
⚒	NORTH CAROLINA	State treasurer	College Vision Fund[15]	187,500
⊘	NORTH DAKOTA	Morgan Stanley	College Save	TBA
✋	OHIO	Putnam	College Advantage Savings Plan	229,000
	OKLAHOMA	TIAA-CREF	Oklahoma College Savings Plan	235,000
✋	OREGON	Strong	Oregon College Savings Plan[17]	150,000
⚒	PENNSYLVANIA	State treasurer	Pennsylvania Tuition Account Program[19]	170,000
✋	RHODE ISLAND	Alliance Capital	CollegeBoundfund	246,023
★	TENNESSEE	TIAA-CREF	Tennessee's Best Savings Plan	100,000
▤	UTAH	Vanguard/state treasurer	Utah Educational Savings Plan	160,000
⚒	VERMONT	TIAA-CREF	Vermont Higher Education Savings Plan[17]	100,000
★	VIRGINIA	State treasurer	Virginia Education Savings Trust	100,000
✋	WISCONSIN	Strong	EdVest Wisconsin College Savings Program	246,000
✋	WYOMING	Merrill Lynch	The College Achievement Plan	120,000

Notes: TBA: To be announced. [1] Lifetime. [2] Expense ratios are for youngest age-based portfolio, unless otherwise noted. [3] Class A SM&R Equity Income Fund; shares also carry a 5% sales charge, which is waived if you buy direct. [4] Maximum contribution varies by age of beneficiary. [5] Equity and fixed-income options expected by year-end 2001. [6] Per beneficiary; can carry forward in OH & VA. [7] Age-3 and Age-10 allocations and the expense ratio are for the moderate age-based portfolio; conservative and aggressive options also available. [8] State residency requirement. [9] Expense ratio and fund options for Client Advisor series; expense ratio is 1.5% if you buy direct by phone or the Web. [10] Allocations and expenses for growth portfolio. [11] There is a tax on unearned income that is waived for the 529 plan. [12] Equity fund options expected by year-end 2001. [13] Plan available for state residents only. [14] Allocations and expenses for managed portfolio.

| STATE TAX BREAKS | | NUMBER OF NON-AGE-BASED FUND OPTIONS | | EXPENSE | | |
MAX. ANNUAL DEDUCTION SINGLE/JOINT	TAX-FREE WITHDRAWALS	EQUITY	FIXED INCOME	RATIO[2]	WEBSITE (WWW.)	TELEPHONE
$10,000 **S** / $20,000 **J**	✓	1	1	0.92%	collegesavingsms.com	800-486-3670
8,000 **S** / 16,000 **J**	✓	1	1	0.65	missourimost.org	888-414-6678
1,000 **S** / 1,000 **J**	✓	3	3	1.01[10]	planforcollegenow.com	888-993-3746
NO STATE INCOME TAX[11]		2[12]	1	1.10	fidelity.com/unique	800-544-1722
0 **S** / 0 **J**	✓	–	–	0.50	hesaa.org	877-465-2378
NO LIMIT	✓	4	4	1.29	theeducationplan.com	877-337-5268
5,000 **S** / 10,000 **J**	✓	1	1	0.65[14]	nysaves.org	877-697-2837
0 **S** / 0 **J**	✓	–	1	0.50	collegevisionfund.org	800-600-3453
0 **S** / 0 **J**		TBA		TBA	TBA	800-472-2166
2,000[6] **S** / 2,000[6] **J**	✓	2	–	1.27[16]	collegeadvantage.com	800-233-6734
0 **S** / 0 **J**		1	1	0.83	ok4savings.org	877-654-7284
2,000 **S** / 2,000 **J**		2	1	2.24[18]	oregoncollegesavings.com	866-772-8464
0 **S** / 0 **J**	✓		1	0.00	patap.org	800-440-400
0 **S** / 0 **J**		3	–	1.25[20]	collegeboundfund.com	888-324-5057
NO STATE INCOME TAX[11]		–	–	0.95	tnbest.org	888-486-2378
1,365 **S** / 2,730 **J**	✓	1	1	0.31[21]	uesp.org	800-418-2551
0 **S** / 0 **J**	✓	1	1	0.80	vsac.org	800-637-5860
2,000[6] **S** / 2,000[6] **J**	✓	–	–	1.00	vpep.state.va.us	888-567-0540
3,000[6] **S** / 3,000[6] **J**	✓	4	2	1.65[22]	edvest.state.wi.us	888-338-3789
NO STATE INCOME TAX		2	1	1.57	collegeachievementplan.com	877-529-2655

[15]Plan available for state residents only; age-based and equity funds expected in 2001. [16]Expense ratio for Class-A shares, which carry a 3.5% sales charge; Ohio residents can buy direct for no commission and pay 1.05% in expenses. [17]State residency requirement; available nationally in 2001. [18]Expense ratio for broker-sold shares includes 0.65% sales charge; if buy direct, expenses are 1.59%. [19]More fund options expected by year-end 2001. [20]Expense ratio for class-A shares, which carry a 3.25% sales charge; R.I. residents can buy direct with no sales charge and pay 1% in expenses; allocations for growth portfolio. [21]Allocations for option two. [22]Expense ratio for class-A shares, which carry 3.5% sales charge; can buy direct and pay 1.25% in expenses.

these accounts. To top it off, many states offer additional tax breaks of their own.

Given the generous tax advantages—plus the opportunity to shelter enough cash to actually make a dent in those six-figure tuition bills—529s are on their way to becoming the collegiate version of the 401(k). Today some 36 states operate 529 savings plans; 29 of them are available to residents of any state. Five more states will launch 529s by the end of 2001. More good news: States are increasingly turning over the operation of their 529s to established money-management firms. TIAA-CREF, with 12 state plans, dominates the field, but others are grabbing a piece of the action—among them Fidelity (three states), Merrill Lynch (three) and Salomon Smith Barney (two)—using the states as launching pads to market plans nationwide. Charles Schwab is marketing the nationally available Kansas savings plan, managed by American Century. With the recent revamp of the Alaska 529 plan, which will eventually be available to residents of all 50 states, T. Rowe Price will have a nationally available 529 plan.

Investors have already stashed $2.5 billion in 529 plans, an amount that could grow to $10 billion by 2002, according to Joseph Hurley, who runs savingforcollege.com, a website that tracks college savings plans. Declares Hurley: "People are starting to realize that 529s are the best college savings plans to come along."

We agree, with a few reservations. Unlike 401(k)s, these new programs—most are no more than a year or two old—may not be right for everyone. One major limitation is the lack of flexibility: Once you select an investment option, you cannot change it—unless you follow an IRA-style rollover procedure. If you need to tap the account for any reason other than education, you will pay a 10% penalty. Another flaw: A 529 account can end up hurting your chances of obtaining financial aid (as we'll explain shortly).

We'll help you determine if a 529 is right for you. If it is, we'll then help you figure out which of the plans best suit your situation. Finally, we will outline how best to manage a 529 plan once you've signed up and answer the most frequently asked questions about 529s in the box on page 216.

First, a quick word about whether you should rely on the new and improved Education IRA or a 529 plan. We think 529s have the edge, especially if you live in a high-tax state whose plan offers generous tax perks, such as New York and Michigan. You can salt away more money (up to $250,000 in some states) in funds run by seasoned managers with no income limits. Yes, the

Least Taxing

The states with the most generous deductions:

Colorado Unlimited

New Mexico Unlimited

Mississippi $10,000 for singles; $20,000 joint

Missouri $8,000, single and joint

Michigan $5,000 single; $10,000 joint

New York $5,000 single; $10,000 joint

tax-free withdrawals sunset in 2010, but this is one reform Congress will likely make permanent. Education IRAs are better, however, if you might use them to pay for elementary and secondary schools. And, like custodial accounts but unlike 529 plans, they allow you total investment flexibility.

SECTION 1: ENTRANCE EXAM

Shortcomings and all, 529 plans are a hard-to-beat way to boost your college savings, especially if you're unlikely to qualify for need-based financial aid.

As adviser Raymond Loewe of College Money, a planning firm in Marlton, N.J., puts it, "The tax savings you get in a 529 plan blow up when it comes time to qualify for aid." Here's why. Under financial aid formulas, 529s are counted as the parents' asset until you withdraw the money. That's when the problem sets in. Gains from a 529 count as the student's income, up to 50% of which is considered available to pay tuition. (Even though 529 earnings are not federally taxable after December 31, 2001, financial aid offices nonetheless expect you to report all non-taxable income.) The income from a taxable fund held in a parent's name is assessed at about the same rate (47%). The key difference is that the fund has been distributing gains all along, which reduces your taxable gain—and the number plugged into the aid formula—when the fund is sold to pay for college. Complicating matters even more is the fact that private schools can set their own rules.

Lowest Fees

Age-based plans with the lowest expense ratios:

Utah 0.31% of assets

New Jersey 0.50%

Michigan 0.65%

Missouri 0.65%

New York 0.65%

All this means is that anyone who might qualify for aid—parents currently earning less than $100,000—may be better off saving outside a 529. If you're in the 31 % bracket, however, you probably won't qualify for substantial need-based aid. (Possible exceptions are families with more than one child in expensive colleges at the same time.) Even if you do qualify, you'll probably receive most aid in the form of loans, not grants. To avoid borrowing later, it makes sense to save in a 529.

What if your financial situation changes after you've begun funding a 529? If you later find yourself in a position where you are likely to be eligible for financial aid, try and wait to take withdrawals from your child's 529 until the last year of college, when it won't be counted against future financial aid.

Such plans are also terrific for grandparents looking to reduce their estates. You can deposit up to $50,000 ($100,000 for a married couple) into a 529 plan without incurring the federal gift tax. A $50,000 contribution is counted against your $10,000 annual gift exclusion over five years, so you won't be able to make another tax-free gift to that beneficiary for six years.

SECTION 2: HEAD OF THE CLASS

Okay, you're sold on 529s. But which one is best for you? As you can see from our state-by-state tables, no two programs are alike and they differ dramatically in many ways.

Your first step should be to look at your own state's plan (if it has one). In five states, you may qualify for a matching grant or scholarship (see "State Aid" on opposite page). More important,

State Aid

If you live in one of these states, you may qualify for a matching grant or scholarship.

New Jersey Up to $1,500 in scholarships, good at a state school, if you invest for 12 years.

Louisiana Tuition grants equal to 2% to 14% of your contribution, depending on income.

Michigan A $1 match for every $3 invested the first year, up to $200, for those earning $80,000 a year or less and with beneficiaries six or younger.

Minnesota A 15% match, up to $300 a year, if earning $50,000 or less; 5%, up to $300, if earning $50,000 to $80,000.

Pennsylvania A 50% match, up to $300, for the first two years if the family earns no more than twice the state poverty level.

---

16 states give residents a tax deduction on 529 contributions, and 25 exempt the earnings on withdrawals (six exempt earnings on out-of-state plans as well). Thirteen states offer both breaks. If your state taxes are high and your local plan offers generous tax benefits, you can stop reading here: You're best off staying at home.

But what if you live in a state with low or no taxes—or with limited tax breaks? Then it's time to shop around. In the tables, we've indicated our five favorite plans—Iowa, Michigan, Missouri, New York and Utah. But your family's specific needs may point you in another direction. We'd suggest that you do your own comparison shopping using the following three rules.

• **Shop for a manager, not a performer.** Given the short track record of 529 plans, you can't glean much from the funds' performance history. So stick with plans run by investment companies with successful records managing retail mutual funds and pension plans, such as Vanguard, Fidelity and TIAA-CREF, to name a few. At TIAA-CREF, for example, the same team that manages retail funds also guides the 529 portfolios.

• **Stick with low-cost plans.** Expense ratios vary considerably, from 0.31% in Utah to 2.24% in Oregon. Some states' plans are

FAQs on 529 Plans

Q. What's so great about 529 plans?
A. Chiefly, the tax breaks. There is no federal tax on the earnings in your account. In 28 states (and counting), residents get additional tax breaks, such as deductions on contributions or a tax exemption on withdrawals.

Q. Can anyone open a 529 account for any child?
A. Generally, you ("the account holder") can open an account on behalf of any child ("the beneficiary"), regardless of your income. Grandparents, for example, can save on behalf of grandchildren. You can even put away money for someone who's not a family member. Six states currently require either the account owner or the beneficiary to be residents (or, in Kentucky, a former resident).

Q. Can two people open an account for the same child?
A. You can open more than one account in a single state for the same child, and more than one person can fund a 529 for the same beneficiary. No matter the number of accounts, the state's maximum contribution limit still applies to the beneficiary. States don't have to count balances in out-of-state accounts when determining whether you've met your limit, but some have started doing so.

Q. What if I need to tap the plan?
A. You can get a refund anytime, but you'll pay a penalty on the earnings of 10% if the money is not used for higher education.

Q. Does my child have to go to a state school?
A. You can use the money at any accredited degree-granting school, private, public, undergraduate or graduate.

Q. What kind of educational costs can the money be used for?
A. The money can be used to pay tuition and, in most cases, to cover other costs as well, including room, board, fees, books and equipment.

Q. What if my child doesn't go to college or has the money left over?
A. You can take out the money, and pay the penalties. In most states, you can leave money in the plan indefinitely, in the hopes that your child will eventually go to college. (The exceptions include, Iowa, Nebraska, Utah and Virginia.) A third option is to name a new beneficiary.

Q. What happens if I move to a different state—can I switch plans?
A. You can leave your money in the plan; you'll lose any state tax deduction on future contributions and state exemptions on withdrawals. You can also

roll the money into another state's plan. Think of it as being similar to an IRA rollover. It is not considered a taxable distribution, and you can do such a rollover once—but only once—every 12 months for the same beneficiary.

Q. Can I switch investment options?
A. Generally, only by moving the money. You can either do a rollover, as described above, or open another account for the same beneficiary and invest new money in a different fund.

Q. Can I also use an Education IRA?
A. Yes. Beginning in 2002, you can put money in a 529 and a tax-deferred Education IRA for the same beneficiary in the same year.

---

sold by brokers, which layers on additional costs. If you buy the Arizona, Ohio, Rhode Island or Wisconsin plans through a broker, for instance, you could pay 3.25% to 5% up front in commissions. With all four plans, you can avoid a sales charge by buying direct, although in Ohio and Rhode Island you must be a resident to do so. The Maine plan run by Merrill Lynch comes in two versions: one with four funds that's sold directly by phone—and a broker-sold series with more funds but higher fees.

You could also pay other fees. About half a dozen states charge to open an account (usually $10—but $85 in Virginia). Fourteen plans tack on $25 or so in annual fees, although you can often get the up-front or annual fee waived if you sign up for an automatic investment program—or if you buy directly by phone or the Web.

• **Look for the right investment choices, not the most.** The typical 529 menu is still fairly limited. In most plans, the key offering is an age-based portfolio, which gradually shifts the asset allocation as your child ages. For children under three, for example, some 80% of the portfolio may be stashed in stocks. As your child grows, the equity portion shrinks, so that by the time he or she is 18, the assets are held mainly in bonds or cash, ensuring that you can meet that first tuition bill.

Increasingly, states are adding conventional stock and bond funds to the original age-based portfolios. Maine, Nebraska and Arizona now offer 10 or more funds, including foreign and technology portfolios. But because you can't switch your money around freely the way you can in a 401(k), a vast number of choices isn't much of an advantage—and potentially riskier.

For most investors, the best choice is an age-based portfolio. In the past, these funds were criticized by financial advisers as being too heavily oriented toward fixed-income assets, even during the child's youngest years. But in light of the recent market bloodbath, a conservative strategy suddenly looks more sensible. "People forget that they usually have fewer years to save for college than for retirement—most often 10 years or less, since they tend to start late," notes TIAA-CREF vice president Timothy Lane. "If you lose a lot in the early years, it's very hard to make it up."

Five states (Kansas, Nebraska, New York, Rhode Island and Utah) also now offer two or more types of age-based portfolio, with allocations designed to suit either risk-oriented or cautious investors. You can also create your own stock and bond mix by opening more than one account in the child's name—one for each asset class—and controlling your own allocation by the amounts you invest in each. Another strategy: If you don't like the asset mix choice designed for your child's age, find out if you can use a portfolio for a different age. Some states, such as Colorado and Virginia, let you pick your own starting point.

SECTION 3: YOUR ASSIGNMENTS

Once you're ensconced in a 529 plan, review its growth twice a year to make sure you're saving enough. When it comes time to make withdrawals, you cannot pay any state taxes with money from the 529, since that's not a higher education expense. So be sure to tuck away enough cash to finance the tax bill.

If you aren't relying on an age-based portfolio to regularly shift allocations, it's important to make those changes yourself so that you don't get caught short in a market downturn. To do so, you may need to roll over your existing account.

One more point to keep in mind, notes Judy Miller, a college financial adviser in Alameda, Calif.: State contracts with money managers to operate 529 plans are typically set for just five to eight years. So your state may switch your manager down the line. But chances are, by that point, 529s really will be the equivalent of 401(k)s, and you will be able to simply pick up the phone and move your money if you aren't happy with the change.

INDEX